THE AMERICAN EXPLORATION AND TRAVEL SERIES

MANSFIELD ON THE CONDITION OF THE WESTERN FORTS, 1853–54

MANSFIELD
on the
CONDITION
of the
WESTERN FORTS
1853–54

Edited and with an Introduction by

Robert W. Frazer

UNIVERSITY OF OKLAHOMA PRESS : NORMAN

Library of Congress Catalog Card Number 63-18072

Copyright 1963 by the University of Oklahoma Press, Publishing Division of the University. Composed and printed at Norman, Oklahoma, U.S.A., by the University of Oklahoma Press. First Edition.

To
William and Rose Burnett

Contents

[ix]

[x]

Illustrations

Introduction

I n 1853 and 1854, Colonel Joseph King Fenno Mansfield inspected the United States military posts in the Oregon country and the territory acquired at the close of the Mexican War. His tour took him through an extensive region at a time when the major aspects of the military policy to be followed in the Far West were beginning to take shape. As late as 1845 a chain of twelve posts, stretching from Fort Jesup, Louisiana, to Fort Snelling, in the present Minnesota, constituted the western military frontier and marked the line between the frontier of settlement and the land occupied by the Indians. The annexation of Texas, the settlement of the Oregon question, and, most particularly, the territorial acquisition resulting from the Treaty of Guadalupe Hidalgo led to a rapid and far-reaching change in the military policy of the United States in the trans-Mississippi West.

Even before the outbreak of the Mexican War, the change had been foreshadowed by the establishment of two posts on the lower Rio Grande and the contemplated establishment of one or more posts along the Oregon Trail. With the addition of western territory, portions of which were already settled, the retention of a permanent military zone between Indian and settler was no longer possible. As soon as New Mexico and California were occupied by United States military forces, it was necessary to provide for their defense against a possible uprising of the Mexican population or an attempted reconquest by Mexico. Lines of communication had to be laid out and guarded, not only along the already existing Oregon and Santa Fe trails, but along new routes across Texas and to California as well. The discovery of gold in California and the resultant increase in migration to the West Coast complicated the problem by multiplying the routes of travel and stirring up the hostility of the Indians. Protection had to be provided for settled areas and for those areas into which settlement was rapidly expanding. Finally, by the terms of the Treaty of Guadalupe Hidalgo, the United States bound itself to restrain the Indians in its territory from crossing into Mexico to commit depredations. For the moment this agreement remained more an obligation recognized than a duty performed.

Both the Oregon country and the Mexican cession contained fairly large settled areas, isolated from each other and from the rest of the United States. Any protection afforded the inhabitants, any control exerted over them, had to be provided on the spot. The closest existing military facilities, Fort Brown on the lower Rio Grande, Forts Towson and Washita in Indian Territory, and Forts Leavenworth and Kearny on the Missouri River, were much too far removed to serve either purpose. In 1846 the populated portion of New Mexico began at San Elizario, some twenty miles below the Mexican town of El Paso del Norte (Ciudad Juárez), and extended north in a broken line up the Rio Grande Valley to the Culebra River in what is now Colorado.[1] In addition, there was a scattering of settlement east and west of the Rio Grande Valley, principally in the mountainous region of northern New Mexico. The settled portion of New Mexico constituted an enclave in an extensive region occupied by hostile Indians who, if sometimes willing to engage in trade, were always ready to run off stock or, when the occasion arose, to perpe-

[1] It is true that the Republic of Texas claimed much of this territory, but it had neither occupied nor established political control over it.

trate more serious damage. Much of the territory surrounding the settled parts of New Mexico remained officially unexplored as late as 1853.[2]

In California the non-Indian population was much smaller and more dispersed. There the settlers lived west of the major mountain ranges, most of them close to the coast, from San Diego in the south to San Francisco Bay and Sutter's Fort in the north. The Indians to the east and north of this area were less menacing than those surrounding the Mexican population in New Mexico, but they either were—or were presumed to be—hostile. In the Oregon country the areas of settlement were west of the Cascade Mountains along the Columbia River below the Dalles, in the Willamette Valley, and, very thinly, along lower Puget Sound. In addition, there were a few mission stations and Hudson's Bay Company posts east of the Cascades. The Indians east of the Cascades were considered unfriendly, if not openly hostile, while those west of the mountains, long under the influence of the Hudson's Bay Company, were generally assumed to be friendly. The other settled area of the newly acquired West, the country in the vicinity of the Great Salt Lake into which the Mormons were moving, was not at the moment of concern to the military.

Almost as soon as the bloodless occupation of New Mexico had been accomplished, the process of providing for military defense and control began. Before he left Santa Fe to participate in the conquest of California, Brigadier General Stephen Watts Kearny ordered the construction of Fort Marcy. On November 3, 1846, "so much of the Mexican province of New Mexico as has been or may be subjected to the arms or the authority of the

[2] See "Map of the Territory of New Mexico," compiled by Brevet Second Lieutenant John G. Parke, Topographical Engineers, Santa Fe, 1851). Parke's map labels much of the area to the west, north, and east of the Rio Grande "unexplored." There had been some additional exploration by 1853, but most official exploration began in or came after that year.

United States" was designated Military Department No. 9.[3] Between 1846 and 1850 garrisons were established at various centers of population, at first to maintain order among the newly conquered inhabitants, then, beginning in 1847, to provide protection against Indian depredations.[4] In April, 1851, Lieutenant Colonel (Brevet Colonel) Edwin Vose Sumner, 1st U.S. Dragoons, was named commander of the department. Secretary of War Charles M. Conrad instructed him to "revise the whole system of defence" within the department, making "such changes as you may deem advisable." In selecting locations for posts, Sumner was to be guided by: "1st. The protection of New Mexico. 2nd. The defence of the Mexican Territory, which we are bound to protect against the Indians within our borders. 3rd. Economy and facility in supporting the troops, particularly in regard to forage, fuel, and adaptation of the surrounding country to cultivation." In what sounds very much like a plea, Conrad added, "You will use every effort to reduce the enormous expenditures of the army in New Mexico, particularly in the quartermaster's and subsistence departments. . . ."[5] Sumner complied vigorously and was soon able to report, "I reached Santa Fé, on the 19th of July and assumed command of the Department. My first step was to break up the post at Santa Fé, that sink of vice and extravagence, and to remove the troops and public property to this place [Fort Union]. I left one company of Artillery there. . . ." The garrisons were withdrawn from all of the other towns except

[3] Raphael P. Thian, *Notes Illustrating the Military Geography of the United States*, 49. Although the official designation was Department No. 9, it was often referred to as the Department of New Mexico, even in official documents.

[4] In addition to the garrison at Santa Fe, troops were stationed at Taos, Albuquerque, Doña Ana, Socorro, Coons' Ranch (opposite El Paso del Norte), Las Vegas, Rayado, Abiquiu, Cebolleta, and San Elizario in 1850. *Report of the Secretary of War, 1850*, in 31 Cong., 2 sess. *Sen. Exec. Doc. 1*, II, facing p. 116.

[5] Conrad to Sumner, April 1, 1851, in 32 Cong., 1 sess, *Sen. Exec. Doc. 1*, pp. 125–26.

[xvi]

Taos, where troops were stationed until the establishment of
Cantonment Burgwin in 1852. Sumner elaborated upon his opinion of the stationing of troops in towns:

> I consider the withdrawal of the troops from the towns, a mat-
> ter of vital importance, both as it regards discipline and economy.
> It is unquestionably true, that most of the troops in this territory
> have become in a high degree demoralized, and it can only be
> accounted for, by the vicious associations in those towns. These
> evils are so great, that I do not expect to eradicate them entirely,
> until I can bring the troops together, in considerable bodies, for
> discipline and instruction.[6]

Under Sumner's zealous direction Forts Union, Fillmore,
Defiance, and Conrad were established in 1851. Cantonment
Burgwin and Fort Massachusetts came into being in 1852. Despite his attitude toward towns and his suspicion of their effect
upon soldiers' morals, Sumner found it expedient to return the
departmental headquarters to Santa Fe in May, 1852, and then
in August to transfer them to a regarrisoned Albuquerque.[7] Los
Lunas also was garrisoned in 1852. Fort Webster was established
in 1851, though not originally by that name, as headquarters
for the United States-Mexican boundary survey. The commission
escort occupied the old private fortifications erected to protect the
Santa Rita copper mine. When the commission moved on in October, 1851, the post was occupied by a detachment of troops previously stationed at Coons' Ranch, opposite El Paso del Norte.
It was at this time that the post was designated Fort Webster.
In 1852 the site was abandoned and a new post, still called Fort
Webster, was erected on the Mimbres River, some fifteen miles
northwest of the copper mine. Hence, all of the posts in existence

[6] Sumner to Jones, October 24, 1851, in Annie Heloise Abel, ed., *The Official Correspondence of James S. Calhoun while Indian Agent at Santa Fé and Superintendent of Indian Affairs in New Mexico*, 417.
[7] Thian, *Notes Illustrating the Military Geography*, 50.

in the summer of 1853, with the exception of Fort Marcy, had been established or re-established during Sumner's tenure as commander of the department.

Politically, New Mexico remained unorganized and subject to military rule until 1850. In emulation of California, New Mexico sought to become a state in 1850, but the effort failed when territorial status was conferred upon it instead. As a territory, New Mexico comprised all of the present states of New Mexico and Arizona, except for the Gadsden Purchase which was added to it in 1854, Nevada south of 37°, and that portion of Colorado west of 103° and south of 38° to the Continental Divide.[8] All of the posts included in Military Department No. 9 lay within this area.[9] Although individual posts in the department had been inspected upon orders from departmental headquarters, the first general inspection of the department was made by Colonel George A. McCall in 1850. Colonel McCall's reports, which have not been published, deal with the individual posts and, as a whole, are less informative than Mansfield's inspection report of 1853. They are limited largely to a discussion of the several military establishments and have almost nothing to say of the people of the territory, the towns, production, and other matters upon which Mansfield touches.[10] McCall did submit two

[8] See Leroy R. Hafen, "Status of the San Luis Valley, 1850–1861," *The Colorado Magazine*, Vol. III (May, 1926), 46–49.

[9] Military Department No. 9 had been redefined several times since it was originally established. On February 15, 1853, it was somewhat ambiguously described as consisting of "New Mexico and the territory north and west of a line commencing at the intersection of the 32d degree of north latitude with the Rio Bravo del Norte, and running due east along the northern boundary of Texas to the intersection of the 103d degree of west longitude; thence to the junction of the Choctaw Creek with the Red River, and down said river to western boundary of Arkansas." The department was abolished on October 31, 1853, and replaced by the Department of New Mexico, which consisted of the Territory of New Mexico east of 110° west longitude. Thian, *Notes Illustrating the Military Geography*, 50, 79.

[10] George A. McCall, "McCall's Inspection Report, Department of New Mexico,

reports of wider interest which have been published. One was a
report in compliance with Secretary of War George Crawford's
request for his "observations and views on their [the New Mexicans'] probable numbers, habits, customs, and pursuits of life."[11]
The other was a report to Colonel Roger Jones, adjutant general, dealing with specific problems of concern to the military,
but containing some information regarding the Indians and the
general population.[12] While McCall did not object to the garri-
soning of towns, which he deemed necessary for the preservation
of lives and property, he recommended that if the Indians were
to be brought under control, it would be necessary to establish
posts "in the heart of the Indian country," one among the Navajo
near the Cañon de Chelly, one in the Apache country on the eastern slope of the Sacramento Mountains, and one on the Gila
River or near the old copper mine.[13]

In 1851, Major Thomas Swords, assistant quartermaster, inspected the affairs of the Quartermaster's Department in New
Mexico. He accompanied Colonel Sumner, who was on his way
to assume command of the department, from Fort Leavenworth
to Rayado, New Mexico. Swords inspected the posts at Rayado,
Taos, Abiquiu, Santa Fe, Albuquerque, Socorro, Doña Ana, El
Paso (Coons' Ranch), and San Elizario, and the quartermaster's
sub-depot at Algodones. He did not visit Cebolleta, and by the
time he reached Las Vegas the troops previously stationed there
had been moved to the site of Fort Union. His primary concern
was with the expense of the military establishment in New Mexico, particularly the cost of forage for horses and mules and the
rental of quarters for troops. Swords' report was highly critical

1850," Records of the Office of the Adjutant General, Records Group 94, the National Archives, Washington, D.C.

[11] Crawford to McCall, November 19, 1849, in 31 Cong., 1 sess., *House Exec.
Doc. 17*, 280–81.

[12] Both reports are published in 31 Cong., 2 sess., *Sen. Exec. Doc. 26.*

[13] McCall to Jones, December 26, 1850, *ibid.*, 19–20.

of past policy and completely in agreement that the stationing of troops in towns had greatly increased expenses. Praising Sumner for his prompt measures to reduce expenses, he commented that it might have been wiser to leave the stores in Santa Fe, where "there were large and secure storehouses belonging to the government," until provisions had been made to care for them properly at Fort Union. Swords wrote:

> It appears to me that the causes requiring the presence of the troops in towns, if they ever have existed, exist no longer, and that Colonel Sumner has now adopted the true policy by occupying positions beyond the present settlements, where there is good grazing and land suitable to agricultural purposes, or where, by their presence in their country, they can control the wild Indian tribes more effectually, than when at a distance from them. The inhabitants of the towns and large settlements should be taught to depend upon themselves as did the first settlers in our western States. By the distribution of arms and ammunition to them under proper restrictions, and the introduction of a suitable militia system, they, with their simple habits, excellent horsemanship, and great powers of enduring fatigue, would soon be made valuable partizan soldiers, and after overcoming their terror of the Indian, be ever anxious and ready to meet him, instead of, as now, fleeing in terror at his approach. Another advantage must result from the location of troops, in their present positions. New sections of country, from which settlers have heretofore been kept out, in consequence of the want of protection, being opened to the labors of the husbandman, and this in a country where but so small a proportion of the land is available for agricultural purposes, is an advantage of paramount importance, as it will tend not only to lessen the expense of maintaining the troops, but to the increase and comfort of the inhabitants.[14]

The military posts in the Department of New Mexico were

[14] Swords' inspection report is in 32 Cong., 1 sess., *House Exec. Doc.* 2, 235–41.

among the most difficult and expensive to supply in the United States. At the same time they were dependent upon sources outside the department for almost everything they required. Arms and munitions, clothing, medical supplies, most foodstuffs, even mounts had to be brought in. Building materials were obtained locally, chiefly because in this period the army constructed its western posts of materials available in the immediate vicinity, making use of the labor of soldiers. Forage, such fresh foodstuffs as could be had, and firewood were procured locally. The bulk of the supplies came over the Santa Fe Trail and were distributed from Fort Union. By 1853 some supplies for Forts Fillmore and Webster were brought across southern Texas from San Antonio.[15] By the time of Mansfield's inspection, the local availability of supplies, particularly flour, forage, and fresh meat, had improved, but the cost of maintaining military posts in New Mexico was still a matter of concern. As late as 1852, Secretary of War Conrad had proposed:

> To protect this small population, we are compelled to maintain a large military force at an annual expense nearly equal to half the value of the whole real estate of the territory. Would it not be better to induce the inhabitants to abandon a country which seems hardly fit for the habitation of civilized man, by remunerating them for their property in money or in lands situated in more favored regions? Even if the government paid for the property quintuple its value, it would still, merely on the score of economy, be largely the gainer by the transaction, and the troops

[15] In 1853 there were supply depots at San Antonio, Austin, Corpus Christi, Indianola, and Brazos Santiago. See M. L. Crimmins, ed., "W. G. Freeman's Report on the Eighth Military Department," *The Southwestern Historical Quarterly*. The report continues through twelve successive numbers of the quarterly, beginning in LI (July, 1947), and concluding in LIII (April, 1950). There were two commonly used routes across Texas, ordinarily referred to as the upper and lower routes, both beginning at San Antonio and reconverging in the vicinity of El Paso del Norte.

now stationed in New Mexico would be available for the protection of other portions of our own and of the Mexican territory.[16]

The military situation in California initially was similar to that in New Mexico. Military Department No. 10, consisting of "the Territory of Oregon, and so much of the Mexican provinces of the two Californias as has been, or may be, subjected to the arms or the authority of the United States," was established on November 3, 1846.[17] There were at the time no United States troops in the Oregon country and, before the first troops arrived, Military Department No. 11, embracing the Territory of Oregon, was created on August 31, 1848.[18] The Pacific Division, made up of Departments 10 and 11, was established on October 10, 1848, then, in 1851, the two departments were dissolved. On October 31, 1853, the Department of the Pacific replaced the Pacific Division. The new department included all of the country west of the Rocky Mountains except the Territory of Utah and that portion of the Territory of New Mexico east of 110°.[19] Politically, California remained under military control until it began to function as a state in December, 1849, some nine months before its

[16] The estimated value of all real estate in New Mexico, as given by Conrad, was $2,700,000. *Report of Secretary of War Conrad, 1852*, in 32 Cong., 2 sess., *House Exec. Doc. 1*, II, pp. 5–6. In the summer of 1851 an experiment was conducted by the Quartermaster's Department to determine the cost of supplying the posts in New Mexico. At that time, including the cost of the military escort, loss of animals, and other incidental expenses, it cost twenty-two dollars a hundred pounds to transport supplies from the Gulf of Mexico and nineteen dollars a hundred pounds to bring them over the Santa Fe Trail from Missouri. Thomas Jesup to Conrad, November 22, 1851, *ibid.*, 221.

[17] Thian, *Notes Illustrating the Military Geography*, 50.

[18] *Ibid.*, 51.

[19] *Ibid.*, 25, 86. However, Secretary of War Davis, in his report of 1854, stated that the Department of the Pacific embraced "the State of California and the Territories of Oregon, Washington, and Utah, and a part of the Territory of New Mexico." 33 Cong., 2 sess., *House Exec. Doc. 1*, II, p. 6. There were no military posts in the Territory of Utah nor was the territory included in any other department.

actual admission. The Oregon country was not provided with
any form of government until the Act of August 14, 1848, created the Territory of Oregon. Governor Joseph Lane arrived
in March, 1849, to inaugurate the territorial government more
than two months before the first troops reached the area. On
March 2, 1853, Washington Territory was created from the
northern portion of Oregon Territory. Isaac I. Stevens, who
headed the survey of the northernmost Pacific railway route,
assumed the territorial governorship in November, 1851.

The United States forces in California took over the existing
military posts[20] and, for about a year, occupied Sutter's Fort. Of
the presidios, only San Francisco became a permanent post. Santa
Barbara and Monterey were occupied for a few years only, although the military reservation at Monterey was retained. At
San Diego, the Mexican earthwork and the mission, rather than
the presidio, were occupied, the mission being the principal military post at San Diego from 1849 to 1858. Sonoma, where a
small Mexican garrison had been stationed, was occupied until
1852. Only one completely new post, Fort Moore in Los Angeles, was immediately established, and it was abandoned in 1849
before it was completed. Once the resistance of the Mexican population had been put down, as it was early in 1847, the problem
of maintaining order and control in California was relatively
simple. Connection with the East, both for the movement of
troops and supplies, was kept up by sea. For the moment, even
the overland routes to California could be neglected by the
military.

The calm of the California scene was shattered by the discovery
of gold in 1848. The vast influx of population, beginning in

[20] These included the Presidio of San Francisco and the associated Castillo de San
Joaquín, the Presidio of Monterey, the Presidio of Santa Barbara, and the Presidio
of San Diego with the associated Castillo Guijarros and Mexican earthworks. The
fortifications at Sonoma, which were not designated a presidio, were occupied also.

1849, brought about a change in military policy as it became necessary to meet the several new situations which arose. For one problem, the desire of the soldier to desert and rush off to the gold fields, no solution was found. Secretary of War Jefferson Davis, in his annual report for 1853, stated, "the excess [of desertions] from that cause, in one year alone, being 530 over the average of the three succeeding years."[21] An attempt was made to discourage desertions by stationing unnecessarily large numbers of troops at Missions San Diego and San Luis Rey, as far away from the mining districts as possible. This was, at best, a temporary expedient, as the mining districts were the very areas in which the services of troops were needed. As the gold seekers moved into regions previously left to the non-mission Indians, clashes inevitably occurred. Even though the Indians had much the worst of it, the army was called upon to protect the mining districts and the routes of supply leading to them. Several years were to pass before a measure of protection was extended to the Indians also. The coast Indians were less aggressive than those of New Mexico and their control less a problem to the military. Fewer posts were required for the purpose, most of them being camps of an impermanent nature. In 1854 only four forts existed in California in direct connection with the mining districts, and two of these, Forts Jones and Reading, were abandoned prior to the Civil War.

One of the problems associated with the protection of the gold fields was the constantly shifting population as new strikes were made and the old mining camps abandoned. The best the army could do was to establish a limited number of strategically located forts, augmented by temporary camps.[22] In the central and south-

21 33 Cong., 1 sess., *Sen. Exec. Doc. 1*, II, p. 6.

22 In general the designation "fort" indicated a permanent post while "camp" implied an impermanent post. However, this policy was not officially set forth until it was so ordered by General Phil Sheridan on November 8, 1878. See General

ern mining districts, the Indian problem did not reach serious proportions. Of the three forts established in the southern two-thirds of the state for the control of the Indians, two, Miller and Tejon, were abandoned in 1864 and were not replaced. The third, Fort Yuma, had a much longer period of usefulness. Located at the most important crossing place on the lower Colorado River, it served both to control the Indians and to guard the southern emigrant route. That it continued to function as an active post for three decades can be attributed to the fact that it came to be the supply depot for the military posts of Arizona and continued to fill that role until the building of the railroads destroyed its usefulness.

Most of the forts designed to control the Indians were in the northern third of the state and most of them existed for fewer than ten years. Only two, Bidwell and Gaston, were garrisoned for as many as thirty years. The Indians of northern California were to be troublesome sporadically at least until as late as the Modoc War of 1873. In 1854 a reservation system was just coming into being in California. The Tejon Reservation had been established in 1853, and, over the next several years, a number of reservations were established in northern California. At the time of Mansfield's inspection neither reservations nor regular Indian agencies functioned in the north.[23] Nonetheless, existing military policy clearly indicated the lines to be followed for the next three decades, namely, strong defense of San Francisco Bay, protection of the principal overland routes, and control of the Indians.[24]

Orders No. 79, 1878, Records of the Office of the Adjutant General, the National Archives, Washington, D.C. It should be noted that some camps had a much longer span of existence than did many forts. Also, some posts originally designated forts later became camps, although the reverse was more common.

[23] See A. J. Bledsoe, *Indian Wars of the Northwest: A California Sketch*, 146.

[24] The Civil War injected new considerations into the policy temporarily, but in no way lessened the emphasis on the long range factors.

Although preparations had been made for the establishment of military posts along the Oregon Trail and in the Oregon country as early as 1846, they were delayed by the Mexican War.[25] As a result, the first United States troops did not reach the Oregon country until May, 1849. Short-lived posts were established at Astoria, Oregon City, and near the Hudson's Bay Company's Fort Hall in the present Idaho.[26] Very soon the policy of providing protection for the settled areas went into effect. Fort Vancouver, occupied by both the army and the Hudson's Bay Company until 1860, guarded the lower Columbia and Willamette valleys and served as a supply depot for the entire northern portion of the department. Fort Steilacoom protected the lower Puget Sound. Fort Dalles occupied a position of major importance at the upper of the two rapids which interrupted navigation on the Columbia and necessitated the transshipment of goods and passengers. It stood, roughly, between the area of settlement and the Indian country, and marked the division between "wild" Indians and those presumed to be friendly, a presumption which was to be drastically revised in 1855. The discovery of gold in southern Oregon in 1851 led to a movement of prospectors into the region between the Cascades and the Pacific and resulted in the founding of both Jacksonville and Scottsburg.[27] The inevitable clash with the Indians followed, leading to the establishment of the Rogue River Indian Reservation and Fort Lane. Fort Orford, too, came into existence as a result of Indian hostilities. It was hoped originally that it would also serve as a sub-depot for the supply of a post to be established in the in-

[25] See the *Report of Secretary of War William L. Marcy, 1848*, in 30 Cong., 2 sess., *House Exec. Doc. 1*, p. 79

[26] Cantonment Loring, which is sometimes referred to as Fort Hall, though it was never so designated officially, existed for less than a year. An account of the post, as well as the other early Oregon country posts, is given in Raymond W. Settle, *The March of the Mounted Riflemen*.

[27] See Charles H. Carey, *A General History of Oregon Prior to 1861*, II, 481.

terior on the Oregon-California route. When it proved impossible to lay out a road suitable for wagons from Trichenor Bay through the coast mountains, Fort Orford was doomed to early abandonment.

The military policy in the Oregon country was the same in over-all objectives as it was elsewhere in the West, protection of the areas of settlement and routes of travel, in other words, control of the Indians.Widespread Indian hostilities did not occur until 1855–56. Hence, the development of a reservation system and a more widely dispersed pattern of permanent posts had not taken place in 1854. Of the posts inspected by Mansfield, Forts Orford and Lane were soon abandoned to be replaced by others more conveniently located for control of the Indians when they were induced to settle on reservations. Adequate protection for the Oregon Trail and for most of the area comprising the Territory of Washington was to be provided only as Indian activities required the erection of additional military posts.

As was true of New Mexico, the Department of the Pacific had been subjected to only one previous general inspection. It too had been carried out by Colonel McCall, who prepared a series of reports which dealt with each of the posts individually. All of the posts inspected by McCall in 1852 were still in existence in 1854, although the Redoubt of Monterey was no longer garrisoned. Three additional posts had been established, Forts Humboldt, Jones, and Lane, and a fourth, Fort Tejon, was in the process of establishment. Comparatively few of the recommendations made by McCall were repeated by Mansfield, even in those cases where they had not been carried out. This can be attributed to two things, the lack of major Indian difficulties in the Department of the Pacific between 1852 and 1854 and the fact that McCall's recommendations were limited chiefly to individual posts while Mansfield's major recommendations were for the department as a whole.

Although the cost of maintaining the posts in the Department of the Pacific was burdensome for the slim military budgets of the day, it was less a cause of concern than the expenses of the Department of New Mexico. Supplies of foodstuffs, fuel, and forage were more readily available locally on the Pacific, while other supplies were sent by sea from the East, a much less expensive mode of transportation than the wagon trains across the plains. Fort Yuma was the only post for which the cost of supply was excessive, with the resultant interest in the development of an all-water route to serve it. Though military policy in both departments had the same general objectives, the problems involved in carrying out the policy in New Mexico were greater. Even though there were fewer posts in New Mexico, there were more officers and men and much more Indian activity. For these reasons, perhaps, both McCall and Mansfield were less critical of the conduct of the Department of the Pacific and made fewer major recommendations in regard to it.[28]

Joseph King Fenno Mansfield, who conducted the inspections presented herein, was born on September 22, 1803, in New Haven, Connecticut. He graduated from the United States Military Academy in 1822, ranking second in his class. On July 1, 1822, he was commissioned a second lieutenant in the Corps of Engineers. Prior to the Mexican War he was engaged primarily in the construction of works for coastal defense. He served in the Mexican War as chief engineer under General Zachary Taylor. In this capacity he supervised the construction of Fort Brown, Texas. He was wounded in the campaign which resulted in the capture of Monterrey, Nuevo León, and later participated in the Battle of Buena Vista. He was three times breveted for his gallant and meritorious conduct. From 1848 to 1853, Mansfield

[28] See George A. McCall, "McCall's Inspection Report, Department of the Pacific, 1852," Records of the Office of the Adjutant General, Record Group 94, The National Archives, Washington, D.C.

was a member of the Army Board of Engineers, engaged in the planning of coastal defenses.

Early in 1853, in anticipation of the forthcoming change of departmental command, Colonel McCall was instructed to carry out a general inspection of Military Department No. 9. The intent was that McCall would conduct the inspection before Colonel (Brevet Brigadier General) John Garland arrived to replace Colonel Sumner. However, McCall submitted his resignation on April 22, 1853, thus making impossible an inspection prior to the change of command. Secretary of War Jefferson Davis, who had served with Mansfield under General Taylor in the Mexican War, appointed Mansfield to fill the vacancy created by McCall's resignation. Now with the rank of Colonel, Inspector General's Department, Mansfield inspected Military Department No. 9 in 1853, the Department of the Pacific in 1854, the Department of Texas in 1856, the Utah Army in 1857, the Department of California and the Department of Oregon in 1858–59, and the Department of Texas in 1860–61. Mansfield was still in Texas during the events leading up to the outbreak of the Civil War and the secession of Texas. He returned to Washington, D. C., where, on May 14, 1861, he was commissioned Brigadier General, United States Army. On July 18, 1862, he became a Major General, Volunteers. On September 17, 1862, Mansfield, then commanding the Twelfth Army Corps, was severely wounded in the Battle of Antietam. He died the following day.[29]

Mansfield's inspection reports cannot be termed models of composition, yet they contain much valuable detail regarding problems and conditions in the departments inspected. Though

[29] M. L. Crimmins, ed., "Colonel J. K. F. Mansfield's Report of the Inspection of the Department of Texas in 1856," *The Southwestern Historical Quarterly*, Vol. XLII (October, 1938), 122–24; Francis B. Heitman, *Historical Register and Dictionary of the United States Army, from its Organization, September 29, 1789, to March 2, 1903*, I, 688; and Robert M. Danford, ed., *Register of Graduates and Former Cadets, United States Military Academy*, 157.

they are concerned primarily with matters deemed to be of interest to the military, they also have much to say, even if indirectly, of the socio-economic conditions of civilian life. They are straightforward accounts, as inspection reports usually are, containing little that is deliberately imaginative or colorful. Nevertheless, here and there is a touch which would seem to indicate that Mansfield took pleasure in the performance of his duties. Invariably he found something of beauty in the setting of the more isolated posts, such as Forts Defiance, Yuma, and Dalles. Rarely does he fail to mention a snow-capped peak, whether on the horizon or near at hand. His private "digressions" into the mining districts of California give further evidence of a healthy curiosity about the region which he traversed. Mansfield's attitude toward the Indians, whether labeled wild, friendly, or civilized, reflects some understanding of their needs and sympathy with their plight. Mansfield is critical of certain characteristics of the Spanish-American population in New Mexico, notably of their lack of education, their prejudices, and their unsuitableness for military service. Here again, he avoids the wholesale condemnation of this segment of the population in which so many visitors from the "states," both military and civilian, indulged. If Mansfield's observations were not always accurate, they, at least, represent the opinions generally prevailing at the time. It must be remembered that the areas inspected had been in the hands of the United States for less than a decade and were still imperfectly known.

In editing the manuscript, certain deviations from the original have been employed throughout, always with due care to preserve the original meaning. The punctuation used by Mansfield is highly inconsistent, and his abbreviations are both numerous and varied. For clarity and improved readability, punctuation has been added or deleted and most abbreviated words have been spelled out. In a very few cases extraneous words have been omitted. Also in the interest of clarity, numbers have sometimes been spelled out or given as numerals, even though they appear differently in the manuscript. In Mansfield's writing it is not always possible to distinguish between upper and lower case letters; hence, no attempt has been made to adhere to the original capitalization. The manuscript is written on both sides of the pages. Unfortunately, the first page of the report of the inspection of Military Department No. 9 was lost or destroyed before it was deposited in the National Archives. In addition, corners of some pages in both reports have disappeared, but the missing words or parts of words are not difficult to determine and have been supplied in brackets.

In order to achieve satisfactory reproduction of Mansfield's original sketches of plans and localities of forts, it was necessary to print them separately from the text. They have therefore been grouped together in a section, which also includes a map, prepared especially for this volume, showing Mansfield's routes. I am indebted to the National Archives for the sketches from Mansfield's reports.

Robert W. Frazer

Wichita, Kansas
July 10, 1963

I

The Department of New Mexico

1853

New Mexico

. . . and turnips, barley, and oats have recently been introduced into the Territory by the Americans so called. The facilities for grazing herds and flocks [are] very great, and the sheep and wool of this Territory would be of immense value if secure against the depredations of the wild Indians. As it is, large droves and flocks of cattle and sheep are annually driven over the mountains to California at great profit. The climate of this Territory is unsurpassed as to healthiness, and it would seem that this Territory only wanted facility of communication with the States to bring all its resources into account. Such communication can be effected readily by a rail road from the western part of the state of Missouri to Santa Fé, and from the southern part of Texas (say, San Antonio) to El Paso. Over either route there can be no possible obstacle to laying one of the cheapest roads in the United States. The level prairie and table lands extend for miles as far as the eye can see; and the distances that now take days to overcome, with the iron horse would be passed over in as many hours. Travellers would with these roads enter New Mexico in the fall via the northern road and in the spring return via the southern.

The advantages of these rail road communications would not be confined to this Territory. Once in New Mexico at Albuquerque, for instance, about half the distance to California is accomplished. Thence a westerly course [is] followed, it is believed, without difficulty by a wag[on or] rail road constituting

[3]

one grand trunk that would [join] the northern and southern branches via Santa Fé and El [Paso,] and goods shipped to Galveston and Indianola in T[exas] would meet other articles from the west of M[issouri] and the upper Mississippi, and travel together [to the] Pacific Coast.

The true boundary of New Mexico where it joins the state of Texas on the east and south, has not been defined by monuments. This subject was brought to my attention by Judge Joel L. Ankrim, who resides at San Elizario in the county of El Paso, Texas. He represents the difficulty of administering justice within certain limits for want of these land marks and informed me that the state of Texas had authorized the Governor to appoint proper agents on the part of the state, to meet corresponding agents on the part of the United States whenever the U.S. shall notify to that effect.[1] It seems to me [that] in a place like this there should be no obstacles to the administration of justice and that the southern boundary of New Mexico as it borders on the county of El Paso in Texas should be run and marked at once. The eastern

---

[1] El Paso County was created in 1849. It included all of the area between the Rio Grande and the Pecos River, south of a line running due east from a point on the Rio Grande twenty miles north of San Diego. San Diego, the point where the wagon road laid out by Major Philip St. George Cooke, Second U. S. Dragoons, in 1846, left the river and headed west, was some fifteen miles above Doña Ana. Hence, El Paso County, as originally established, included a considerable area which lies in the present New Mexico. See William C. Binkley, "The Question of Texan Jurisdiction in New Mexico Under the United States, 1848–1850," *Southwestern Historical Quarterly*, Vol. XXVI (July, 1920), 23. On February 11, 1854, the Texas state legislature approved an act appropriating ten thousand dollars and making other provisions for "running and marking the boundary line between the State of Texas and the Territories of the United States, from the point where it leaves the Red River to the point where it intersects the Rio Grande. . . ." The act was made contingent upon the enactment of suitable legislation by the United States Congress. *Boundary Between Texas and the Territories*, 33 Cong., 2 sess., *House Exec. Doc. 89*, pp. 2–3. Not until June 5, 1858, did the United States Congress provide the necessary legislation to permit the boundary survey.

boundary probably will run through the wild Indian country and may not now be readily established by land marks.

This Territory is inhabited by two distinct races of people besides the American. The most civilized of the two is the Mexican, who speaks the Spanish language, being a cross with the Spanish and Indian, and this class is the most numerous being about fifty thousand souls.[2] They are located almost entirely along the valley of the Rio Grande del Norté where they [obta]in a subsistence by planting the bottom lands of the [river] and by raising stock

[2] In 1844, General Mariano Martínez de Lejanza, then Governor of the Department of New Mexico, placed the population, including Pueblo Indians, at 100,064. "Report of Lieut. J. W. Abert, of His Examination of New Mexico, in the Years 1846–'47," in 30 Cong., 1 sess., *House Exec. Doc. 41*, pp. 477–79. Major George A. McCall, when he inspected the Department of New Mexico in 1850, believed Martínez' figure to be too high. In his opinion, not more than 1,200 Mexicans had withdrawn from the territory following its cession to the United States. He considered the population little more than enough "to give one seat in the House of Representatives of the United States." He estimated the number of persons of United States or European birth who had become citizens of New Mexico at 1,200, and the number of Pueblo Indians at more than 10,000. The number of wild Indians he estimated at 47,600, including, however, some Indians in areas not within the limits of the Territory of New Mexico as it was organized later in the year, and excluding some which did fall within its jurisdiction. McCall to Crawford, July 15, 1850, in 31 Cong., 2 sess., *Sen. Exec. Doc. 26*, pp. 2–3, 16. Charles Bent, in 1846, had estimated the population of the same wild tribes as 36,950. Bent to William Medill (commissioner of Indian affairs), November 10, 1846, in 31 Cong., 1 sess., *House Exec. Doc. 17*, p. 193. The census of 1850 recorded for New Mexico a population of 61,574, including 7,867 Pueblo Indians. The Hopi pueblos were not included nor were the so-called wild Indians, their combined number being estimated at 45,000. James S. Calhoun, Superintendent of Indian Affairs in New Mexico and later first territorial governor, wrote on February 16, 1851, that the population of New Mexico had decreased during the past year. Further, excluding the military, he believed there were fewer than 300 persons from the United States in the territory. Calhoun to Luke Lee (commissioner of Indian affairs), in Abel, ed., *The Official Correspondence of James S. Calhoun*, 294. The Indian population of New Mexico in 1853 was estimated to be 45,000. J. D. B. DeBow, *Statistical View of the United States*, 191. The Census of 1860, however, increased the estimate to 55,000. Joseph C. G. Kennedy, *Preliminary Report on the Eighth Census: 1860*, 37 Cong., 2 sess., *Sen. Doc.*, 136.

such as mules, cattle, sheep, and goats [which] the extensive table lands and mountains that are worth [less] for any other purpose, enable them to do by the abundance [of graz]ing they afford— but few horses or hogs are raised. [These people] as a body are ignorant, and as a community jealous, [and t]heir priests look on American missionaries and school masters with distrust. There are not more than two schools in the whole Territory of a population of fifty thousand Mexicans. One of these is organized by the Catholic bishop[3] for the children of the most influential persons, and the other is kept by the Reverend Henry Smith, a Baptist missionary, who has 12 or 14 scholars, the children of American fathers and Mexican mothers; and both [are] located in Santa Fé. Only one Protestant church is organized in the whole Territory, and that a Baptist,[4] in Santa Fé under the charge of the Reverend Henry Smith—but very few people attend this, as the Mexican race know little or nothing of the Bible, and the American population in the Territory are few. There probably are not over six females from the States in Santa Fé.

The impressions I have formed in relation to this population are such, that I think I can safely say, that no reliance whatever can be placed on them as militia to defend the Territory in a war with Mexico, the only nation from their locality they can be brought in contact with. Their peculiar location however, bounded on the east, west, and north by the American race and Indian tribes, precludes their ever undertaking the hopeless task

[3] Jean B. Lamy, the first Bishop (and later the first Archbishop) of Santa Fe.

[4] Smith, whose first name was Louis rather than Henry, had been sent to New Mexico by the Baptist Board of Home Missions in 1851. The first Baptist minister in New Mexico was the Reverend Henry W. Read, who arrived in Santa Fe in July, 1849. He opened a school in which English was taught and which the Reverend Louis Smith continued. In 1853, Read was minister in Albuquerque. The first Baptist church, which was also the first Protestant church in New Mexico, was dedicated in Santa Fe on January 15, 1854. See W. W. H. Davis, *El Gringo: or New Mexico and Her People*, 238, 270; and Ralph Emerson Twitchell, *The Leading Facts of New Mexican History*, II, 350.

of aiding Mexico in any war that may at any future day have place with that country. They are not warlike and are incapable of defending their property against the Indians as a general thing.

The next race are the civilized Indians, known as Pueb[los], the original occupants of the soil, when the Mexican race ca[me] among them. They number about ten thousand souls in twenty-eight vill[ages][5] located mostly in the valley of the Rio Grande del Norté [and] scattered from the extreme north to the extreme south [and] the extreme west of the habitable parts of New Mex[ico and], although incorporated with the Mexicans, speak [seven] languages as follow: the Pueblos of Zuñi & Jemis, one language of the seven; [those of the] Moquis villages, one language; of Taos, Picuris, Sandia, [and] Isleta, one language; of San Juan, Santa Clara, San Ildefonso, Pujuaqui, Tesuque, and Nambe, one language; of Santo Domingo, San Felipe, Cochité, Santa Anna, Cilla,[6] Laguna, Acoma, and Lentis,[7] one language;

[5] There were twenty-eight pueblos, though not exactly as Mansfield listed them. There were the seven Hopi (Moqui) pueblos in the present Arizona (Mansfield apparently allowed for only six), the two pueblos on the Rio Grande in Texas, and nineteen pueblos in the present New Mexico. (Mansfield lists a twentieth. See note 7 on this page.) All are still in existence except the two pueblos in Texas, which are now simply towns, and Pojoaqui, which became extinct in 1922. See Edgar Lee Hewett, *Ancient Life in the American Southwest*, 76–93. Calhoun was instructed to take an accurate census of the pueblos but found it impossible. In lieu of this he estimated the population, excluding the Hopi pueblos, at not less than 12,000 and possibly as much as 15,000. Calhoun to Medill, October 15, 1849, in 31 Cong., 1 sess., *House Exec. Doc. 17*, p. 223. Abbé Domenech, who was in New Mexico a few years later, gives a population of 16,000 for the New Mexico pueblos and 7,000 for the Hopi, but these figures would seem to be too high. *Seven Years' Residence in the Great Deserts of North America*, I, 186.

[6] The name of this pueblo is usually given as Zia or Sia and sometimes Cia. Hewett renders the Indian name as Tsi-ya. *Ancient Life in the American Southwest*, 88. In Hodge it appears as Tsia. Frederick W. Hodge, ed., *Handbook of American Indians North of Mexico*, II, 562.

[7] Lentis, though sometimes referred to as a pueblo, was probably a village established for the benefit of *genízaros*. It was located on the right bank of the Rio Grande,

of Islata [Isleta del Sur; Isleta, Texas], and Socorro,[8] one language. They obtain a subsistence by planting the bottom lands and by raising stock like the Mexicans. As good wheat, corn, onions, pumpkins, and fruit are raised by these people as by the Mexicans. Like the Mexicans, they have no schools except one established by the Reverend Mr. Gorman,[9] a Baptist missionary at Laguna, and as a matter of course are extremely ignorant and primitive in all their ways. No reliance what ever can be placed on this class of the population for national defence as militia, or even against the wild Indians. Yet they are free from the prejudices against the Americans that the Mexicans possess and being naturally acute and quick of comprehension, might be made a very reliable population in a few years by proper means by the Government, and philanthropy should prompt the Government

---

about a mile and a half above Los Lunas. Hodge, ed., *Handbook of American Indians*, I, 764; and "Report of Lieutenant J. W. Abert," 30 Cong., 1 sess., *House Exec. Doc.* 41, p. 480. Calhoun, in July, 1849, listed Lentis as a pueblo but three months later, in another listing of pueblos, omitted it. Calhoun to Orlando Brown (commissioner of Indian affairs), July 1, 1849, in Abel, ed., *The Official Correspondence of James S. Calhoun*, 177; and Calhoun to Medill, October 4, 1849, in 31 Cong., 1 sess., *House Exec. Doc. 17*, p. 211. Mansfield, obviously, did not obtain his information regarding the pueblos by personal observation, though he undoubtedly visited some of them.

[8] Isleta del Sur and Socorro, sometimes called Socorro del Sur, were located on the Rio Grande in Texas, below the present El Paso. Both were established after the Pueblo Revolt of 1680. They exist today as towns, but are no longer Indian.

[9] Samuel Gorman came to New Mexico in 1852, arriving at Laguna on October 5. He remained in Laguna until February, 1859, when he moved to Santa Fe. In Santa Fe he conducted a school and served as minister until April, 1862, when he left New Mexico to return to the East. Mrs. Samuel Gorman, "Samuel Gorman," *Old Santa Fe*, Vol. I (January, 1914), 308–31. Apparently Gorman was both popular and reasonably successful in his work at Laguna. Davis wrote in this respect, "They have elected him a member of their community, with all the right and privileges of a full-born Indian. He sits with them in the *estufa* in council when affairs of state are discussed, and preaches to them on the Sabbath in the village church, and, upon the whole, he is exercising a good influence over this simple-minded people." *El Gringo*, 393.

to improve their condition if practicable. And here I would recommend that Government send into each of the above named villages a sound moral man with his family—a mechanic with tools would be preferable—and let [it] be his business to teach these people the English language [not] by reading and writing, but by learning them the English [na]mes of every thing about them and also teach them the [mec]hanic and useful arts, and in process of time finally [stamp] out the Indian languages entirely by the substitu[tion of] the English. Mr. Gorman with his family at [Laguna] is effecting a great reformation by the small means afforded by the Baptist Society and should be aided by useful tools and a small amount of funds furnished by the Government.

Of this race there are the wild or uncivilized Indians who live in lodges and move about the Territory in tribes and bands, and as a matter of course at times when in want of food in the absence of game, commit depredations on all the rest of the population. These Indians are often highwaymen who murder small parties, when found in their power, to obtain their animals and supplies. In large bands they cross over to the Mexican Territory and rob the people near Chihuahua of droves of cattle, and mules, and horses &c. In short by their nomadic habits [they] are a great evil to the country and a constant drawback to the industrious population, and have almost destroyed the grazing interests by their attacks on hurds men and [their] seizing of the herds. If these Indians could be induced to settle down and build permanent villages and plant and have a permanent interest in a locality, there would be no further trouble with them, as in such cases, they could always be reached by a military force; whereas now it is very difficult to punish their aggressions, and under their present roving and thieving habits they are destined to be finally exterminated by the sword as an inevitable consequence. This is an unhappy prospect in view for them, and if practicable should be averted by the philanthroply [*sic*] our Government can extend to the wild man and the original possessor of the soil. It seems to me that the Indian Agents could aid immeasurably the cause of civilizing these Indians by gathering the [old] and infirm into villages where the land can be cu[ltiva]ted. Such a locality for instance as Fort Webster on the [Mimbres] with the aid of a small amount of funds to assist them in building houses and paying the young for planting the fields of the old would gradually bring them into industrious habits and to the supply of their wants by planting and raising domestic animals in preference to the laborious and uncertain life of the hunter. Certainly this plan would bring the aged and the very young to the influences of such a method as a nucleous which would be a great point gained. With such asylums in the country offering reward for labour among them, they would soon acknowledge the benefits of industry over the risk of life in committing depredations on the other races and the uncertainty of hunting.

These wild Indians are known by different names, and seem to have a claim among themselves to different ranges of country for hunting. There are the Chayons and Arrapahoes on the Arkansas River, of about 500 warriors; the Comanches on the Cimarron, of about 1,000 warriors; the Utahs, who occupy the country from Taos north and west of the Rio Grande del Norté under different specific or local names to the Grande River,[10] of about 500 warriors; the Hickeray[11] Apaches, who occupy the country from Santa Fé to Taos, of about 100 warriors; the Navahoes, who occupy the country west of the Rio Grande del Norté and south of the Utahs to the dividing lands between the sources of the little Colorado and the Gila, of about 1,000 warriors; [and] the

[10] The Grand River is the name formerly given the Colorado above its junction with the Green. The name is perpetuated in the Grand River Valley and Grand County, Utah.

[11] Jicarilla. In discussing Cantonment Burgwin (see p. 17) Mansfield places the number of Jicarilla Apache warriors at about 150.

Apaches, who occupy the region of the Copper mines and the Gila and stretch eastward across the Rio Grande del Norté and occupy the country east of that river to the White and Sacramento [mountains] and to the northward under dif[feren]t specific local names, of about 1,000 warriors. Thus shewing [bands] of warriors scattered over New Mexico to the num[ber of 4,1]00[12] and upwards, constituting a population say of 6,000 souls dependent for support on hunting and fishing and plunder.[13]

The American race so called in this Territory is quite limited and merely nominal besides the troops that occupy the several posts—there is but little to invite the American here—but little is done at mining, and trade is quite limited; and the labour of cultivating lands that are inferior to lands in the States and the great distance from a profitable market preclude the settlement of Americans. It is quite probable however that the facility of a rail road communication would lead to a more complete exam-

[12] The corner of the manuscript containing the first two numbers has been destroyed; however, the number of warriors listed by Mansfield in the paragraph totals 4,100.

[13] Mansfield's figures for the number of warriors are appreciably smaller than the estimates of McCall, Calhoun, and Bent for the same groups. The figure six thousand for the total population of these groups is incomprehensible. John Russell Bartlett, who was greatly interested in the Indians, believed that there were fewer than twelve thousand Comanches and not more than five thousand Apaches, and he had traveled through much of the Apache country in his capacity as commissioner for the United States-Mexican boundary survey in the years 1851–53. Bartlett, *Personal Narrative of Explorations and Incidents in Texas, New Mexico, California, Sonora, and Chihuahua, Connected with the United States and Mexican Boundary Commission during the Years 1850, '51, '52, and '53*, II, 386–87. The difficulty of arriving at a reasonable population for even the friendly Indians was considerable. Lieutenant Colonel Philip St. George Cooke, who, with the Mormon Battalion, passed through the Pima and Maricopa villages in November, 1846, estimated the number of these Indians as "15 or 20,000." "Report of Lieutenant Colonel P. St. George Cooke of His March from Santa Fé, New Mexico, to San Diego, Upper California," 30 Cong., 1 sess, *House Exec. Doc. 41*, p. 561. Yet Captain Abraham R. Johnston, who was with Cooke, said that the Pimas and Maricopas "number over 2,000 souls." "Journal of Captain A. R. Johnston, First Dragoons," *ibid.*, 599.

ination of the mineral lands and to the discovery of valuable gold and silver mines, of which there are great indications. Such discoveries in a short time would change the character of its population and lead to immediate changes in the moral and political condition of this Territory. As it is, I doubt if that population will think serioulyy [*sic*] of taxing themselves to support a state Government for many years to come. At present a valuable trade is carried on through the county of El Paso Texas with the Mexicans in Chihuahua and Sonora & c, that will in due time lead to the occupancy of all the bottom lands of the Rio Grande del Norté from El Paso about one hundred miles down the river, provided the Government afford suitable protection against the Indians by the establishment of posts at convenient distances.

The bottom lands of the Mesilla Valley directly opposite Fort Fillmore, and about forty-five miles above El Paso on the Rio Grande del Norté, comprising about thirty square miles, have latterly been occupied by the Mexicans, although the village was laid out by Major E. Steen[14] of the U.S. Dragoon, and a flourishing population of about three thousands souls produce [*sic*] as good crops as are to be found in New Mexico. A map of these lands is hereunto appended marked A [No. 1, Plans and Sketches

[14] For brief biographies of the military personnel mentioned herein see p. 198. The Mesilla Valley was settled in 1848 by Mexicans and a few United States citizens. Many Mexicans from the nearby portions of New Mexico and Texas, unwilling to remain under United States rule, moved to the Mesilla Valley, more than half of the population of Doña Ana doing so within a year. In October, 1852, the population of the valley was estimated at one thousand nine hundred. Probably not more than twenty United States citizens, all of them traders, had settled there. Bartlett, *Personal Narrative*, II, 391. Mansfield places the population of the town of Mesilla alone at three thousand. W. W. H. Davis, however, wrote, "The glowing accounts that have been written about the beauty and fertility of La Mesilla are not sustained by the reality, and were gotten up by those who were entirely ignorant of of the subject. The population is much less than represented. . . . at the highest estimate, not more than about twenty-five hundred." *El Gringo*, 385–86. The Mesilla Valley passed into the hands of the United States as a result of the Gadsden Purchase treaty, the ratifications of which were exchanged in Washington on June 30, 1854.

section]. There are other bottom lands capable of cultivation and will be occupied as soon as the country is secure against the depredations of the Indians.

I have thus given the character of the country and population generally with a view to consider the location of the military posts and their strength; and in order to [gain] a full understanding of these, a more particular account of the Indian tribes seems necessary in connection. Santa Fé, the capitol of New Mexico, is about 800 miles from Independence. To reach this place the road crosses the great plains and via Fort Atkinson[15] on the Arkansas River, and the Cimarron River and Fort Union, which is about 700 miles from Independence. Along this route the mail and traveller are exposed to the exactions, depredations, and attacks of the Arrapahoe Indians, who number about 275 warriors; the Cheyenne and Kiowa Indians, who number about 400 warriors on the Arkansas River; and Comanche Indians on the Cimarron River, who number about 1,000 warriors. From Fort Leavenworth to Council Grove is 118 miles; thence to Fort Atkinson, 165 miles without a single settlement; thence to Fort Union, 325 miles; and thence to Santa Fé, about 100 miles. At Fort Union the settlements in the bottom lands commence on the Moro River.

Fort Union is situated at the foot of the Mesa opposite Gallinas Mountain on the west side of a valley stretching nearly north and south say thirty-five miles. About seven miles to the southward is Barclay's Fort[16] on the Moro River, where the old road to

[15] Fort Atkinson was located west of the present Dodge City, Kansas, on Walnut Creek. The original post was moved to this site in June, 1851. It was abandoned in the summer of 1853, temporarily reoccupied in the summer of 1854, and finally abandoned on October 2, 1854.

[16] Barclay's Fort was built in 1849 by Alexander Barclay, an Englishman, at the present town of Watrous. It was both a trading post and a defensive position. Colonel McCall described Barclay's Fort at the time of his inspection of the department in

Santa Fé crosses the valley. About fifteen miles to the northward the road from the Valley of Moro crosses this valley, and five miles farther is Ocaté Creek, and three miles further still in a "Cañon" of the mountain is the farm attached to this post. This valley is well adapted to grazing, and large quantities of hay are annually cut on the Ocaté for the public animals. This post is now directly on the shortest road to Santa Fé. A change having been effected through the exertions and reconnaissance of Major J. H. Carleton, U.S. Dragoons, to open the road to the northward of Wagon Mound and Gallinas Mountain, thereby saving in distance about thirteen miles—and by the exertions of Major E. S. Sibley, U.S. Quartermaster, to open the road from the post to Las Vegas direct thereby saving several miles in distance westward. Thus situated, it is well located for a depot for the supply of the northern posts direct to Burgwin and Fort Massachusetts through the Valley of Taos, and to Santa Fé and Albuquerque either via Burgwin or Las Vegas. It is well adapted for keeping beef cattle and supernumerary dragoon horses and mules & c & c.

1850, apparently because some thought had been given to acquiring it for use as a military post.

Barclay's trading house, or fort as it is called, situated at the point where the Bent's-fort road & the Cimaron road come together, & 18 miles from Vegas, has been much extolled as an advantageous position, both for the location of a depôt & the establishment of a Military Post. But there are undoubtedly objections to this position, which should not pass unnoticed. . . .

Of this fort the outer walls are a square of 64 yards, with some circular bastions or towers at two opposite angles. Against the N. wall is a range of two-story buildings—against the S. wall, one of one-story. Detached from the E. & W. walls are one-story buildings, & between these and the walls are sheds for horses. The buildings, either for quarters or for store houses are one room deep, about 15 feet in the clear. The whole structure is of *adobe*, with roofs of the same. Mr. Barclay demands $20,000 for the fort together with 700 *varas* of land fronting on the water (the Mora) & extending back to the hills—would probably take $15,000. The rent he fixes at $2,000 per annum.

"Report of Troops and Staff Department at Las Vegas," September 13, 1850, in "McCall's Inspection Report, Department of New Mexico, 1850."

[14]

The supplies of flour, corn and hay and fuel are obtained from the neighbouring valleys as conveniently as at other posts in New Mexico and on reasonable terms. The buildings of all kinds are as good as at any post and there seems to be enough of them to satisfy the demands of the service. It is important however that a good wagon road be opened to cross the Moro Mountain directly to Burgwin about twelve miles south of Don Fernandes de Taos, and a distance of about fifty miles. For this object I would recommend an appropriation of 2,000 dollars. For a sketch of this valley and a plan of this post see C and D hereunto appended [Nos. 2 and 3, Plans and Sketches section].

This post is established on a reservation of eight miles square and like the farm is claimed by citizens. It was commenced in 1851[17] by Brevet Lieutenant Colonel E. B. Alexander of the 8h Infantry and continued successively by Brevet Major J. H. Carleton, 1t Dragoons, and Major G. Morris of the 3rd Infantry and Brevet Lieutenant Colonel H. Brooks, 2d Artillery. It is too close under the Mesa for a tenable position against an enterprising enemy, unless the immediate heights can be occupied by a block house which could readily be done. It seems to have been selected on account of a good spring of water and will undoubtedly answer a very good purpose and should be retained.

This locality like that of the Moro Valley and the sources of the Pecos River is exposed to the depredations of the Hickeray Apache and the Utah Indians who frequently are quite annoying and troublesome.

Cantonment Burgwin[18] is located on the Rio Grande,[19] an

[17] Fort Union was established July 6, 1851. It was abandoned in 1891.

[18] Cantonment Burgwin was established August 14, 1852. It was named for Captain John H. K. Burgwin, First U. S. Dragoons, killed in the Taos uprising of 1847. The post was abandond on May 18, 1860.

[19] The Rio Grande de Ranchos, which flows north into the Rio Taos. The cantonment, which has been reconstructed, was located approximately at the mouth of the Rio de la Olla. The site may be reached by New Mexico State Highway 3. Geo-

eastern tributary of the Rio Grande del Norté and about twelve miles from the latter in the Valley of Taos and about twelve miles southward of Don Fernandes de Taos, on the only wagon road to Santa Fé. It lays about fifty miles west of Fort Union which is separated from it by the Moro Mountain and the Moro River with its beautiful and fertile valley of about four thousand population, where wheat, corn, and beans grow luxuriently.

From this point, troops can move directly to Fort Union, Fort Massachusetts, Fort Marcy at Santa Fé, and west to Abiquiu, and supplies of wheat, corn, beans, fuel &c [are] convenient and abundant at reasonable rates. Further, it is on the only wagon road from Taos to Santa Fé, and about twelve miles from Sienega, the crossing of the Rio Grande del Norté at Taos,[20] a more northern crossing being about forty miles further up the river.[21] The river in this distance runs at the bottom of a very deep cañon with precipitous and impassible sides except at half a dozen places where mules have crossed it. Hence it is well located to intercept the passage by Indians of the Rio Grande del Norté

graphical nomenclature, including spelling, is taken from the most recent Geological Survey Maps of the United States, scale 1:250,000 (United States Geological Survey, Washington, D.C.), unless otherwise noted.

[20] The ford of Cienega was near the point where the New Mexico State Highway 96 bridges the Rio Grande today, more nearly opposite Ranchos de Taos than Taos. The ford, more commonly called Cieneguilla, was a little below the mouth of the Taos River while the present bridge is a little above. See "A Map of the Territory of New Mexico," compiled by Brevet Second Lieutenant John G. Parke, Topographical Engineers (1851); and "A Map of the Territories of New Mexico and Arizona," prepared in the Office of the Chief of Engineers, U.S.A. (1879).

[21] Mansfield did not himself visit the more northerly ford, hence his figure of "about forty miles" is simply an approximation. It does indicate that the first commonly used ford north of Taos was in the vicinity of the present Colorado state line. As late as the early years of the present century, there was a crossing place on the Rio Grande just above the mouth of the Costilla River. It fell into disuse when the Stateline Bridge was built about the year 1910. Information provided by Professor William Meyer and Professor Emeritus Luther Bean, Adams State College of Colorado, Alamosa.

in the Valley of Taos. The Indians that occupy the Taos mountains and extend down to Santa Fé are the Hickeray Apaches who number about 150 warriors. This valley however is also exposed to the depredations of the Utahs, who occupy the country from Taos to the Grande River and the Salt Lakes and can bring into the field in one week about 500 warriors, and are warlike. The tillable lands in the Valley of Taos, that are irrigated by four small streams issuing from the mountains, extend north and south about ten miles and will average about eight miles in breadth, thus affording abundant crops for the population which numbers about 7,000 souls. Under such views of this post, I can speak favourably of it, and believe the location a good one, and should not be dispensed with. For a plan of this post see E hereunto appended [No. 4, Plans and Sketches section]. The post was planned and the buildings put up under the direction and command of Lieutenant Robert Ransom, Jr., U.S. 1t Dragoons; and for its size, being calculated for a company of dragoons, deserves commendation as well adapted to the service. The wagon road to Santa Fé from this post over the mountain to La Joya[22] is precipitous and impassible for loaded wagons, and requires an appropriation by Congress of 4,000 dollars.

Fort Massachusetts[23] is situated in latitude 37° 30' north, in the Valley of San Louis, eight thousand feet above the sea, and about ten or fifteen miles east of the Cañon of the Rio Grande del Norté, and directly north of the Valley of Taos—say one hundred five miles from Burgwin and ninety-two miles from Don Fernandes de Taos. It is seated at the foot of the White Moun-

[22] La Joya is the present town of Velarde.

[23] Fort Massachusetts was established on June 22, 1852. It was located in the present Colorado and was the northernmost post in the Department of New Mexico. It was abandoned in 1858 when it was replaced by Fort Garland, located about six miles to the south. Mansfield underestimated the distance from the Rio Grande, which has not yet descended into a cañon at its nearest approach to Fort Massachusetts. It was about twenty-three miles from the post.

tain,[24] which is perpetually snow topped, and on Utah Creek at the mouth of a ravene out of which the creek flows, a cool limpid stream. There is abundance of wood, and in summer the grazing is good; but the warm season is short, and it is doubtful if corn will ripen here. The nearest settlement is thirty miles to the southward on the Coulubre River where there are about 25 families engaged in planting of corn and wheat. The next settlements south are as follow: on the Costille River eighteen miles further, about 25 families; on the Colerado River seventeen miles further, about 50 families; at San Cristobal thirteen miles further, about 12 families; on the Rio Hondo four miles further, about 80 families. At all of which corn, wheat, beans &c grow. Thence twelve miles to Don Fernandes de Taos. The road throughout the whole distance is from three to ten miles from the Rio Grande del Norté, and the rivers crossed run westward to that river. This road is good and passible for loaded wagons, with the exception of six steep and difficult hills between the rivers Colerado and Hondo which will require an appropriation by Congress of 6,000 dollars.[25]

The design of this post was to keep the Utah Indians in check and it is calculated for dragoons and infantry. It was commenced in June, 1852, and built under the direction and command of

[24] On present maps this appears as Blanca Peak. It rises to an altitude of 14,363 feet, immediately to the west of the site of Fort Massachusetts. Ute Creek flows south between Blanca Creek and Buck Mountain.

[25] The route described by Mansfield is approximately that followed by Colorado State Highway 159 and New Mexico State Highway 3 between Fort Garland and Taos. The first settlement mentioned, on the Culebra River (Creek), was the farming community established in 1851 in the vicinity of the present town of San Luis. The settlement on the Costilla River is the town of Costilla, just south of the Colorado line. The settlement on the Colorado (Red) River is the present Questa. San Cristobal is on San Cristobal Creek, about a mile east of the modern highway. The settlement on the Rio Hondo is the present Arroyo Hondo. The total distance given by Mansfield is nine miles more than the present distance by highway, allowing six miles from Fort Garland to Fort Massachusetts.

Major George A. H. Blake, U.S. 1t Dragoons, and the buildings are good and suitable as well as abundant. They are however placed too near the spur of the mountain for a good defense against an enterprising enemy. All supplies for this post come from the settlements at the south as far as Taos Valley and Fort Union, which may be called 165 miles distant. In winter the snow falls here to the depth of four feet.

My impressions are that this post would have been better located on the Calubre River, the most northern settlement in New Mexico, where access could be had to the troops by the population of the valley, without the hazard of being cut off by the Indians. The home of the Utah Indians is here, and particularly on the west of the Rio Grande del Norté. A post therefore is necessary in this quarter, and this valley may before long be a good route of communicating with the States in the summer season, and it probably is the best route of communicating between New Mexico and the Great Salt Lake and Northern California. For a plan of this post see F hereunto appended [No. 5, Plans and Sketches section].

Fort Marcy[26] is the only real fort in the Territory and is located at Santa Fé, and is seated on a spur of the mountain one-fourth of a mile long and about one thousand yards to the north east of the plaza, and commands the city perfectly. It is well planned and provided with a magazine, and its entrance is commanded by a block house within musket range. See plan hereunto appended marked G [No. 6, Plans and Sketches section]. The troops do not occupy this fort, but it can be occupied by the troops at short notice. It has the disadvantage of no water, but its guns will readily supply that deficiency and control a city of about four thousand population, mostly of the Mexican race. Fort Marcy is accessible from Fort Union by two routes: the most

[26] Fort Marcy, named for Secretary of War William L. Marcy, was established on August 23, 1846, by Brigadier General Stephen Watts Kearny. It was abandoned on October 10, 1894.

direct via the sources of the Pecos and Las Vegas and may be called one hundred miles, and the other via Cantonment Burgwin which is seventy-five miles and thence over the Moro Mountain fifty miles. I have already referred to the necessity of an appropriation for the road over the mountain from La Joya to Burgwin and from Burgwin to Fort Union. The other road via Las Vegas also requires an appropriation of about 2,000 dollars to make it suitable for military purposes and supplies. The communication of this fort with Albuquerque is good by two routes. The troops that occupy this post live in the public buildings in Santa Fé, and, as this is the seat of government in the Territory, seems indispensable to preserve order and sustain the authorities in cases of domestic excitements, and are conveniently placed here to undertake any expedition against the Indians, although there are no troublesome Indians near this place. I look upon this post as desirable and should not be abandoned.

Albuquerque[27] is about 65 miles south of Santa Fé on the Rio Grande del Norté. It is the head quarters of the commanding general of this department and well located therefor. At this

[27] The Post of Albuquerque was established on November 17, 1846. Troops were withdrawn for about a year, 1851–52. When regarrisoned it became department headquarters on August 31, 1852. It was discontinued on August 23, 1867.

Albuquerque in 1853, according to Heinrich Balduin Möllhausen, had a population of between seven and eight hundred, and has "a rather ruinous aspect." All of the buildings of the town, including the barracks and stables of the garrison, were built of adobe with earthen floors. Möllhausen was in Albuquerque from October 3 to November 8, 1853, with the expedition commanded by First Lieutenant Amiel W. Whipple, Topographical Engineers, engaged in the survey of a Pacific railroad route along the thirty-fifth parallel. A portion of Whipple's party, which numbered seventy at the time, was quartered in the town while the rest encamped on its outskirts. Möllhausen himself was provided with a room in the home of Major Surgeon Eugene H. Abadie. Balduin Möllhausen, *Diary of a Journey from the Mississippi to the Coast of the Pacific with a United States Government Expedition*, II, 7–10. The Abbé Domenech, who visited the town a few years later, placed the population, including the native rancheros, at 2,500. *Seven Years' Residence*, I, 202. Davis said that the population in 1854 was not more than 1,500. *El Gringo*, 353.

place communication is had directly with Fort Union, 135 miles; Santa Fé, 65 miles; Fort Defiance, 200 miles; and other posts south: and here news of the doings of the Apache Indians on the east and Navahoes on the west are readily obtained. The troop [*sic*] here are quartered in hired buildings of the usual style in this Territory. This post therefore should be retained and is probably well selected and is suitable for a second depot for the supply of the posts south and last [west]. At this place the road comes in from Fort Defiance and San Francisco via Zuñi.

Fort Defiance[28] is located in the middle of the Navahoe Indian country which is about 150 miles square, and is about 200 miles west of the Rio Grande del Norté, and of Albuquerque, and in latitude 35° 44′ north and longitude 109° 25′ and is seated at the eastern entrance of the Cañon Cito in a beautiful valley about 55 miles north of Zuñi, and so far west that the waters of the neighbourhood flow into the Pacific. It was commenced by Major E. Backus commanding in September, 1851, who put up about six-tenths of the building before he relinquished command in August, 1852, when Brevet Lieutenant Colonel Joseph H. Eaton was left in command until 8h September, 1852, when the work was continued to the present time under the command of Brevet Major H. J. Kendrick who put up about four-tenths of the buildings. The buildings are good and mostly of logs and mud, but some good stone store houses have recently been completed. The grazing in this locality is excellent and hay and wood abundant, and the soil affords good garden produce, and the seasons favorable to corn, wheat, beans, cabbages, turnips, potatoes &c &c, and the Indians bring in peaches abundantly. The post has the disadvantage of being commanded within musketry range by a

[28] Fort Defiance was established on September 18, 1851. It was located west of Black Creek near the mouth of Quartzite Canyon in the present Arizona, immediately west of the New Mexico line. It was abandoned as a military post on April 25, 1861.

rocky ridge on the east; but this evil can readily be remidied [*sic*] by the erection on the ridge of two small block houses.[29] This is the most beautiful and interesting post as a whole in New Mexico. There are two roads leading from it to Albuquerque— one via the Pueblos of Zuñi, which is 35 miles the longest and in the aggregate 200 miles, and the other via Bear Creek,[30] which was adopted and made under the direction of Brevet Major Kendrick. This road however requires an appropriation of 1,000 dollars to make it a suitable military road at all seasons. They both unite at the River Gallo[31] and thence through Corvero,[32] a

[29] In 1858 a blockhouse was completed on the hill east of the post, prior to the beginning of the campaign against the Navaho in the fall of that year. Lieutenant Colonel Dixon S. Miles to Major William A. Nichols (assistant quartermaster general, Santa Fe), September 8, 1858, in 35 Cong., 2 sess., *House Exec. Doc. 2*, II, p. 309.

[30] Bear Creek, though it does not appear on maps of the period nor on current Geological Survey maps, was probably the stream flowing north from Ojo del Oso, near Fort Wingate, into the Rio Puerco of the West. Both of the routes from Fort Defiance described by Mansfield are shown on "Map No. 2. Reconnaissance and Survey of a Railway Route from Mississippi River near 35th Parallel North Lat to Pacific Ocean," by Lieutenant A. W. Whipple, in *Report of the Secretary of War Communicating the Several Railroad Explorations*, 33 Cong., 1 sess., *House Exec. Doc. 129*, atlas, n.p.

[31] The Rio Gallo does not appear on present Geological Survey maps. On the Whipple map cited in the preceding note, it is shown as the Cañon del Gallo, entering the Rio de San Jose south of Mount Taylor.

[32] Cubero is north of the Rio San Jose and about ten miles west of Laguna Pueblo. The Whipple party encamped for the night of November 13, 1853, at Cubero. Möllhausen described the town as follows: ". . . the houses were stuck to the rocky walls like swallow' nests. . . . Near the spring the houses, crowded closely together, presented a melancholy picture of poverty and dirt, and such of the population as we saw about gave the impression of people who would only work just as much as necessary to keep them in existence, and enable them to dance an occasional fandango." Without realizing it, Möllhausen also gave some explanation for the condition of the town and people. "The town of Covero lies at the eastern end of a wide plain, which is also again enclosed by rocks and mountains; the soil is sandy and barron, so as scarcely to afford sufficient nourishment to the flocks and herds of the inhabitants; and small fossils, oysters and other shells lie about on it, which have evidently been washed down from the mountains." *Diary of a Journey*, II, 60–61.

Mexican Village, and the Pueblos of Laguna and across the Rivers Puerco and Rio Grande del Norté. The supplies of this post are all obtained through Albuquerque with the exception of corn which is obtained of the Pueblos of Zuñi, Laguna & c.[33] It is calculated for three companies, the least force that should be kept here. It appears well located to watch over the doings of the Navahoe Indians, who number about one thousand warriors, and no doubt will one day be found on or near the best overland route to San Francisco. It should be preserved in the system for regulating the Indian tribes and protecting traders to California. For a plan of this locality see H and for a plan of the post see J hereunto appended [Nos. 7 and 8, Plans and Sketches section].

Los Lunes[34] is merely a temporary station for a company of dragoons on the west bank of the Rio Grande del Norté. It is twenty-four miles south of Albuquerque and eighty-five miles north of Fort Conrad, and in direct communication with Fort Defiance, and conveniently located to intercept and influence the movement of the Apaches and Navahoes in their depredations in driving off sheep and cattle & c, and affords protection to the inhabitants in this neighbourhood who otherwise would be much exposed. This post can be changed up or down the river at will, to a view to having in view the thwarting of the movements of the Indians. The supplies are convenient here and the soil good and cultivated by the Mexicans.

[33] The pueblo of Laguna seemed to have a peculiar fascination for many of the Americans and Europeans who visited it during this period. Möllhausen described it as having "not only an interesting, but even a picturesque and beautiful effect." *Ibid.*, 56–57. Abert, who, generally speaking, took greater delight in slaughtering the New Mexican fauna than in examining the native Indian population, was something of an exception. See "Report of Lieutenant J. W. Abert," 30 Cong., 1 sess., *House Exec. Doc. 41*, p. 469.

[34] The Post of Los Lunas, located at the town of the same name, was established on January 3, 1852, and abandoned in October, 1862.

Fort Conrad[35] is on the west bank of the Rio Grande del Norté [and] was commenced in August, 1850, under the command of Major W. S. Howe, 2d Dragoons, and is opposite the locality called Val Verdé and 24 miles south of the flourishing town of Soccorro, 88 miles south of Las Lunes, 135 miles north of Fort Fillmore and 150 miles northeast of Fort Webster. Grazing, hay, and wood are abundant here, and other supplies convenient. To the northward of this post along the bottom lands of the river there are settlements, and the lands generally improved. But at this place and along the bottom lands south through the locality of Santa Barbara[36] to the vicinity of Dona Aña and Mesilla, the Indians have devastated the country. The buildings that were erected here for the accommodation of the troops are falling down, and a claim has been set up for the land by individuals. A better site, I have no doubt, can be found some 10 miles further south, between this post and Fra Cristobal,[37] that will more effectually intercept the trails of the Indians; and I would accordingly recommend the breaking up of this post and [the] building [of] an entire new one. A post in this neighbourhood seems necessary to complete the chain of communication along through this country to El Paso, particularly as from this point there are two roads to Fort Fillmore, one following the west bank of the river, via Santa Barbara which requires an appropriation by congress of 1,000 dollars to make it suitable as a military road, [and] the other over the famous Jornada [del Muerto] on the east side of

[35] Fort Conrad was established in August, 1851. It was named for Secretary of War Charles M. Conrad. It was abandoned on March 31, 1854, as a result of Mansfield's recommendation, and replaced by Fort Craig.

[36] Santa Barbara was located on the right side of the Rio Grande immediately above the present town of Hatch. It no longer exists.

[37] Fra Cristobal was located on the left side of the Rio Grande at the base of the Fra Cristobal Mountains at the north end of the Jornada del Muerto and opposite the site of the later Fort Craig. Originally a rancho, established in the early years of Spanish occupation, it later developed into a settlement, but was abandoned because of Apache raids. In 1853 it was only a camping place.

[24]

the river where murders by Indians residing at the White Mountains and on the Gila River are frequent. The route on the west side of the river is certainly the best although the longest, as wood, water, and grazing are abundant and it forms part of the route to Fort Webster; whereas the route of the Jornada in dry seasons is without water for 80 miles. This post was designed for two companies and is not too large. For a plan of this locality and of the fort see K and L hereunto appended [Nos. 9 and 10, Plans and Sketches section].

Fort Webster [38] is in latitude 33° on the River Mimbres about 14 miles east of the [Santa Rita] copper mines. It was commenced in October, 1852, under the command of Major G. Morris of the 3rd Infantry, but in November, Brevet Major E. Steen of the 1t Dragoons was in command. Grazing, hay, and wood are abundant here, and the soil on the bottom lands good. It is among the Apache Indians, and dependent for supplies on Fort Fillmore, 135 miles [distant] and Fort Conrad, 150 miles [away]. The distance however to Fort Fillmore via the Jornada where the road forks at Cooks Spring,[39] and in dry seasons 50 miles without water, is 30 miles less. This route strikes the Rio Grande del Norté opposite Dona Aña at the commencement of the cultivation in the Mesilla Valley, and it is usual to pass through the village of Mesilla and cross the river directly over to Fort Fillmore. This road is very good with some minor exceptions. The buildings of this post are made of logs and mud and quite indifferent and not sufficient for the command as one company and the sick were in tents.

[38] Fort Webster, in the location visited by Mansfield, was established on September 9, 1852. Apparently it was named for Secretary of State Daniel Webster. It was abandoned on December 20, 1853.

[39] Cooks Spring is located in the Cooks Range some forty-five miles west of the Rio Grande. The main emigrant route from Mesilla through Tucson to southern California passed by the spring. Fort Cummings was established there in 1863.

The old post at the copper mines[40] has nothing at all to recommend it, and was judiciously abandoned. All posts through an Indian country should be placed on, or near the great thoroughfares where aid and protection can be had by the traveller in case of necessity. Such positions would be equally convenient to overawe the Indians, and their depredations and murders would sooner come to the knowledge of the troops there stationed, and therefore protection or assistance [would be] readily afforded. My opinion is that this post is not properly located, that it should be on the Gila River, on the route travelled by the traders to California, and thus form one in a chain of posts that must eventually be extended across to the Pacific, and that the present post should be given up to the Indian Agent, Mr. J. M. Smith,[41] who resides here, and encouragement given to these Indians thereby to settle permanently where they can be reached (See sketch of locality M and plan of post N appended [Nos. 11 and 12, Plans and Sketches section]).[42]

Fort Fillmore.[43] Is on the east bank of the Rio Grande del

[40] The "old post at the copper mines" was the private defensive post erected, probably in 1804, by Francisco Manuel Elguea to protect the Santa Rita copper mines, discovered in 1800. Both the post and the mines were abandoned in the fall of 1838 because of the hostile incursions of the Apaches. The post was garrisoned by United States troops from April, 1851, until September, 1852, when it was replaced by Fort Webster. See Thomas A. Rickard, *A History of American Mining*, 252–57; and Bartlett, *Personal Narrative*, I, 178–79, 227–29. The fort was built of adobe in the shape of an eqilateral triangle with round towers at the three corners. The walls were four feet thick. See "Journal of Captain A. R. Johnston," in 30 Cong., 1 sess., *House Exec. Doc.* 41, p. 578. A portion of the fort, including one of the towers, still stands, the rest having been torn down in 1910.

[41] James M. Smith arrived in Santa Fe on August 8, 1853, and received his instructions from Governor David W. Merriwether on August 11. See Annie Heloise Abel, ed., "Indian Affairs in New Mexico Under the Administration of William Carr Lane," *New Mexico Historical Review*, Vol. XVI (July, 1941), 356.

[42] The parenthetical statement, which is not in Mansfield's writing, apparently was added later.

[43] Fort Fillmore, named for President Millard Fillmore, was established on Sep-

Norté in latitude 32° 13′ 33″ north and longitude 106° 36′ 30″, and forty-two miles to the northward of El Paso [del Norte, Chihuahua] with a good road of communication therewith. It is directly opposite the town of Mesilla of 3,000 souls and fourteen miles south of Dona Aña. This post was commenced in September, 1851, under the command and direction of Lieutenant Colonel D. S. Miles of the 3rd Infantry who was succeeded by Major E. Backus of the 3rd Infantry in August 1853. The buildings and store houses here are good. Grazing, hay, and wood [are] abundant and the soil, where cultivated, good. All supplies such as corn, flour and beans and beef [are] readily obtained in the neighbourhood and at El Paso, and all other supplies through Albuquerque and Fort Union. A post just south of the Jornada is necessary, and is convenient to operate against the Apaches at the White Mountains &c, and the Gila River. These Apaches are very troublesome at times and number 300 warriors. And as this post is already established [it] will answer that object well. For a sketch of this locality see A [No. 1, Plans and Sketches section], and for a plan of the post see O hereunto appended [No. 13, Plans and Sketches section].

« *Posts Recommended* »

I found no post at San Elizario.[44] While on this subject it may not be out of place to recommend the establishment of other

tember 23, 1851. It was evacuated on July 26, 1861, at the time of the invasion of New Mexico by a Confederate force from Texas. The Confederates held the post until July 8, 1862, and it was not thereafter permanently garrisoned.

[44] San Elizario, located on the Rio Grande below El Paso, Texas, was originally a Spanish presidio named Nuestra Señora del Pilar y Gloriosa San José. The capilla de San Elizario was located nearby. The presidio was occupied from September 15, 1849, to September, 1851, by United States troops. At that time San Elizario was located on an island some twenty miles long which has since become a part of the mainland as a result of changes in the channel of the Rio Grande. Isleta del Sur and Socorro del Sur were on the same island.

posts, according to the importance of protection to the citizens of the country.

1t. A post is indispensable opposite the town of El Paso, either at Maguffins Ville or Smiths Ranch. The former would be preferable, see sketch hereunto appended marked Q [No. 14, Plans and Sketches section]. There are but four settlements on the American side of the river at this place towit, Harts Mill, Smiths Ranch, Maguffins Ville, and Stevensons Ranch.[45] These few families are exposed at all times to the depredations of the Indians, and since the troops were removed in September, 1851, many depredations have been committed. See list hereto marked L. Further a post established here would have the effect to protect the American citizen against any excitement in El Paso, where there is a Mexican population of 7,000 souls and a small garrison under the command of a captain of the Mexican Army.[46] By a post here, the bottom lands of the river at this place would be occupied,

[45] Of the four settlements on the United States side of the Rio Grande, Magoffinsville was the most important. Established in 1849 by James W. Magoffin, a Kentuckian long prominent in the Santa Fe and Chihuahua trade, it consisted of Magoffin's home, stores, warehouses, and other buildings, surrounded by a substantial adobe wall for protection against the Indians. Hart's Mill, also called El Molino, was established in 1851 by Simeon Hart of New York and included Hart's home, flour mill, and other buildings. Hart's mill supplied flour for Forts Fillmore and Webster. Stephenson's Ranch, also known as Concordia Ranch, was the property of Hugh Stephenson of Kentucky. Stephenson also had mining interests in southern New Mexico. Smith's Ranch was the oldest ranch on the left side of the river (see note 69 below) but was not occupied by William T. Smith until 1853. Smith, who was also a Kentuckian, was killed in 1860 when he was thrown from a stagecoach. White's Ranch, also called Frontera, was about eight miles farther up the Rio Grande. It was established by a T. F. White in 1848 at a point where the river was sometimes forded. These settlements are described in Roscoe P. and Margaret B. Conkling, *The Butterfield Overland Mail, 1857–1869*, II, 69–91. See also M. H. Thomlinson, *The Garrison of Fort Bliss, 1849–1916*, 3; and Martin Hardwick Hall, *Sibley's New Mexico Campaign*, 10–11. Fort Bliss was established in January, 1854, at Magoffinsville, in part as a result of Mansfield's recommendation.

[46] Colonel Emilio (Emil) Landberg, military inspector of the frontier, was in command of the Mexican garrison at El Paso in August, 1853.

and cultivation entended down the river to Isleta, and a trading town would soon spring up with an American population capable of self defence. At this point the mail comes in from San Antonio, and as I returned to head quarters over this mail route, it may not be out of place here to express an opinion as to additional posts in Texas

From El Paso to San Antonio is 674 miles via Fort Clark[47] on the Mora River and Fort Inge[48] on the Leona River. To Fort Clark is 544 miles without a settlement of *any description* after leaving San Elizario, 20 miles from El Paso, and exposed to Indian attacks at all times. The trade that is carried on over this route is great: it is one of the overland routes to California and to Chihuahua, and across this route the Indians travel at different points to commit their depredations on the Mexicans. There should be at least three posts established along this road as places of protection and resort to travellers in distress. One should be established where the road leaves the Rio Grande del Norté, 83 miles below El Paso.[49] Another at the head waters of the Limpia,[50] about 138 miles from the last mentioned place, and another at Live Oak Creek,[51] 148 miles further and 174 miles from Fort Clark. These points are selected for the abundance of grazing, wood, and *good* water they afford, and as excellent locations to overawe the Indians. By the establishment of these posts too, the mail contractor would be enabled to have relays of mules, and the mail might then be readily carried twice a month with much greater ease than it can now be done once a month.

The entrance into New Mexico from the north, I doubt not after a suitable reconnaissance by an officer of engineers, might be very much improved and facilitated and rendered safer by a

[47] Established June 20, 1852.
[48] Established March 13, 1849.
[49] Fort Quitman was established near this point on September 28, 1858.
[50] Fort Davis was established at this point on October 7, 1854.
[51] Fort Lancaster was established near this point on August 20, 1855.

route from Fort Riley to cross the Arkansas River west of Choteau's Island.[52]

« *Command of the Department, Troops &c* »

Colonel E. V. Sumner of the 1t Dragoons assumed command of this department on the 19h July, 1851, and remained in command till the 30h June, 1853. During this period he established the posts of Fort Union, Fort Massachusetts, Cantonment Burgwin, head quarters at Albuquerque, Fort Defiance, Fort Conrad, Fort Webster, Fort Fillmore, and the post of Las Lunes, and retained Fort Marcy at Santa Fé, but broke up all other stations held by his predecessor.[53] These forts are merely stations with buildings and store houses for the accommodation of troops with the exception of Fort Marcy which is a real fort.

Brevet Brigadier General John Garland assumed command of this department on crossing the Arkansas River 20h July, 1853, while with troops and supplies marching across the plains. I entered this department with this command and marched with it as far as Fort Union. Thus it appears that the original design of the order to Colonel McCall, my predecessor, for the inspection of this department before General Garland shall reach the command could not be accomplished for want of time. The march was well conducted: General Garland placed Major E. Backus on 28h June at Council Grove in command of the troops of the column, who conducted it with strictly military propriety to the comfort and convenience of the whole. Lieutenant William D.

[52] Chouteau's Island, which is now part of the mainland, was in the Arkansas River about thirty miles above the present Dodge City and ninety miles below Bent's New Fort.

[53] The only fort in the department when Sumner assumed command was Fort Marcy. All garrisons at that time were located in towns or settlements, a matter which Sumner strongly disapproved. The garrison at Fort Marcy was greatly reduced for a time and all other posts abandoned, although Albuquerque was re-established within a year.

Smith, 2d Dragoons, in charge of a large number of dragoon horses, managed the same with skill and energy to the benefit of the service. The train, consisting of 51 baggage and commissary six-mule wagons and teams, was under the command of Captain L. C. Easton of the Quartermaster's Department, and systematically and well conducted. The Medical Department, under the direction of Assistant Surgeon David C. DeLeon, was skilfully and well conducted, and his skill as a physician entitles him to a high stand in his profession. Although the number of cases that he administered to amounted to 361 exclusive of officers' families and servants, he did not lose one, and in several instances to my personal knowledge his subjects were very sick. Although unwell himself at times, he attended cheerfully to his duties, and here it would seem that two physicians would be desirable on such long marches exposed to attacks of cholera &c.

It may not be remiss to remark here relative to marches across the plains that this command started as early from Fort Leavenworth as it would be prudent, to avoid exposures to heavy rains and consequent sickness and death to men and officers. Not earlier than the 20h of June probably, is the best time to start from that post. By this time, the grass on the prairies after the rainy season is sweet and large, and the command will reach New Mexico just as the refreshing showers there have started up the grass, and when the animals after a long march without corn need it most. The roads too that are excellent when dry are extremely heavy on teams when wet. I must here remark as to the profanity of the citizen teamsters as a general thing. If there be any thing shocking to the moral sense, it is the awful and hearty swearing bestowed by them on their mules. On the most trifling occasion, the whole vocabulary of "billingsgate" is poured out to the anoyance [*sic*] of every person within hearing. I have no doubt this evil can be corrected by making it a matter of sufficient importance to be noticed by wagon masters and others in authority. The employment of soldiers too, as teamsters is very desirable on account of their better discipline, and accordingly I would recommend that at least three soldiers in each company in the service be instructed wherever practicable to drive teams, to be ready at hand on emergencies. We reached Fort Union on the 31t July.

« *Fort Union—1t to the 6h August* »

This is the general depot of supplies for this department and was commanded by Captain and Brevet Lieutenant Colonel Horace Brooks, 2d Artillery. This command consisted of his own Company D but not a subaltern officer present with it, 79 in the aggregate: 10 on detached service, one on furlough, one officer, 1t Lieutenant Lloyd Beall, on leave of absence for six months, leaving 67 present for duty of which one was confined and 6 were sick. 1t Lieutenant W. C. Adams on detached service and 2d Lieutenant J. C. Moore on detached service as commissary and quartermaster at Santa Fé.—Company D, 3rd Infantry, Captain N. C. Macre [Macrae] commanded by 1t Lieutenant and Brevet Captain George Sykes, the only officer present with this company, 73 in the aggregate: 13 on detached service, 2 on furlough, Captain N. C. Macrae on detached service and 2d Lieutenant J. E. Maxwell on detached service as quartermaster and commissary at Santa Fé, leaving 56 present for duty of which 9 were sick. —And Company K, 1t Dragoons, commanded by Captain and Brevet Major J. H. Carleton, the only officer present with this company, 53 in the aggregate: 5 rank and file on detached service, one rank and file absent confined, 3 rank and file on furlough, 1t Lieutenant R. Ingalls detached service acting quartermaster in California and 2d Lieutenant L. Graham detached service at Carlisle Barrack and had never been with this company, leaving 42 present for duty of which 2 were sick—37 horses and 5 ponies.

Thus the line of the army present consisted in the aggregate of 3 officers and 164 rank and file for duty. It must be remarked here that Captain Macrae of Company D, 3rd Infantry, and Lieutenant Adams of Company D, 2d Artillery, reached this post at the close of the inspection. The staff of this command consisted of Captain and Brevet Major E. S. Sibley, chief of the Quartermaster's Department in New Mexico; Captain Isaac Bowen, chief of the Commissary Department in New Mexico; Military Store Keeper Wm. R. Shoemaker, chief of ordnance supplies in New Mexico; and Assistant Surgeon John Byrne, chief of the Medical Depot in New Mexico on detached service since 28h March, 1853, and place supplied by Dr. O. W. Blanchard,[54] a citizen of respectable standing in his profession.

I found this post in a high state of discipline and every department of it in good order and highly creditable to the gallant and distinguished officer, Colonel Brooks, in command. The artillery, infantry, and dragoon companies were found in excellent efficient order. Of course they were all in the old uniform such as the Government had provided—their arms and equipments in excellent serviceable condition although much worn, and the arms and equipments and clothing in the particular charge of the commanders of companies in a good state of preservation. The quarters occupied by the respective companies were in a good state of police, and the comfort of the troops studied in all the details. The whole number of men on the sick list amounted to 17 and the hospital comfortable. The horses of the dragoons well provided with safe and good accomodation [*sic*]. It was necessary to condemn 8 horses and 5 ponies of Major Carleton's company which were recommended to be turned over to the Quartermaster's Department. The Mexican Poney is wholly unfit for the dragoon service.

The troops here have been well instructed in the drill. Colonel Brooks formed the artillery and infantry companies in a batal-

[54] Dr. Blanchard has not been further identified.

lion with the sergeants acting as commissioned officers [and] gave a very handsome batallion drill, taking them through all the changes of position & c. He also took his own company through the artillery drill with a mountain howitzer battery of four pieces, and closed with his company by a very complete drill at the rifle, thus exhibiting his own company competent to duty at the three arms of service. Brevet Captain Sykes took the company he commanded very handsomely thro the heavy and the light infantry drills very much to the credit of that young and excellent officer and to the men he commanded. The dragoons commanded by Major Carleton were well drilled and appeared to great advantage. Much credit is due to these officers for the fine condition of the troops under their particular command, when it is taken into consideration that the labour of building quarters, getting timber, wood, [and] hay, farming, escorting trains, and pursuing Indians is all performed by them. On my arrival at the post, I found Major Carleton was absent and had been for two days with most of his command after a party of Indians who had committed depredations on his horses. I must here call the attention to the fact of their being but one officer to a company at this post. The consequence is that heavy duty is thrown upon a few, and posts are left or detachments sent off without a commissioned officer.

The troops cultivate a garden which is irrigated by raising water by mule and hand power, and thus they are supplied with vegetables in part. A farm is also cultivated under the regulations established by the Honorable Secretary of War Conrad. This farm as heretofore described is 25 miles distant. About 50 acres of corn was planted which looked well and about 75 tons of hay was cut off the natural meadow. A citizen is employed to take the charge of this farm at the rate of 65 dollars per month and one ration, and a detachment of troops are kept at it to cultivate it. Although the farming interest in New Mexico is about 14,000 dollars in debt, I would recommend the keeping up of this farm as it is well irrigated, but without the citizen employed in superintending it, more as a convenient locality to recruit horses and fat cattle for beef, and gather hay, than profit to be divided among the soldiers; and let the whole be under the direction of the quartermaster and the detachment paid as on ordinary extra service when required to work.

The troops are well fed and clothed at this post with the exception of shoes. There was a deficiency of shoes except some large sizes nos. 11 and 12 which had to be cut down at much expense. There is a good bakery here. The post fund on the 30h June amounted to 300$^{69}/_{100}$ dollars.

Quartermaster's Department. Here is the general depot for supply of all the troops in the Territory. It has been for the last two years under the command of Brevet Major E. S. Sibley, an officer of distinguished merit who attends personally and strictly to every branch of his business. His duties have been arduous. The buildings that have been put up are as good as circumstances would admit, and the public stores and property is in a good state of preservation, and the corrals and stables for public animals, suitable and secure. His books are kept according to the regulations of his department and his accounts properly rendered and his cash, which is obtained by drafts on the quartermaster at St. Louis, is kept in the usual iron safe. On the 30h June, 1853, his account current showed the U.S. his debtor [by] 21,375$^{62}/_{100}$ dollars, which was covered by a temporary loan from the paymaster at Santa Fé. The supplies obtained via Fort Leavenworth are transported by contractors by the pound, a very good arrangement and the cheapest for the Government. Corn is had here at 1$^{40}/_{100}$ dollars the bushel of 56 lbs. delivered inclusive of the sack, and I doubt not the price will be lower still the present year. Hay is had by the cutting at the farm and on the Ocaté River, which should be accomplished at the expense of the extra duty allowance to the soldiers. Major Sibley has erected an excellent mule power circular saw mill which supplies all the boards, planks, and scantling required, and charcoal is obtained by the burning and wood by the hawling. This department had a year's supply on hand for the service of all articles but soldiers' clothing, in which it was particularly deficient in soldiers' shoes, a very important article of which nos. 7, 8, [and] 9 are particularly required. There were twenty-eight citizens employed in this department—one clerk, one carpenter, one wagon and forage master, one principal teamster, one saddler, and twenty-three teamsters and hurders. The soldiers employed were thirty-nine in the aggregate, consisting of two artificers, carpenters, smith, wheelright, sawyers, hay cutters & c, at an extra per diem of 18 cents. The system of employing soldiers is an excellent one, when the officer in charge is active and energetic. It prepares them for every description of duty in the field and as teamsters in particular; more reliance can be placed on them, and a more perfect control had over them. Care should be had to change the labourers where practicable as often as once in twelve days to give all the men an opportunity and to keep them well instructed in their military duties proper. It is a great advantage to the soldier, as well as officer to be engaged habitually at some occupation that will improve his physical ability.

Commissary Department. This post is the depot of supplies in this department under the command of Captain I. Bowen who attends personally to his duties, and this department is well conducted by him. He has abundant supplies on hand with the exception of coffee and rice which were entirely out, so as to compel him to borrow coffee of the sutler to meet his daily issues. This state of his coffee supply is no fault of his but the result of his estimates having been cut down. The articles of flour, beans, and salt are readily obtained here by contract. A good flouring mill is established at the village of Moro and in the Valley of Taos by Mr. St. Vrain,[55] and beans and salt are also the productions of the Territory. Beef cattle are readily obtained here, and some are driven across the plains from Missouri. Captain Bowen obtains his funds by drafts on the commissary at St. Louis and keeps his money in the usual iron safe. His books and accounts are in excellent order. He has by order made large advances on account of [the][56] farming interests and such accounts have been suspended by the auditor of the Government. The farming interest in this Territory is represented to be 14,460⁰⁸⁄₁₀₀ dollars in debt to this department. The supplies are well stored and in a good state of preservation, and an excellent slaughter house has been built.

Medical Department. Has its depot of supplies here in a good state of preservation and abundant, and the sick [are] well cared for in hospital. It was temporarily under the charge of Dr. O. W. Blanchard, a citizen, in the absence of Assistant Surgeon John Burne on detached duty.

Ordnance Department. Has its depot of supplies for the whole Territory here under the charge of the Military Store Keeper William B. Shoemaker. The supplies of this department are ample under the present aspect of affairs, and all in good order and state of preservation. There were here two brass six-pounder field pieces with caissons and traveling forge left by Lieutenant J. N. Ward of the 3rd Infantry more than a year ago for which receipts had not been passed, and which from neglect and exposure required refitting. Also at Barclay's Fort about seven miles southward was a brass six-pounder field piece and carriage that had been loaned by authority of the Secretary of War and [was] no longer required there, which, from exposure and neglect required refitting and painting. These guns on being by me brought to the notice of General Garland were ordered to be taken by the military storekeeper and immediately put in order.

[55] Ceran St. Vrain, formerly associated with the Bent brothers, had extensive business interests and property holdings in northern New Mexico.

[56] In the original manuscript the word is not clear but would appear to be an "a."

The buildings for store houses and quarters with the gun shed being erected, are all sufficient for this depot. The force here in the employ of this department consists of one citizen armorer and 12 enlisted men, and were occupied as follows, one in charge of the garden and 5 haying on the Ocaté for public animals; and the remaining 7 were building gun shed, in the shops, and at the "current" service of the depot. In addition this department has a six-mule team which has hitherto been at work in erecting buildings &c &c. It would seem, now that the buildings are completed, that this team should be dispensed with and turned over to the Quartermaster's Department, which by regulations will do all the transportation of ordnance stores &c. The time of the armorers and mechanics should not be applied to haying, driving teams, and taking care of mules. This force would then be ample for the whole Territory at repairs of arms and making cartridges &c &c.

Attached to this branch of the service is a good garden about three-fourths of a mile off, irrigated by a spring, which affords the men good vegetables and is an absolute necessity in this place where vegetables cannot be bought. More care should be taken in the enlistment of men in this department: I observed one ignorant German who could not understand English when spoken to; such men are not fit for this service.

Pay Department. The troops at this post had not been paid for five months. There seems to be no good reason for so much delay.

Chaplain. This is a chaplain post, but the council of administration have not succeeded in getting a chaplain to conform to their peculiar views.

« *Cantonment Burgwin—11h to the 13h August, 1853* »

This post is commanded by 2d Lieutenant Robert Ransom, Jr., of the 1t Dragoons, in command of Company J, Captain and

Brevet Major W. N. Grier, 1t Dragoons, 75 in the aggregate: captain, 1t lieutenant and 30 rank and file on detached duty, 2 rank and file absent on leave, of these 3 non-commissioned officers and one bugler and 21 privates left by Lieutenant Ransom temporarily at Abiquiu, having been after the Indians, one non-commissioned officer and 2 privates on detached duty at Fort Leavenworth with Colonel Sumner since 25h May, and 2 privates at Don Fernandes de Taos in charge of corn, leaving 41 in the aggregate at the post of which 3 were sick and one confined—58 horses belonging to this company. Lieutenant Ransom had just returned from Abiquiu having left his command of necessity in charge of a non-commissioned officer. This post is in good discipline and police, and the comforts of the troops, both sick and well, cared for. The quarters and store houses are good, and [there is] a safe and commodious corral for the horses and mules, and a good garden is cultivated. The supplies of corn, flour, beans, fresh meat, wood, fodder &c are abundant here—other supplies are obtained from the general depot at Fort Union. Lieutenant Ransom also performs the duty of quartermaster and commissary. There is no physician here. The troops are well instructed in the drill, and the arms and equipments [are] in good serviceable condition although much worn and the uniform of course old, no other having been provided. I was obliged to condemn 8 horses and 6 ponies as unserviceable and unfit for the dragoon service and recommended they be turned over to the Quartermaster's Department. This post is well supplied except in the articles of horse and mule shoes, where there was a deficiency. One dollar the bushel is paid for corn, and flour is furnished by contract thro' Captain Bowen of the Commissary Department. A flouring mill however is not two miles off. There is a good bakery here, but no post fund. Of ten recruits recently joined this company, one is near sighted and one left handed. It is a misfortune to have men that cannot understand English when spoken to; but it is still worse to have them near sighted, and a left handed man is quite awkward in the ranks.

The troops had not been paid here for five months.

« *Fort Massachusetts—18h to the 21t August* »

The post was commanded by Major George A. H. Blake, 1t Dragoons. His command consisted of Company F, 1t Dragoons, Captain P. R. Thompson, but [was] commanded by 2d Lieutenant R. Johnson [Johnston], the only officer present with this company, in the aggregate 81, of which 12 were on detached service, Captain Thompson absent without leave, and one absent sick, thus leaving 67 for duty of which one was confined and 3 sick—49 horses.—And Company H, 3rd Infantry, Captain William H. Gordon, commanded by 2d Lieutenant A. Jackson, the only officer of this company present, 74 in the aggregate, of which 1t Lieutenant W. H. Wood and 13 rank and file were on detached service, Captain Gordon on leave for 6 months, and one rank and file on furlough, leaving 58 for duty, of which one was confined and 5 sick. Lieutenant Jackson also performed the duty of quartermaster and commissary—And Assistant Surgeon D. L. Magruder.

Thus the line of the army present for duty consisted of three commissioned officers and 125 rank and file.

This command was in a good state of discipline. The arms and equipments of the dragoons and the infantry were in good serviceable order although much worn and a deficiency of spurs. I was obliged to condemn six poneys as unfit for dragoon service and recommended they be turned over to the Quartermaster's Department and one six-pounder iron gun and carriage as unfit for service. These troops have been very little instructed in the drill for the past year, in consequence of the constant labour within the year in building the post. The whole command is entitled to great credit for the work they have done in so short a time. The quarters occupied by the troops were abundant and good. The comfort of the troops, both well and sick, cared for. A good bakery exists for each company and the supplies of food [are] good. All supplies here of corn, flour, beans, fresh meat &c must come from the settlements south as far as the Valley of Taos, and all other supplies from Fort Union over roads in several points impassible for loaded wagons. This I presume has been one cause of a great deficiency in many articles. The men of those companies have been obliged to purchase shirts, draws, socks, and shoes of the sutler at very high rates because the Government failed to have these articles on hand for several months past, and it has born heavily and unjustly on them. The sutler's prices, in consequence of the great cost of transportation from the States, are exorbitant and much beyond the ability of the soldier to pay. The troops were in the old uniform as no other had been furnished. Public property was in a good state of preservation and the hospital and medicines, in the hands of Assistant Surgeon D. L. Magruder, well conducted. A large corral well calculated for horses, mules, and cattle of this post has been built and a garden made for the use of the troops and an effort made at farming which, owing to the seasons and other causes, has not been successful. There was a post fund on the 30h June last of 208 $^{68}/_{100}$ dollars.

The Troops had not been paid at this post for more than five months.

« *Fort Marcy at Santa Fé—27h to the 31t August* »

The troops for the defence of this post are quartered in Santa Fé, there being no suitable quarters in the fort which is on an elevated spur of the mountain and one thousand yards distant, and only fit to be occupied in time of war. This post was commanded by Brevet Major and Captain William T. H. Brooks, 3rd Infantry. The only troops here were his own Company G,

84 in the aggregate, of which 6 were on detached service, one absent confined, [and] one commissioned officer, the 1t lieutenant, and one private, absent with leave, leaving 75 for duty of which 3 were confined and 3 sick. The only subaltern officer present at this company, 2d Lieutenant L. H. Marshall, performed also the duty of quartermaster and commissary. Under this command is stationed Assistant Surgeon D. C. DeLeon. This company is in a high state of discipline, arms and equipments in the best serviceable order, and the rank and file extremely well instructed. Major Brooks carried his company through the heavy and light infantry drill in handsome style. It was in the old uniform fatigue dress, no other having been furnished. The quarters were in a good state of police and the public property in a good state of preservation in suitable store houses—except some field pieces and carriages, which required the attention of the Ordnance Department, which on my representation, General Garland ordered the military store keeper at Fort Union to correct. A good garden is attached to the post, and other supplies good and abundant except soldiers' shoes. A good hospital exists, and the sick are well attended and cared for under the particular direction of Assistant Surgeon DeLeon. There is a good saw mill about one and one-half miles out of the city on the Santa Fé River and attached to it a miller's house. This although new, having been erected soon after General Kearney took possession of the country, it seems difficult to sell and a soldier is constantly quartered there to keep charge of it.

Major Brooks sustains here the high reputation the army officers have for their gentlemanly deportment in their intercourse with citizens, and I think him peculiarly well qualified for this post.

Santa Fé. In this city is also stationed Major F. A. Cunningham and Major C. H. Fry, paymasters. Major Cunningham shows a statement of 73,371^{59}/100 dollars in his hands at this time, inclusive of 45,161$\frac{19}{100}$ dollars in the hands of Assistant Quartermaster Brevet Major E. S. Sibley loaned to that department; 2,802$\frac{5}{100}$ dollars in the hands of Captain I. Bowen, commissary of subsistence, and loaned to that department; and 1,294$\frac{5}{100}$ dollars in the hands of Captain John Pope, topographical engineer, and loaned to that department. Thus leaving but 24,113$\frac{99}{100}$ dollars actual money in his own hands. These several loans I was verbally informed by Major Cunningham were made at the desire of Colonel Sumner then in command of the Territory. The loan to the Topographical Department not being indispensable to the transportation of supplies and the *subsistence?*[57] of the troops seems entirely too irregular for a time of peace.

Major Fry brought into the Territory 100,400 dollars and turned over to Major Cunningham 50,000 dollars. Thus leaving in his own hands 50,400 dollars which was kept in an iron safe in his office, and none of it had been expended.

The division of duties of these officers is to the effect that Major Cunningham will pay off the posts north of Santa Fé, towit, Forts Union, Burgwin, and Massachusetts, and Major Fry the posts south, towit, Albuquerque, Fort Defiance, and Los Lunas &c.

This city may be convenient for the Pay Department to sell drafts on the States, and obtain the funds required to pay the troops, and therefore may be convenient for two paymasters, but in other respects, it is inconvenient to obtain suitable escorts and transportation in the performance of their duties.

« *Albuquerque—3rd to the 8h September* »

This post is at the head quarters of the commanding officer of this department, Brevet Brigadier General John Garland, who

---

[57] The underlining of the word printed here in italics and the question mark were added later.

had attached to his staff Assistant Adjutant General Brevet Major W. A. Nichols and Lieutenant S. D. Sturges [Sturgis] of the 1t Dragoons, acting aid. The senior medical officer, Assistant Surgeon E. H. Abadie, is attached to head quarters and attends on the post here also. These officers all live in hired quarters. Here the records of the department are kept with order and regularity. I found at this post, but not on duty in this department, Captain John Pope of the Topographical Engineers, who had been relieved 15h May from duty here and who was waiting further order from Washington.

This post was temporarily under the command of Brevet 2d Lieutenant K. Gerrard [Garrard], 1t Dragoons, in consequence of the sickness of 2d Lieutenant D. Bell of the 2d Dragoons. These two young officers [were] the only commissioned officers in authority present. The troops at this post consisted of Company H, 2d Dragoons, Captain O. F. Winship. This company has been commanded since the 1t January, 1852, by five different lieutenants: towit, 2d Lieutenant T. Bingham, 2d Dragoons; 2d Lieutenant R. Johnson, 1t Dragoons; 2d Lieutenant B. H. Robinson [Robertson], 2d Dragoons; 2d Lieutenant K. Guerrard, 1t Dragoons; and 2d Lieutenant D. Bell, 2d Dragoons; and has been much engaged in escort duties, and without a complement of commissioned officers; and as a necessary consequence has fallen off very much. This company is 80 in the aggregate, of which the captain, on detached service [as] assistant adjutant general; 1t Lieutenant E. K. Kane, 2d Dragoons, on detached service Quartermaster's Department; Brevet 2d Lieutenant D. S. Stanley on detached service; and 17 rank and file on detached service [are absent], leaving 60 present for duty, of which Lieutenant Bell and 4 rank and file were sick and 2 confined.—62 horses. The company of course was in the old uniform and their arms in good serviceable order. The men and horses required instruction and training. There was no farrier to this company and the horses unshod and not in a fit condition to move off at an hour's notice after Indians. In short the company required a complement of officers, and much attention, and accordingly has subsequently been ordered by General Garland to Fort Union for that purpose, and Brevet Major Carleton's company ordered to take its place. I condemned 7 ponies as unfit for the dragoon service and recommended they be turned over to the Quartermaster's Department.

The quarters for the soldiers and the public stores were quite indifferent and insufficient for the post. As this position is excellent for the convenience of its location as respects southern and western posts for a depot of supplies, and as the buildings are hired by the Quartermaster at over 2,000 dollars per annum, an effort should be made to lease land at a nominal rent and erect buildings in this vicinity that would remove the troops from the close contact with the citizens and afford a better state of discipline. I believe the commanding general of this department might effect a great improvement in the condition of things here, at no material expense, over the aggregate expense of hiring quarters for two years.

Lieutenant Guerrard also performs the duty of quartermaster and commissary which are quite arduous here and well performed. The supplies and ordnance of this post are as well stored as practicable under present facilities, and abundant except in the article of shoes for the men which were deficient. The supply of corn, flour, beans, mutton &c readily had at reasonable rates. Corn costs $12\%_{00}$ dollars the bushel of 56 pounds. Hay costs 30 dollars the ton and flour 8 cents the pound. Other supplies readily obtained from Fort Union &c except wood which is brought a distance of twenty-five miles.

There are thirteen citizens in the employ of the quartermaster, towit, one clerk, one forage master, one ferryman, one hurder, four teamsters, and five laborers. The monthly expenditure being about 3,500 dollars, making about 42,000 dollars per annum.

The balance of funds in the hands of Lieutenant Guerrard was 4,636⁰⁹⁄₁₀₀ dollars as quartermaster, and 331²⁴⁄₁₀₀ dollars as commissary. A farm of 30 acres has been undertaken here, but failed entirely so far as it was conducted under the conditions of the order on that subject. The expenses were borne by the Quartermaster's Department, and the proceeds accordingly assumed by that department. The farm was hired and the land was good but will not pay the cost. The post garden, except that assigned to the commanding officer of the department, proved almost a failure this year.

Lieutenant Guerrard deserves credit for his great exertions here, but there was too much for any one officer to perform, and more than should ever be expected of an officer. A change has subsequently been made.

« *Fort Defiance—15h to the 20h September* »

This post was under the command of Captain and Brevet Major H. L. Kendrick, 2d Artillery. The force consists of his own Company B, commanded by 1t Lieutenant Charles Griffin, 87 in the aggregate, of which 15 rank and file [are] on detached service, leaving 72 for duty, of which Major Kendrick, in command of post; 2d Lieutenant A. L. Long, acting quartermaster and commissary; and 2d Lieutenant J. C. Tidball, adjutant of the post; and 4 rank and file [were] sick and 3 confined.—Company F, 3rd Infantry, Captain and Brevet Lieutenant Colonel J. H. Eaton, commanded by 1t Lieutenant H. B. Shroeder [Schroeder], 3rd Infantry, in the aggregate 85, of which Colonel Eaton was absent and 25 rank and file on detached service, one absent sick and 2 rank and file absent confined, thus leaving 56 for duty of which one commissioned officer, 2d Lieutenant A. E. Steen, and one rank and file [were] sick and 5 rank and file confined.—Company B, 3rd Infantry, Captain and Brevet Major O. L.

[46]

Shepherd in command, 81 in the aggregate, of which 1t Lieutenant J. Trevitt is on general recruiting service and 21 rank and file on detached service and 2 rank and file absent sick, leaving 57 for duty inclusive of 2d Lieutenant J. W. Alley and 2 rank and file sick. Thus constituting a force present of 8 officers and 167 rank and file of the line of the army. Attached to this command was Assistant Surgeon J. H. White, and Chaplain and Schoolmaster Rev. J. M. Shaw.

This post was in a high state of discipline, and every department of it unexceptionable and highly creditable to the distinguished officer, Major Kendrick, in command. The troops were all in the old uniform, no other having been furnished. The arms and equipments of the respective companies were in good serviceable condition. The drills at the artillery and heavy and light infantry showed that the instruction of the troops was not lost sight of notwithstanding the great labour that had been performed in erecting quarters & c & c in this locality where every thing had to be originated. The quarters of the officers and men were good and the comfort of the troops studied as far as practicable, and the store houses good, and all public property in a good state of preservation. The Medical Department under Assistant Surgeon White was exceptionable, the comfort of the sick well cared for. The Quartermaster's and Commissary departments in the hands of 2d Lieutenant A. L. Long, 2d Artillery, well conducted and the supplies good and abundant with the exception of the article of shoes and socks which the soldiers have been obliged to purchase of the sutler at high rates. All supplies for this post must come from Albuquerque, two hundred miles off, with the exception of corn which is purchased of the Pueblos of Zuñi and Laguna and the people of Corvero & c, distant say one hundred miles, at about $1^{35}\!/_{100}$ dollars the bushel. Hay is had by the cutting, there being four good natural meadows within ten miles, and this year 100 tons have been cut and brought in, and wood is abundant; and Major Kendrick has recently discovered mineral coal about eight miles distant.

The warm season here is long enough to bring all vegetables to maturity, and there is an excellent garden attached to this post irregated by the spring that exists in the Cañon. [Water][58] is found good and abundant by wells. There are no great facilities for farming here, but notwithstanding it has been tried and proved a failure. Only one citizen is employed at this post besides the chaplain, and he an Indian interpreter. Twenty-two rank and file were on quartermaster's duties and 11 on commissary duty and on the legal extra pay.

There is no post fund here. The troops had not been paid for about six months.

The Chaplain gives satisfaction. There are no children that would make a school necessary.

The Indians are freely admitted in and about the post during the day and are friendly and bring peaches to sell. There is a building devoted to them where they must remain over night if they do not leave before Tattoo. These Indians are Navahoes and can bring into the field not over 1,000 warriors. Their chiefs are numerous, and they sometimes commit depredations on the New Mexicans. In May last, eleven of them drove off five armed New Mexicans and captured 5,000 sheep—2,800 of which were afterwards restored. A party of five Indians—Navahoes—lately murdered at Abiquiu one New Mexican and captured two others to get their animals.

« *Los Lunes—25h to the 27h September* »

This post was under the command of Captain R. S. Ewell, in command of his own Company G, 1t Dragoons, and the only

[58] The last word on page 39 of the manuscript has been blocked out but appears to be a repetition of "Cañon." This probably accounts for the omission of the first word or words in the following sentence.

commissioned officer present for duty. The Company number 84 in the aggregate, of which 1t Lieutenant and Brevet Captain O. H. P. Taylor was absent on detached service as regimental quartermaster and 2d Lieutenant I. N. Moore never joined, and 7 rank and file on detached scervice and two rank and file absent sick, leaving 73 present for duty of which 6 rank and file were confined and 3 sick—59 horses. The discipline of this post is good. The troops in the old uniform as a matter of course, no other having been furnished. The arms and equipments in good serviceable order, although the horse equipments were much worn. I was obliged to condemn 17 ponies and 2 horses as unfit for the dragoon service, and recommended they be turned over to the Quartermaster's Department. This company was well instructed and drilled handsomely. The quarters were good and all the public property in a good state of preservation. The supplies were good and abundant at present although until recently and for some time past, the soldiers had been obliged to purchase shoes and socks and shirts of the sutler at high prices in the absence of Government supplies. All supplies at this station can be readily obtained: corn can be purchased at one dollar the bushel of 56 lbs., and beans and flour abundant; mutton and beef readily obtained, and all other supplies from Fort Union via Albuquerque. There is a good garden attached to this post, and Captain Ewell has been successful with a small farm, the use of the land and irregating ditch having been given the command in consideration of the protection afforded.

Captain Ewell performs the duty of quartermaster and commissary. There is no medical officer at this station, and there is no post fund.

« *Fort Conrad—30h September to 4h October* »

This post was under the command of Captain and Brevet Lieutenant Colonel D. T. Chandler, 3rd Infantry. The Troops consist

of his own Company I, 83 in the aggregate, of which 1t Lieutenant J. N. G. Whistler on leave of absence, 2d Lieutenant M. L.
Davis on detached service, and 25 rank and file on detached
service and 2 rank and file absent sick, thus leaving 54 for duty,
of which 3 rank and file were confined and 4 sick.—Company K,
2d Dragoons, Captain W. Steel [Steele], commanded by 2d
Lieutenant H. F. Delano of the 2d Dragoons, 51 in the aggregate, of which Captain Steel is on leave of absence for 40 days,
Brevet 2d Lieutenant G. B. Anderson is on leave of absence and
absent from his company since 1t July, 1852, 1t Lieutenant A.
Pleasanton on general recruiting service, 5 rank and file on detached duty, and one rank and file on furlough, leaving 42 for
duty of which Lieutenant Delano was dangerously sick, 2 rank
and file sick, and 2 rank and file confined—54 horses.

Under this command was 2d Lieutenant J. E. Maxwell, 3rd
Infantry, acting quartermaster and commissary. Assistant Surgeon E. P. Langworthy was attached to this command, but has
recently been ordered to Fort Defiance to exchange stations with
Assistant Surgeon W. J. H. White, and his place has been temporarily supplied by a citizen physician in consequence of the dangerous illness of Lieutenant Delano. Thus for duty there were
present Brevet Lieutenant Colonel Chandler and 2d Lieutenant
Maxwell and 2d Lieutenant Delano and 96 rank and file.

This command was in a good state of discipline. The troops of
course in the old uniform: no other had been furnished. Their
arms and equipments in good serviceable order. I was obliged to
condemn 6 horses as unfit for service and recommended they be
turned over to the Quartermaster's Department. The Dragoons
were drilled by the 1t sergeant and appeared well instructed.
The infantry company was drilled by its 1t sergeant at heavy and
light infantry and appeared well; the musicians of this company
were at Fort Fillmore for instruction. There however were in-

dications in both companies of the want of sufficient number of commissioned officers on duty.

The quarters of both officers and soldiers are falling to pieces. The timbers had rotted away—some of the troops were in tents. The hospital in a good state for the sick and the public store houses worthless. A good corral exists for the horses and mules & c. There is a good garden at this post and a farm had been in operation on hired ground, where 37½ bushels of wheat and 50 bushels of corn were raised the past year, at a cost of 100 dollars for the use of the farm and 102 dollars for repairs of "acequia" and 45 dollars for hired labour and repairs and other expenses besides the loss of one quartermaster's mule. In short it had proved a failure. The supplies of this post are readily obtained from the places north and from Albuquerque. Corn is abundant at about $1^{35}/_{100}$ dollars the bushel, flour at 8 to 10 cents the pound, and hay by the cutting. A supply of about 80 tons had been cut this season. The public property is all of it as well protected and preserved as the condition of the buildings would allow. In describing this post I recommended that it be broken up and another substituted.

The duties of quartermaster and commissary were well performed by Lieutenant Maxwell. The funds in his hands as quartermaster on the 30h September, $545^{05}/_{100}$ dollars and as commissary, $430^{98}/_{100}$ dollars.

On the 1t September there was a post fund of $147^{08}/_{100}$ dollars.

« *Fort Webster—1oh to the 13h October* »

This post was under the command of Major E. Steen, 1t Dragoons. It consisted of his own Company H, 1t Dragoons, 69 in the aggregate and 43 horses, of which the three subalterns, 1t Lieutenant and Brevet Captain A. Buford, on detached service at Harrisburge, Kentucky, [and] 2d Lieutenant J. D. Sturgis and

2d Lieutenant K. Guerrard, on detached staff service at Albuquerque, [were absent], leaving 65 for duty of which one rank
and file was sick.—Company K, 3rd Infantry, Captain and Brevet Major I. B. Richardson, 77 in the aggregate, of which 1t
Lieutenant and Brevet Captain B. E. Bee was absent on furlough, leaving Major Richardson and 2d Lieutenant L. W.
OBannon and 74 rank and file for duty—And Company E, 2d
Dragoons, Captain R. P. Campbell, commanded by 1t Lieutenant William D. Smith, 69 in the aggregate and 42 horses, of
which Captain Campbell was absent sick since 30h September,
1851, and one rank and file absent sick at Fort Leavenworth, and
2d Lieutenant N. G. Evans on detached service at Fort Leavenworth, leaving 65 for duty, of which Brevet 2d Lieutenant C. E.
Norris and 6 rank and file were sick and 2 rank and file confined.

Attached to this command was Assistant Surgeon T. C. Henry.

The strength of this command was therefore 5 commissioned
officers and 201 rank and file for duty.

This Command was in a good state of discipline, and the distinguished and experienced and gallant officer Major Steen commanded the respect which his position entitled him to. It was
gratifying to learn that most of the men of his own company had
joined the Temperance Society.

The troops were in the old uniform [as] no other had been
provided and their arms and equipments in good serviceable order, although the horse equipments were much worn. The muskets of Major Richardson's company were quite old, and there
was a great deficiency of pistols in Company E, 2d Dragoons,
and many sword knots wanted. These troops, considering the
hard labour they had to perform in moving and erecting quarters
within the year, were well instructed. Lieutenant W. D. Smith,
who was acting adjutant of the post, had but recently joined in
command of Captain Campbell's company, and here I regret to

say the complaint with which this highly meritorious and ambitious officer is afflicted obliges me to recommend his recall from the arduous duties of the frontier stations to some duty in some other branch of the service. I have seen him in so much pain as to bring drops of water from his face, and he cannot unless cured do the duty of a dragoon officer. His complaint is that of the gravel.[59]

I was obliged to condemn 2 ponies of Company H, 1t Dragoons, and 5 horses and 9 ponies of Company E, 2d Dragoons, as unfit for the dragoon service.

The quarters and buildings of the command were in a good state of police, but quite indifferent and insufficient, the post not having been completed. Major Richardson's company were in tents, and the sick were in a tent as there was no hospital. The comforts of the troops, however, both sick and well, studied and suitable corrals for the horses and public animals. All public property of every description was in a good state of preservation. The supplies were all obtained thro' Forts Fillmore and Conrad, and the supplies were abundant with the exception of horse shoes and horse shoe nails and horse brushes and curry combs. A good garden was cultivated and a corn and oats farm planted which looked well. Hay is cut from the natural meadows for the animals.

The Medical Department is well managed by Assistant Surgeon T. C. Henry who stands high in his profession and is also actively engaged as a naturalist very much to the advancement of that science in the number of new variety he has collected.

The Quartermaster and Commissary departments are in the hands of Lieutenant C. E. Norris and well conducted. He had no

---

[59] Captain Campbell recovered from the "gravel" sufficiently to become a Colonel in the Confederate Army. He was killed on June 27, 1862, in the Battle of Gaines's Mill, Virginia. The gravel is described as a deposit of crystalline dust or concretions of crystals in the kidneys and bladder.

quartermaster's funds on hand and 522 $^{75}\!/_{100}$ dollars of commissary funds. There is a post bakery here and a post fund of 524 $^{32}\!/_{100}$ dollars on the 30h September.

At this post is the residence of Mr. J. M. Smith the Indian Agent and seems well located for his purposes.

In the description of this post, I recommended it be changed to the Gila.

« *Fort Fillmore—17h to the 28h October* »

This post was under the command of Major E. Backus, 3rd Infantry, with 1t Lieutenant W. H. Wood, 3rd Infantry, acting adjutant; Assistant Surgeon Charles Southerland [Sutherland], medical officer; Major W. B. Brice, Pay Department; and 1t Lieutenant J. C. McFarran [McFerran], acting quartermaster and commissary.

There are four companies of this command: towit, Company D, 2d Dragoons, Captain and Brevet Major L. P. Graham, commanded by 1t Lieutenant J. C. McFarran, 3rd Infantry, 69 in the aggregate and 51 horses, of which Major Graham was absent on general recruiting service since 2d August, 1852; 1t Lieutenant P. Calhoun, transferred to this company in August, 1852, has never joined; 2d Lieutenant B. H. Robinson, on detached service at Fort Leavenworth since April, 1852; 5 rank and file on detached service, leaving 61 for duty, of which 5 rank and file were sick and one confined.—Company C, 3rd Infantry, Captain W. E. Johns, 81 in the aggregate, of which 10 rank and file [were] on detached service, leaving Captain Johns and 2d Lieutenant W. D. Whipple and 69 rank and file for duty, of which 5 rank and file were sick and 4 confined.—Company A, 3rd Infantry, Captain A. W. Bowman, commanded by 1t Lieutenant J. N. Ward, 76 in the aggregate, of which Captain Bowman was on detached service at Washington City, 2d Lieutenant D. C. Green on detached service since March, 1853, 3 rank and file on detached service, 2 rank and file on leave, and 3 rank and file absent sick, leaving 1t Lieutenant Ward and Brevet 2d Lieutenant R. V. Bonneau, and 64 rank and file for duty, of which 5 rank and file were sick and 3 confined.—Company E, 3rd Infantry, Captain and Brevet Major J. Van Horn [Van Horne], commanded by 2d Lieutenant J. Daniel, 84 in the aggregate, of which Major Van Horn was on recruiting service since July, 1852, and 1t Lieutenant J. D. Wilkins on leave of absence for 6 months, 3 rank and file on detached service, one rank and file on leave, and one absent sick, leaving 2d Lieutenant Daniel and Brevet 2d Lieutenant A. M. D. McCook and 75 rank and file for duty of which 7 rank and file were sick and 8 confined.

The strength of this post therefore consists of 8 commissioned officers of the line and 269 rank and file for duty.

This post is in a high state of discipline in every respect, and the commanding officer, Major Backus, enjoys the high respect of his whole command, [to] which his distinguished services in the field, combined with his individual character entitle him; and he is peculiarly well fitted for the command where so much discretion, as well as firmness, is necessary, within two miles of a Mexican population directly on the opposite side of the river, at Mesilla, and the nearest post at this time to El Paso.

The troops were in the old uniform of course, no other having been furnished them. The arms and equipments [were] in excellent serviceable order. They were well instructed in view of the great labour they have performed in building this post. Major Backus took the infantry through the batallion drill handsomely and the companies afterwards went through the company drills under their respective commanders creditably. An impetus has been given to the military duties of this post since the arrival of Major Backus, Captain Johns, and Lieutenants Daniel and Mc-Cook in August, 1853. The dragoon company was under the command of an infantry officer, Lieutenant McFarran, who commands it well and to the advantage of the company in addition to his other duties. Yet it is to be regretted [that] the dragoons do not have sufficient officers at their posts. 1t Lieutenant P. Calhoun has been under orders to join his company more than a year and yet has never reached it. There is a good regimental band here, and the guard mounting is done in very handsome style and other duties performed with great regularity.

I was obliged to condemn one horse as unfit for the dragoon service, and recommended it be turned over to the Quartermaster's Department.

The quarters for this post for both officers and men are the best in the Territory. There is a good hospital and magazine and store houses, and all public property is in a good state of preservation. The supplies of corn, flour, beans, beef, and mutton readily obtained in the neighbourhood: other supplies are brought from Fort Union via Albuquerque. Corn costs 75 cents the bushel and flour 10 to 12 cents the pound. Beef and mutton are reasonable.

1t Lieutenant J. C. McFarran performs the duty of quartermaster and commissary very well. There was due him as commissary on the 30h September, 1853, 10,524^{32}⁄₁₀₀ dollars which was covered by a loan from the Pay Department of 8,169^{06}⁄₁₀₀ dollars and the Quartermaster's Department of 2,355^{28}⁄₁₀₀ dollars; and at the same time the farm interest owed the Subsistence Department 2,078^{7}⁄₁₀₀ dollars. On the 31t December, 1851, the farm interest owed this department but 1,747^{98}⁄₁₀₀, thus shewing an accumulation of debt which no doubt will go on increasing if this business be continued. Also at that date he had in his hands of Quartermaster's funds 16,682^{94}⁄₁₀₀ dollars less the above loan. His funds are kept in an iron safe in the same room with the paymaster's funds.

Major B. W. Brice, paymaster at this post, has been assigned to the payment of the district comprising Fort Fillmore, Fort Webster, and Fort Conrad, and has made his payments according to the requirements of the law. On the 20h October, he had on hand of Government funds 35,576⁸⁸⁄₁₀₀ dollars kept in an iron safe in his office at this post where also is kept the quartermaster's and commissary's funds, and a sentinel is posted in front of the building.

The Medical Department is well conducted by Assistant Surgeon C. Southerland and well supplied.

A good garden and bakery are attached to this post and a farm is cultivated. There is a post fund of 1,008⁰⁵⁄₁₀₀ dollars.

It was at this post that Ex Governor W. C. Lane[60] met with a refusal on the part of the commanding officer, Lieutenant Colonel D. S. Miles, to take forcible possession of the Disputed Territory [No. 15, Plans and Sketches section], the Mesilla Valley, on his requisition and in consequence accused "some 350 U.S. troops who were unemployed and within 5 miles of the scene of action" of folding "their arms in frigid tranquility and thereby sustaining the enemies of their country" (See copy of Governor Lane's letter annexed [on page 76]. The propriety of the course of the commanding officer on this occasion cannot be questioned and the subject needs no further notice from me.

« *Close of the Command and Troops* »

Thus having completed the inspection of all the military posts in this department, I hereunto append a table of the strength of the military posts in this Territory with the serviceable small arms and cannon, amounting in the aggregate to 1,624 officers

---

[60] William Carr Lane, Territorial Governor of New Mexico in 1852, Lane arrived at Santa Fe on September 9, 1852, and the following day assumed charge of civil affairs. Sumner to Colonel Samuel Cooper (adjutant general), September 24, 1852, in 32 Cong., 2 sess., *House Exec. Doc. 1*, II, p. 26.

and soldiers, 1,743 muskets, 1,583 rifles, 940 pistols, 1,106 musketoons, 430 colts revolvers & c. The supply of ammunition in
the Territory is commensurate with the arms. It will be seen that
the supply of dragoon horses are quite too limited, being but 383
horses to 483 rank and file.

« *General Remarks Applicable to the Whole Command* »

Quartermaster's Department. The clothing of the troops is
defective in the cut. The complaint is quite general. First soldiers'
pantaloons [were] generally too short in the leg, and too small
at the foot, and too large in the waste. Coats too narrow across the
back and breast and too long in the collar. Draws too small and
short in the leg. Few of no. 2 pantaloons but nos. 3 and 4 mostly
required and as to shoes, nos. 7, 8, 9 and a few 10's and 6's required. It costs the soldier from one and a half to three dollars
to have his clothes altered. These remarks are applicable to the
old uniform only.

The article of knapsack is quite unsatisfactory; reasonable objections are made to the painted canvas and the gum elastic on
account of their effects in this climate on the soldiers clothes. My
own opinion is that stout canvas alone would be best, and they
might probably be manufactured whole. The canteen is still a
desideratum.

While at Fort Defiance my attention was called to see pitched
the French bell tent as established under the existing regulations
of the uniform & c of the army—also a tent made by the Quartermaster's Department according to a plan of Brevet Major
H. L. Kendrick of the 2d Artillery, and the ordinary common
tent heretofore in use by the army; and [I] now submit for consideration the following remarks before much expenditure be
made for tents. The French bell tent on the ground covers a surface of 180 square feet as per diagram, towit,

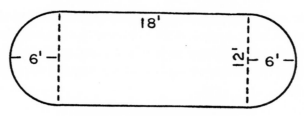

A - French Bell Tent

and requires 22 pins, and weighs 67½ pounds inclusive of the pins. Its ridge pole is supported by one king pole 7 feet long and two braces secured to the pole by hinges as per diagram, towit,

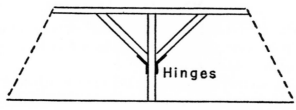

B - French Bell Tent

and will probably accommodate 15 men. The tent of Major Kendrick on the ground covers a surface of 115 square feet as per diagram, towit,

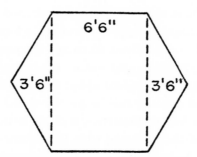

C - Major Kendrick's Tent

and requires 18 pins, and weighs 53 pounds, inclusive of the pins. Its ridge pole is supported by two common tent poles 6 feet long in the usual way, and will probably accommodate 9 men. The old common tent covers a surface of 49 square feet as per diagram, towit,

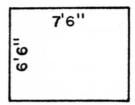

D - Common Tent

and requires 14 pins and weighs 42 pounds inclusive of the pins. Its ridge pole is supported on two poles 7 feet long, and will probably accommodate 5 men.

There are several objections to the French bell tent for the field. First, it covers too much ground, as it is generally difficult to find many large level spots in the field for a camp. Second, it requires several men to pitch it. Third, it is not well adapted to the field on account of the ventillation required in the top. Fourth, the hinges to the braces will be broken at once in the transportation and thereby rendered useless. It is however well enough and perhaps the best for an intrenched camp to supply the place of buildings at posts to stand for a long time.

The tent of Major Kendrick has many advantages. It requires but three men to pitch it, and has no hinges to be broken; it is portable and can accommodate about twice as many as the old common tent, and is not so tall by one foot, and yet tall enough. It is not too large for small parties, and yet large enough for the general service of the rank and file. These tents were examined by the officers at Fort Defiance, and they concur generally with me in opinion.

This department have adopted an excellent system as to transportation wagons. The wheels are all of a size and the axels steel, but for this climate it is difficult to prevent motion in the joints of connexion between the spokes and felloes and hub. I would recommend a thicker tire than any I have seen for these wheels as it often happens the wheel on a march must either be caulked or wedged between the tire and felly, and in such cases as well as on passing down steep and stoney roads, it is important to prevent any permanent alteration in the tire which will inevitably take place in a weak one.

The use of gum elastic in any shape but the water bucket meets with general objection in this climate. It is worthless as a wagon whip.

Subsistence Department. The articles of coffee, sugar, and salt to the one hundred rations are generally complained of as too small. The complaint for salt is owing I presume to the fact of their being more fresh meat and less salt used. Coffee should be increased in the ration about one-third and suger and salt in proportion. The ration of fresh beef is also complained of as too small. These complaints I presume are particularly applicable to this Territory where men have laboured so hard. The troops would prefer more salt provisions—yet the supplies of bacon and ham are excellent although limited. There is no salt pork in the Territory except a few barrels at posts condemned. I have heard no material complaint on this account. The bacon sent into the country although well packed is nevertheless exposed to great wastage for want of boxing. When put up in large piles, the understrata are subjected to a heavy pressure, which no canvas can relieve, and which in a warm climate forces out the grease to waste; and here where butter and lard are scarce is a great disadvantage to the consumer. It is this grease that is mixed with the soldiers flour, and enables him to make buiscuit on the road. If bacon, after being put into canvas, were boxed with but two or three sides in a box and filled in with cut straw or rice chaff, the box would relieve the bacon of any weight that might be placed on it in store or transportation and thereby prevent wastage.[61]

The article of coffee in this department has been out so as to occasion purchases at high rates to the Government, but this was but a temporary deficiency resulting from too small a requisition on the States. The article of flour is no longer obtained from the States at a cost of about 30 dollars the barrel. It is now purchased at the several small mills in the northern part of the Territory in abundance, but is a little gritty yet otherwise excellent and at a saving in price of from 10 to 14 dollars the barrel, and the southern part of the Territory at Harts Mill it is had entirely free of grit and excellent.

Farming Interests.[62] This duty of the troops seems to have

[61] Colonel McCall had complained, three years earlier, that the packing of bacon in barrels for shipment across the plains was inefficient and expensive. Much space was lost, and the weight of the barrels was excessive. He recommended that square boxes, made to fit the wagon bodies, be employed. McCall to Roger Jones (adjutant general), December 26, 1850, in *Report of the Secretary of War, Communicating, in Compliance with a Resolution of the Senate, Colonel McCall's Reports in Relation to New Mexico,* 31 Cong., 2 sess., *Sen. Exec. Doc. 26,* pp. 22–23.

[62] The farming program, of which Mansfield was so critical, was instituted in 1851 as a measure to improve the health of the troops and reduce the cost of subsisting men and animals. It provided that "the commanding officer of every permanent post and station where the public lands are sufficient, or private lands can be leased on reasonable terms, will annually cultivate a *kitchen garden* with the soldiers under his command, to enable him to supply the hospital and men with necessary vegetables throughout the year." In addition, in all military departments west of the Mississippi River, the posts and stations were to maintain farms for the purpose of producing, "as far as practicable, grains for bread and forage, and long forage." All of the profits resulting from these activities were to be divided equally, each quarter, among the enlisted men of the various garrisons. General Orders No. 1, January 8, 1851, Roger Jones (adjutant general), in 32 Cong., 1 sess., *House Exec. Doc. 2,* p. 164. In his report for the year 1851 Secretary of War Charles M. Conrad said only that insufficient time had elapsed to determine the success of the farming experiment. *Ibid.,* 111. The following year he was forced to admit that "the attempts to cultivate farms by the troops has, but in a few instances, during the past season, been attended with beneficial results." *Report of the Secretary of War, 1852,* in

proved a failure generally. The mode of cultivation in this Territory is necessarily so different from that to which the American and European, who constitute the rank and file of our army, have been accustomed, and the business so entirely different from the pursuits of an officer and soldier, that it is not at all astonishing it did not succeed. There are probably many officers and soldiers too who have never had the least practice at planting not even an ordinary garden, and certainly the subject at the Military Academy has never been introduced as one of the essentials of an officer in defence of his country, however pleasant and agreeable it may be to possess information and have practice in farming. The system of farming as now organized I feel it my duty to report as injurious to the discipline of a command. Its tendency, that of dividing the proceeds among the "enlisted men" in addition to their pay, is to excite the cupidity of the soldier, to the neglect of other duties. All military instructions, drills, and expeditions after an enemy will become onerous and distasteful and neglected, in view of the all absorbing love of gain. If a command is to be marched, it cannot be done till the crops are gathered and the spoils divided. If a post possesses enriching qualities, the soldiers of other less favoured posts are dissatisfied. Its effect is to detach and separate the aims and views of the soldier from the officer instead of uniting them both in the honourable career of defending their country. Hitherto the aims and the feelings of the officer and soldier were united: here they are separated— the soldier in pursuit of gain and the officer, honor. In short it is contrary to the design and intention of an army to make farmers of them.

This interest in this Territory is in debt over 14,000 dollars. The result is that the soldiers have been compelled to work

Fillmore's *Message from the President* . . . , 32 Cong., 2 sess., *House Exec. Doc. 1*, II, p. 4. Jefferson Davis, who replaced Conrad as secretary of war in 1853, made no reference to the farming activities in any of his annual reports.

hitherto without any dividends from his labour which bears particularly hard on him. The allowance provided by law for such extra service should be paid them.

My impressions are that the instruction of the troops in every branch of military duties in New Mexico, and the protection of the population against the Indians, and the building of their own quarters and making their gardens will if properly executed occupy all their time, and leave them but little recreation.

Officers' and Soldiers' Pay. At Forts Union, Massachusetts, Defiance, and at Contonment Burgwin the troops had not been paid regularly; and there seems no good reason why they should not have been paid as often as the law requires. Merchants in this Territory are always desirous of cashing drafts on the States in preference to transporting hard money, and thus there need never be a want of ready funds.[63]

The troops stationed in this department and the county of El Paso Texas can none of them be nearer than 675 miles, and some as far as 1,000 miles, from the nearest trading town in the States; and the transportation of merchandise and sutlers' goods costs from 8 to 15 cents the pound, independent of the profits these traders must make on their goods in order to live—thus, as will be seen, raising the price of all articles brought from the States say from 100 to 400 per cent. There is but little competition in trade in consequence of the limited sales and the danger attending transportation across the country infested with Indians, and hence this state of the market compared with other places in the U.S. will exist for some time to come. I am of opinion there are no posts in the U.S. so peculiarly situated. The officers are in some degree relieved by the authority to purchase of the commis-

[63] Colonel McCall reported in 1850 that funds were readily obtainable in Chihuahua and that there was no difficulty in getting drafts cashed in Santa Fe or Taos. "Report of Troops and Staff Departments at Santa Fe," August 31, 1850, in "McCall's Inspection Report, Department of New Mexico, 1850."

sary beef, bacon, ham, sugar, coffee, and other articles of the soldier's ration at the contract price in the States, and this is a great help to them. Yet the other necessaries and comforts of life to both officers and soldiers have to be purchased at the advanced prices above stated, or they are obliged to deny themselves what the troops at other posts enjoy.

I would recommend that the law giving to the officers and soldiers stationed under the above disadvantages additional pay, and which expired by limitation in March last, be renewed.[64]

Armament of the Troops and Practice in the Use of Their Arms &c &c. The musketoon[65] as an arm for the dragoon or

[64] Commissioned officers had received no increase in pay for more than fifty years prior to 1857 when they received an increase of twenty dollars a month. Between 1833 and 1854 enlisted men were paid six to eight dollars a month. By a law enacted on August 4, 1854, troops in the various branches of the service were to receive eleven to twelve dollars a month. Congress, on September 28, 1850, provided a small additional pay for officers and soldiers stationed in California and the Territory of Oregon, but this provision expired on March 1, 1852. *Report of the Secretary of War, 1851,* in 32 Cong., 1 sess., *House Exec. Doc. 2,* p. 115. Quartermaster General Thomas S. Jesup reported in 1853 that 1,560 soldiers had been employed during the past year on extra duty, "and were each paid a per diem of fifteen cents and commutation for the whisky ration authorized by law." He recommended an increase in extra duty pay to twenty-five cents a day for laborers and teamsters and forty cents a day for mechanics employed anywhere east of the Rockies, and to thirty-five cents and fifty cents, respectively, for those employed west of the mountains. In 33 Cong., 1 sess., *Sen. Exec. Doc. 1,* II, pp. 133–34.

[65] The musketoon was a short-barreled weapon, forty-one inches in length, weighing six and one-half pounds. Ordnance reports distinguished between dragoon (cavalry), sapper, and artillery musketoons. Major General Zenas R. Bliss wrote of the musketoon: "The most worthless of all the arms with which we were supplied was that called the musketoon, a sort of brevet musket. It was nothing but an old musket sawed off to about two-thirds its original length, and the rammer fastened to the barrel by a swivel to prevent its being lost or dropped when loading on horseback; it used the same cartridge as the musket, kicked like blazes, and was only used because it could be more conveniently carried on horseback." "Extracts from the Unpublished Memoirs of Major General Zenas R. Bliss, U.S.A., Soldiering in Texas, 1854–55," *The Journal of the Military Service Institution,* Vol. XXXVIII (January–February, 1906), 127, quoted in Arthur Woodward, ed., *Journal of Lt. Thomas W. Sweeny, 1849–1853,* 248, n. 67.

mounted man in any way is almost worthless. The shackle that secures the ram rod to the barrel is entirely too delicate and is constantly breaking. When slung it is liable to lose its ball and load. It is too light for the ball and cartridge necessary to execution with it. There is no probable certainty of hitting the object aimed at, and the recoil too great to be fired with ease. There appears to be *at present* nothing better for the dragoon than the carbine and Sharps rifle. Both load at the breech, and will not of course lose their loads when slung. They can be fired with rapidity and with suitable practice with great certainty. The dragoon can feel safe with one of these pieces dismounted, and alone, with a pocket full of cartridges and caps in the midst of Indians. But with the musketoon he is uneasy; it takes so long to load; he loses his ramroad, or his load out: he gets disconcerted and will probably be whipped if hard pushed. With Sharps rifle the case is different, and the pistol and sword can at once be dispensed with, whenever the horse is to be lightened and speed be necessary in the pursuit of Indians. I would therefore recommend that the musketoon be dispensed with and the rifle and carbine substituted in stead.

At present among the dragoons, there are few Sharps rifles, some Harpers Ferry rifles, more carbines and most musketoons, and the ordinary pistols and colts revolvers with the broad sword.

The dragoon requires a stout and hardy and fast horse, and his horse should always be well shod on the hind feet as well as the fore. The American horse so called is the only animal able to endure the service required of the dragoon, and one of the most important things in preserving its usefulness is proper care of its feet. A mistaken idea exists among some in this Territory that it is only necessary to shoe the fore feet, and many an horse is ruined in usefulness by this neglect. The same remark is applicable to the mule. Hard labour cannot be performed by animals without good feet. The practice of the Mexican is no criterian for animals in the service of the U.S.

The infantry soldier is well armed with the musket and bayonet. There can be very little call for the mountain howitzer and field piece among the Indians. Hence the artillery soldier should understand thoroughly the infantry and light infantry drills.

My impressions are that the practice of firing at the target with ball and buck shot is not sufficient. The mere discharge of the guard of the previous day at the target to get rid of the load is not sufficient practice, and there is not interest enough taken in it by the men to produce any real improvement. It requires great use of the ball cartridge to make the soldier confident in what he can do with his musket. It requires a good sized cartridge to throw a ball to produce effect at long range, and light as the musket now is the soldier frequently flinches at the recoil, which practice alone can correct.

Here it is proper to remark that there has been too few officers at their companies to secure instruction to the rank and file and to perform the duty. There were eleven companies with only one officer at a company for duty and in four cases out of the eleven, that officer commanded the post and did quartermaster and commissary duty at the same time, and in one other instance a dragoon company with an infantry officer in command and he also quartermaster and commissary.

It is therefore apparent that these officers were over worked and nothing but their extraordinary merit, combined with the high character of the other officers, has kept up the character of the army to the high standard it should always maintain of honor and sobriety.

Communications between Posts. The trains from Fort Union to all places are necessarily under the protection of an escort, otherwise they would be exposed to Indian depredations. Letters however are sent by express from Fort Union to Santa Fé, Burgwin, Fort Massachusetts, Albuquerque, Los Lunas, and Fort Conrad of one to three men, and they are sent from and to Forts Defiance, Webster, and Fillmore by express of two to five men. The Great Mail from the States moves from El Paso to Santa Fé once a month and returns once a month. Here I would recommend an addition to the mail facilities not only for the accommodation of the posts, but of the inhabitants, and in some measure to dispense with some of the special expresses for officers' and soldiers' letters. A mail to leave Santa Fé for El Paso and return from El Paso to Santa Fé once a week, under the direction of the Post Office Department, would be very beneficial and is really wanted, and in due time, a line of stages would be established between those two places, which would facilitate travel and the transmission of small packages. With this arrangement the Great Mail could start at El Paso and Santa Fé monthly for the States.[66]

« *Recapitulation of Such Matter as Requires Immediate Consideration* »

First, appropriations are recommended for the following military roads:[67] from Fort Union over the Moro Mountain to Can-

[66] The first regular mail service was established over the San Antonio-Santa Fe route in 1850. It was a monthly service carried on horseback. The first stagecoach mail service, over the same route, began in July, 1854. In 1858 the Santa Fe-El Paso section became a separate route, connecting at El Paso with the San Antonio-San Diego route. Conkling, *The Butterfield Overland Mail*, I, 90–91.

[67] In the next several years following Mansfield's inspection a number of roads were constructed or improved in New Mexico, including the road from Taos through Santa Fe and Albuquerque to Doña Ana and the road from Fort Union through Las Vegas to Santa Fe. Averam B. Bender, *The March of Empire: Frontier Defense in the Southwest, 1848–1860*, 70. A congressional act of July 17, 1854, appropriated twenty thousand dollars for the construction and repair of the road from Taos to Santa Fe and twelve thousand dollars for the road from Santa Fe to Doña Ana, including the sinking of wells. Secretary of War Jefferson Davis was forced to point out that when "a comparatively small amount of money is appropriated for a long

tonment Burgwin of 2,000 dollars; from Cantonment Burgwin to Fort Massachusetts on six hills, impassible for loaded wagons between the Rivers Hondo and Colerado, 6,000 dollars; from Contonment Burgwin to La Joya on the road to Santa Fé over the mountain is precipitous and impassible for loaded wagons, 4,000 dollars; from Fort Union to Santa Fé direct, 2,000 dollars; from Albuquerque to Fort Defiance, 1,000 dollars; from Fort Conrad following the Rio Grande del Norté to Fort Fillmore, 1,000 dollars.

Second, the southern boundary line between the county of El Paso Texas and New Mexico recommended to be immediately established by monuments.

Third, a weekly mail recommended to be established between Santa Fé and El Paso.

Fourth, one or two sound moral mechanics recommended to be stationed in each of the Pueblos Indian Villages to teach them.

Fifth, three or four new posts recommended to be established in Texas on the mail route between El Paso and San Antonio in addition to a post at El Paso.

Sixth, the boxing of bacon in a particular manner deemed indispensable to prevent wastage.

Seventh, a limit is recommended to the number of the French bell tents—and attention called to the cut of soldiers' clothes.

Eighth, the officers' and soldiers' pay for New Mexico and the county of El Paso Texas recommended to be increased.

Ninth, the armament of dragoons with musketoons recommended to be changed.

Tenth, farming by troops regarded unfavourably.

line of road" the first duty was to make the road passable for wagons throughout its entire length, then, if any of the appropriation remained, to expend it in improving the more difficult portions. Davis to Captain Eliakin Parker Scammon, Topographical Engineers, November 28, 1854, in 33 Cong., 2 sess., *House Exec. Doc. 1*, II, pp. 42–43.

Eleventh, the enlisting of near sighted men and men that cannot understand English unfavourable.

Twelfth, more officers with a company recommended to be kept at their posts.

All of which is respectfully submitted,
Jos. K. F. MANSFIELD
Colonel and Inspector General

1t March, 1854

« *L. Statement of Indian Depredations* »

committed in the Valley of El Paso, El Paso County, state of Texas, from the month of September, 1851, to the month of October, 1853, inclusive—drawn up by the Honorable Joel L. Ankrim, Judge of the District Court.

I submit the following statement of depredations committed by Indians in this valley and vicinity within the two years last past, that is since the U.S. troops have been withdrawn from us. Should you find any error either in date or otherwise please correct it.

Previous to 1849 the Americans had but little interest and expected but little influence in the Valley of El Paso. In that year the emigration to California commenced, and in September the 3rd Infantry, commanded by Major Van Horn, arrived. In August the Indians swept the valley of stock, and in an effort to recover it Major E. Steen was seriously wounded, being stationed at that time at Doña Ana. Major Van Horn stationed a portion of his command in front of El Paso and at San Elizario, and the troops remained with us till about the month of September, 1851, when they were withdrawn by order of Colonel Sumner to the point now occupied at Fort Fillmore. During the two years that the troops were with us, the only outrage perpetrated or attempted was an attack on Mr. Coon's[68] train in November, 1849,

[68] Benjamin Franklin Coons, a Missourian who had been engaged in the Santa

at the Guadalupe Mountains,[69] about 100 miles from the Valley of El Paso: Mr. Coon lost some stock, had one man killed and one wounded, which constitutes the entire loss of life and property sustained by the inhabitants of this valley and travellers on this side of the Pecos River during the two years ending in September, 1851, during which time the troops were with us, and it may be observed that these troops were infantry and the effect was the result of their presence, for they were powerless for Indian difficulties.[70]

Fe trade, purchased Ponce's Ranch in June, 1849. Ponce's Ranch, located on the left side of the Rio Grande opposite El Paso del Norte, was the first establishment on that side of the river. It belonged to Juan María Ponce de León, who received a grant of 599 acres opposite El Paso on August 13, 1827. J. Evetts Haley, *Fort Concho and the Texas Frontier*, 28, 51; Thomlinson, *Fort Bliss*, 2–3; and Conkling, *The Butterfield Overland Mail*, II, 69. Coons purchased the ranch when he foresaw that the establishment of military posts in the vicinity would attract settlers. It was at Coons' Ranch that Major Jefferson Van Horne established the post, on September 8, 1849, which was the forerunner of Fort Bliss. When a post office was established in 1850, Coons selected his own middle name for it. Hence, Franklin, or Franklin City, was the immediate predecessor of the American town of El Paso. Until it was incorporated as El Paso in 1873, the town was called both Franklin and El Paso. John R. Bartlett, who visited Coons' Ranch, stated that it "was the military post for about three years, under the command of Major Van Horne." *Personal Narrative*, I, 192–93. This would make it the same as Mansfield's Smith's Ranch. Smith first occupied the ranch in 1853. According to Conkling, he purchased it from Ponce de León's heirs on March 25, 1854. *Butterfield Overland Mail*, II, 70. Why Coons disposed or was deprived of the ranch is not clear. Anson Mills, who arrived in El Paso in 1858 and apparently did not know Coons personally, wrote in his reminiscences: "Franklin Coontz turned out an undesirable citizen, and it was suggested that I rename the city." *My Story*, 52. In 1852, Bartlett met Coons near Tucson, in what was still a part of the Mexican state of Sonora. Coons was on his way to San Francisco with a flock of fourteen thousand sheep. He had a party of sixty men, primarily to guard the sheep against Indians. *Personal Narrative*, II, 293.

[69] The Guadalupe Mountains run north and south, extending from New Mexico into Texas. The northern route from El Paso to San Antonio ran by way of Waco Tanks and Guadalupe Pass to the Pecos River.

[70] Bartlett, to the contrary, relates that on January 8, 1851, while he had his quarters at Magoffin's house, Indians stole forty of Magoffin's mules which were grazing about three miles from the house and the same distance from the military

Let me now review the occurrences in the El Paso Valley during the two years since the troops were withdrawn. In February, 1852, about four months after the troops left us, the Indians began their depredations by taking stock: [they] broke down Captain Skillman's[71] corral wall at his residence, and therefrom took various mules and horses. At the same time some Indians attacked his party carrying the mail about 100 miles from this valley and took a greater part of the animals.

About the same time like depredations were committed at Socarro.

In about the month of May, San Elizario suffered in like manner to the amount of 80 head of stock.

About the same time Mr. Maguffin's corral was broken open, and animals taken therefrom to the number of 43.

About August 12h, Messrs. Hoppin and Hubbell[72] lost all

---

post. The Indians were pursued but not overtaken. *Personal Narrative*, I, 152–53. A few days later "the Indians made another descent upon the inclosure near Mr. Magoffin's house in which he kept his mules, and stole thirty." *Ibid.*, 155. Bartlett does state that "the Apaches had been more bold than usual during the spring and summer of 1852; and the whole frontier had suffered from their inroads." He cites various instances of depredations and adds, "When I went to take a ride, if it was extended as far as three miles [from Magoffinsville], I felt it necessary to be accompanied by several friends." *Ibid.*, II, 384.

[71] Captain Henry Skillman was a Kentuckian who had engaged in the Santa Fe trade. During the Mexican War he served as a scout with Colonel Alexander Doniphan in the invasion of Chihuahua. He is usually credited with opening the first mail service through western Texas from San Antonio to El Paso and Santa Fe, although "Big Foot" Wallace is sometimes given that honor. In any case, Skillman maintained a monthly mail service between San Antonio and Santa Fe until 1856. Later he was associated with the Butterfield Overland Mail in West Texas. See Haley, *Fort Concho*, 75–76, 87–90; Conkling, *Butterfield Overland Mail*, I, 90; and Ralph P. Bieber, ed., *Exploring Southwestern Trails*, 311–12.

[72] Messrs. Hoppin and Hubbell were probably Charles A. Hoppin and Jarvis Hubbell. Hoppin had served for a time as aide-de-camp to Governor Calhoun of New Mexico. Bartlett, *Personal Narrative*, I, 207. Hubbell was appointed the first postmaster at Franklin (El Paso) on July 26, 1852. Conkling, *Butterfield Overland Mail*, II, 75.

their mules and horses (between 40 and 50 head) while grazing in sight of the former station of the troops at Mr. Smith's place.

About the same time two men were killed at Mr. White's Ranche, 8 miles above El Paso, and emigrants were robbed of their stock near the Guadaloupe Mountains. Shortly afterwards Captain Skillman again had his corral broken down at his dwelling and animals taken. In or about September, 4 men were killed in the road between this place and the Pecos River and about the 15h day of October, Captain Skillman's corral was again broken down and robbed of stock. This closes as far as now occurs to me the catalogue for the year 1852 which I will leave with merely the statement in which I believe I am correct, viz., that during the months of August and September of that year the Indians virtually held possession of this valley from El Paso to the boundary of our state and that such was the general condition of things that the United States Boundary Commissioner, for the safety of the public documents, was compelled to accept of an escort of Mexican soldiers to go to the Coast. He did not feel justified in travelling from here to San Antonio with the same party which would a year before have been considered amply sufficient.[73]

[73] The troops stationed at Fort Fillmore were barely sufficient to provide an escort for Lieutenant Amiel W. Whipple, who was to complete the survey of the southern boundary of New Mexico. Bartlett's party consisted of twenty-three men, including himself. Bartlett wrote:

> In this position, I was at a loss what course to take, or how to get out of the country. Every small party coming through from San Antonio had been attacked by the Comanches; and accounts had reached El Paso that bands of three hundred warriors had been seen. At no time had there been so much alarm felt; and I was advised, by the army officers and others, who knew the state of the country, not to attempt the journey, with so small a party as mine, without an escort.

Colonel Emilio Landberg, of the Mexican army, offered to provide Bartlett with an escort of Mexican soldiers if he would go through the city of Chihuahua then on through Mexican territory to the lower Rio Grande. This offer Bartlett accepted. The escort, as it turned out, consisted of five soldiers. *Personal Narrative*, II, 396–97, 404.

1853. The depredations of this year commenced in March at San Elizario: a large amount of stock was driven off and a few animals recaptured by the citizens.

In May a herd of sheep belonging to Mr. Hart was destroyed and the shepherd killed within one-half mile of his dwelling.

Smith's train was robbed of 60 head of animals on the road from San Antonio to this place about the same time.

Captain Wallace[74] with the mail at this time had a man mortally wounded, who barely lived to be brought to San Elizario.

Captain Wallace was again attacked on the same trip.

On the 4th July last great loss was sustained at Isleta.

The last day of July the Indians were discovered in the settlement of San Elizario and being pursued fled towards the mountains, and the night of the 1t August stole stock from Benjamin Ryan at the Cornudas[75] and, being followed by 13 well armed men, on the morning of the 2d gave battle and killed 10 out of the 13 of our people.

In the month of August, 1853, Mr. Maguffin had the whole of his stock stolen from his ranche.

The property of the U.S. Mexican Boundary Commission was taken about the same time.[76]

[74] Captain Wallace is undoubtedly William A. "Big Foot" Wallace who, like Skillman, was long associated with the San Antonio-El Paso mail service. He had served with the Texas volunteers in the Mexican War.

[75] The Cornudas de los Alamos, now called Cornudas Mountains, are a group of detached peaks, lying in Texas and New Mexico. Cornuda Mountain, one of the four prominent peaks in the group, is in New Mexico. Thorne's Well, located in a cave in this mountain, was a frequent watering place for travelers. Bartlett, *Personal Narrative*, I, 130; Conkling, *Butterfield Overland Mail*, I, 398–400.

[76] Bartlett said that on two occasions during his stay at Magoffinsville, August 17 to October 7, 1853, the Indians attempted to run off the animals belonging to the boundary commission but were prevented from doing so. *Personal Narrative*, II, 384. His party was attacked in Chihuahua and a herdsman killed and the spare animals stampeded and lost. Bartlett said that this was the only occurrence of the kind which befell the commission in more than two years in the field. *Ibid.*, 411–14.

In March of this year Mr. Maguffin's corral was broken down and stock taken therefrom numbering 11 animals.

In September the Indians made an attack on Mr. Maguffin's herd of mules whilst grazing at Canutille[77] and 6 were stolen.

About [the] same time while two men in the employment of Dr. Raphael Armijo were searching for some lost animals they were attacked by Indians within one-half mile of Mr. Smith's place and one of them seriously wounded in the leg with an arrow.

In the month of October, 5 animals were stolen from Mr. Maguffin's ranche, Indians were pursued and traced to the vicinity of the Sacramento Mountains.

The summary will read as follows: in the 24 months since the troops left us, we have had in the Valley of El Paso, or in the roads approaching it, 23 attacks from Indians, all of which have been attended with loss of property and some loss of life, in the same space of time we have lost 18 men and I believe the average value of property taken by the Indians during the same period may safely be estimated at $2,000, to say nothing of the general interruption of business from these repeated attacks, and the non-security of life and property.

Very respectfully yours,
JOEL L. ANKRIM

Addendum. In September, 1851, Judge Hart of El Paso Mills was employing his train in transporting flour which he was furnishing the U.S. Commissary Department on the road to this place from the city of Chihuahua, 120 miles from El Paso: his train was attacked and the water cut off from his men and animals by a number of Indians 200 strong. The flour was in sacks and was taken from the wagons and a barricade made to fight the Indians from; after fighting two days, as the train was encamped two-thirds of the mules were killed in the corral, 2 men killed, and

---

[77] Canutillo is a valley a short distance above El Paso.

some 10 were seriously wounded and all famished for water. The Majordomo was compelled to treat with the Indians, and for want of animals was compelled to leave two-thirds of his cargo of flour on the ground for the Indians. Several old Mexicans employed in the train knew the Indian chiefs engaged in this encounter and conversed with them: they belonged to the White and Sacramento Mountain tribes on the confines of Texas and New Mexico east of the Rio Grande.

The loss of property in this affair in mules and flour was $7,000 (seven thousand dollars).

I certify the foregoing to be a correct copy.
Jos. K. F. Mansfield

« *Copy of Governor Lane's Letter* »

Fort Fillmore, 19h March, 1853

Colonel Miles, U.S.A. Commanding
Dear Sir:

Please excuse me for not waiting upon you, this evening. I am fatigued and covered with dirt.

I have sent you my proclamation in relation to the *disputed* (but not neutral) Territory, and send you herewith, another copy of the same.

As the army is subordinate and auxiliary to the civil authorities of the U.S.—in all the states and territories, the Governor of New Mexico is certainly not accountable to the army for his acts as civil magistrate. I therefore do not hold myself accountable to Colonel Sumner, or yourself, for what I have done, in relation to this disputed Territory. I am sincerely desirous to please you both: but I have failed to do so—I cannot help it. I have acted under the best legal advice in the Territory—and do not fear that my action will be disapproved, either by the President or the people. I have done my duty and nothing more; and if others have failed to do their duty, also let them take the responsibility of their ill advised acts.

The Government and the people of the U.S. have disapproved and repudiated Mr. Bartlett's line: the Board of Commissioners have been disolved, and we know not when another Board will assemble: the authorities of the state of Chihuahua have usurped authority, in the acknowledged Territory of New Mexico, and trampled upon the rights of the citizens of the U.S. The Executive Department of New Mexico (in the exercise of an undoubted right and plain duty) has asserted the rights of the U.S. and of the citizens, and some 350 U.S. troops, who are unemployed and are within 5 miles of the scene of action, fold their arms in frigid tranquility and thereby sustain the enemies of their country!

I thank you for the extract from Colonel Sumner's order, but would have preferred a copy of the entire communication, as far as it relates to myself, personally or officially.

I will accept your escort, provided you will allow it to accompany me, upon the road which is usually travelled, which is 60 miles nearer and much better than the other road. But if the escort will not be allowed to accompany me upon this near route, I must decline to accept it, as altogether unnecessary for my safety.

I have the honor to be, Dear Sir,
Your Obt. St.
Wm. C. Lane
Gov. Ter. N. Mexico

P. S. I write in haste: please allow me a copy of this note, and also a copy of your proclamation.

W. C. L.

II

The Department of the Pacific
1854

The Pacific

Brevet Lieutenant General and Major General Winfield Scott Commanding the Army of the United States
SIR:

Agreeably to your special order no. 45 dated 18h March, 1854, requiring me to Inspect the Pacific Department minutely, and to exhibit the true state and condition of the commands at the time of the inspection, "as well as the location of the several posts, and stations, the object they were designed to accomplish, and to what extent thus far the purposes in view have been attained; their distances from each other, the practicability of the routes leading to them, the nature of the country in which they are situated, and to what extent they may be relied on, in obtaining supplies; specifying also the nearest settlements, and the number of population capable of bearing arms; what Indian tribes reside in the vicinity and the number of warriors they could bring into the field, with such other general information, as in a military view may be deemed important to be communicated," I have the honor to report that I have performed the duty as follows:

I sailed from New York on the 5h April and, via the Nicaragua Route, reached San Francisco on the 4h May when I reported to Brevet Major General Wool, commanding the department, and received all facilities desirable in the execution of my duties, and entered on them accordingly. In consequence of the great distance to be passed over of uninhabi[ted] and wild country, and the advantage it would be to head [quarters] of this department that one of the officers there stationed should see the country, he ordered his aid, Lieutenant T. Moore, 2d Infantry, to accompany me thro' my tour south of San Francisco and Lieutenant G. H. Mendell of the Topographical Engineers to accompany me thro' my tour northward of that city. I travelled by stage from San Francisco[1] thro' the Valley of San José 50 miles; San Juan [Bautista], 42 miles, and Salinas, 30 miles, to Monterey; thence by steamer, touching at San Louis O'Bispo, Santa Barbara, [and] San Pedro, to San Diego—in all 460 miles by water from San Francisco. From San Diego[2] we

[1] Mansfield's route, throughout the entire portion of his inspection trip south of San Francisco, was over established roads and trails and, except for the sea voyage from Monterey to San Diego and the digression into the southern mining district, can be followed on the "General Map of a Survey in California," prepared by Second Lieutenant Robert S. Williamson, in 33 Cong., 1 sess., *House Exec. Doc. 129*, atlas, n.p. From San Francisco, Mansfield went south along the eastern side of the peninsula, then inland through the towns of Santa Clara and San Jose, past the mission of San Juan Bautista, then southwest through Salinas to Monterey.

[2] From San Diego to Fort Yuma, Mansfield traveled over the established emigrant route which ran from the mouth of the Gila River into southern California. There were at least two more direct trails farther to the south which were less used because of the even greater scarcity of grass and water. The San Pascual battle site is some nine miles east of the town of Escondido by present highway. The Rancho de Santa Isabel was a Mexican grant which included the present town of Santa Ysabel. (For the ranchos mentioned, see Robert G. Cowan, *Ranchos of California; A List of Spanish Concessions, 1775–1822, and Mexican Grants, 1822–1846*; and R. W. Brackett, *A History of the Ranchos of San Diego County, California.*) Santa Isabel was originally a Cahuila Indian village. It became an *asistencia* of the Mission San Diego in 1818. Zephyrin Engelhardt, *San Diego Mission*, 168–69. The Rancho del Valle de San José, another Mexican grant, was originally a large grant to the north of Santa Isabel. Warner's Ranch, or the Rancho de San José del Valle, also called the Rancho Agua Caliente, was originally part of the Rancho del Valle de San José. Buena Vista, which no longer exists, Warner's Ranch, by which Mansfield means the headquarters of the ranch, and Agua Caliente, the present Warner Springs, were all within the confines of Warner's Ranch. San Felipe was an Indian village located on the Rancho del Valle de San Felipe, also a Mexican grant, southeast of

proceeded via San Pasqual (the battle ground of General Kearney) where there was a friendly settlement of Indians of about forty-seven families, engaged in planting the soil, some few willows and cotton wood here; San Isabel, 61 miles from San Diego, which is a good hacienda comprising about 8 miles square —here too is a small settlement of friendly Indians of about fifty families planting. This is an excellent grazing locality with abundance of oak wood—San Jose, Buena Vista, Warners Ranch, which was destroyed by the Indians, and all his stock driven off.[3]

Warner's Ranch. Mansfield's "Cañon" is the Canyon of San Felipe Creek, which flows southeast, then in a generally eastward direction into the Salton Sea. Mansfield's route left San Felipe Creek at about the point where the creek turns eastward, and followed Vallecito Creek which flows along the southern base of the Vallecito Mountains and into Carrizo Creek. It should be noted that the flow of these creeks was largely underground except after a rain. Vallecitos was about midway between San Diego and Fort Yuma and was the last place, before entering the desert, where grass was reasonably abundant. It was the site of a Diegueño Indian *rancheria* and, until it was broken up in June, 1853, had been a sub-depot for army supplies. See Woodward, ed., *Journal of Lt. Thomas W. Sweeny*, 217–18, n. 11. Carrizo Creek, after flowing east, turns north into the Salton Sea. The route ordinarily followed dipped into Lower California at about 115° 30′ west longitude, running east by south then east by north, still in Lower California, to Algodones on the west bank of the Colorado River. Algodones is mentioned frequently in contemporary accounts. It was a Yuma Indian village about eleven and one-half miles downstream from Fort Yuma, some five miles into Lower California. The present Mexican village of the same name is not the Algodones of Mansfield's day. See "General Map of a Survey in California," *loc. cit.*, which shows the complete trail from San Diego to Fort Yuma but does not name all of the places mentioned by Mansfield. The route from Warner's Ranch to the mouth of the Gila River is described in *Reports of Explorations and Surveys to Ascertain the Most Practicable and Economical Route for a Railroad from the Mississippi River to the Pacific Ocean*, 33 Cong., 2 sess., *Sen. Exec. Doc. 78*, V, pp. 38–40. The total distance from the Mission of San Diego to Fort Yuma, according to Lieutenant Williamson's survey, was 208.25 miles. All of Mansfield's distances for this portion of his route are several miles greater than those determined by Williamson. See *ibid.*, Appendix A, 4.

[3] Warner's Ranch was the property of Jonathan T. Warner, a native of Connecticut, who came to California in 1831. In 1844 the rancho was granted to Warner by Governor Manuel Micheltorena. In 1851, Antonio Garra, an educated Cupeño Indian living on one of the Indian *rancherias* on Warner's Ranch, organized a revolt

—here another settlement of friendly Indians about 3 miles northward, at the hot spring, engaged in planting—Agua Caliente; San Philipe, which is 87 miles from San Diego—here another settlement of friendly Indians, about thirty families, very little planting, and limited soil, and here the desert may be said to commence—the Cañon; and Vallecita, 105 miles from San Diego. Here is another settlement of friendly Indians of about six families with very little planting. A Government reservation is here and a log house now occupied by an American family. It was formerly a post and sub depot for Fort Yuma. And the desert of 100 miles without grass and bad water to Algodones on the Rio Colerado. Here a store is kept by   Hooper,[4] the sutler, and the wild Indians plant a little. Thence 12 miles to Fort Yuma at the junction of the Gila with the Colerado—in all 220 miles from San [D]iego.

From Fort Yuma we retraced our route to San Pasqual and here took the road, via San Luis Rey[5] (where were another friendly settle[ment] of Indians planting), 40 miles from San

against the attempt to collect taxes on Indian herds. Apparently Garra hoped to wipe out the entire white population in the area. Warner's ranch house was attacked early on the morning of November 22, 1851. Aware of the Indian unrest, Warner had already sent his family to San Diego. After a brief attempt to protect his property, he too fled. The Indians then sacked and burned the buildings and drove off the stock. Warner's title to the grant was confirmed by the United States land commission, but he apparently spent little time on the ranch after the Indian attack. The last of the property passed out of his hands in 1861. Brackett, *A History of the Ranchos*, 35–37.

[4] George F. Hooper. Mansfield left a space in the manuscript to insert the first name but neglected to do so, though he gives it later in the report. Hooper had served in the Mexican War and, in 1849, on the United States-Mexican Boundary Commission. He became sutler at Fort Yuma in 1852. Woodward, ed., *Journal of Lt. Thomas W. Sweeny*, 263–264, n. 113.

[5] Mansfield distinguishes between the Mission of San Luis Rey and the Indian settlement located about a mile from it. From the mission he proceeded north, presumably following the old Camino Real, by way of the Mission of San Juan Capistrano, crossing the Santa Ana River, and on to Los Angeles.

Diego; the Mission of [San Luis];[6] the Mission of San Juan Capitano; [and] Rio Santana to Los Angelos, 140 miles from San Diego and say 300 miles from the mouth of the Gila. From Los Angelos[7] we proceeded via the old Mission of San Fernando —here were some friendly Indians and planting—San Fernando Mountain; the Cañon San Francisco; Elizabeth Lake; [and] Pass de las Uvas to the Terjon Reservation[8] at the southern ex-

[6] The corner of the page containing the name of the mission has been destroyed. As there were no missions between San Luis Rey and San Juan Capistrano, it seems probable that the missing name was San Luis.

[7] Mansfield's route from Los Angeles to the San Joaquin Valley was indirect. He proceeded by way of San Fernando Pass into the valley of the Santa Clara River then up San Francisquito Canyon. This took him in a northeasterly direction along the eastern side of Red Mountain. He then crossed San Francisquito Pass to Elizabeth Lake, which is dry throughout most of the year. From Elizabeth Lake the route was west and a little north, skirting the southern edge of Antelope Valley, then north across Cañada de las Uvas Pass into the San Joaquin Valley. This was the route commonly followed at the time, except that Old Tejon Pass, rather than Cañada de las Uvas, was frequently used. Uvas Canyon, or Cañada de las Uvas, is the present Grapevine Canyon. The present Tejon Pass was then called Cañada de las Uvas Pass. What was then called Tejon Pass was the route into the valley of Tejon Creek. See 33 Cong., 1 sess., *House Exec. Doc. 129*, III, p. 69; and "General Map of a Survey in California," *loc. cit.*, which shows the route taken by Mansfield from Los Angeles to the San Joaquin Valley.

[8] The Tejon, or Sebastian, Indian Reservation, consisted of thirty thousand acres. It was established in the fall of 1853 and abandoned in 1863. Mansfield confuses Tulare Lake with either Buena Vista or Kern Lake. Kern Lake no longer exists and Buena Vista Lake and the Kern River, in its lower reaches, are now intermittent. The streams mentioned north of the Kern River are properly Posa Creek, White River, Deer (not Deep) Creek, and Tule River. Within the next eighteen miles, more than a dozen creeks are crossed before Elbow Creek is reached. Mansfield's Four Creeks emerge from the mountains as a single stream, now called the Kaweah River, shown on the "General Map of a Survey in California," *loc. cit.*, as "Pipi-yuma or Four Creeks." Once in the valley, the river breaks up into a number of smaller streams, of which Deep Creek is the most southerly and Elbow Creek the most northerly, and one of which, in Mansfield's day, was called Kah-wee-ya Creek. Mansfield's Woodville, which was located on Kah-wee-ya Creek, no longer exists. The present town of Woodville is south of the Tule River about ten miles west of Porterville. Between Kings River and the San Joaquin River, there are a number of creeks, one of which

tremity of the Tulare or San Joaquin Valley, and east of Tulare Lake—say 130 miles from Los Angelos. From Tejon Reservation we proceeded along the Tulare Valley, crossing Kern River 26 miles from Tejon Reservation—here the first American settlement north of Los Angelos—Pose Creek, 10 miles; White River, 10 miles; Deep Creek, 15 miles; Tule River, 6 miles— here are four American's settlements—Four Creeks, 6 miles; Woodville, 6 miles—here the American population number about four hundred and one hundred Indians—Elbow Creek; King River; [and] Dry Creek to Fort Miller on the San Joaquine, say 175 miles from Tejon Reservation. From Fort Miller[9] we proceeded and, at Millertown by ferry, crossed the San Joaquine River; [and then came] Cotton Wood Creek, 4 miles; Fresno River, 11 miles; Cowchilla River; Marriposa River; Bear Creek; [and] Merced River; thence to Stockton it is 70 miles—say 130 miles from Fort Miller to Stockton.

At Shroders Tavern on the Merced River made a digression, on my private account, from the direct route to the military posts.[10] I parted company with Lieutenant Moore, who proceeded to San Francisco, and took a mule and proceeded alone thro' the mining regions via Quartzburg and Mount Ophia to Mariposa, thence across the mountains via Simpsonville, the crossing of the Merced, Coultersville, Maxwell's Creek, Black

---

is Dry Creek. There seems to be no reason why Mansfield chose to mention certain streams by name but not others. The choice was not based on relative importance.

9 The site of Fort Miller is now covered by Millerton Lake, which is formed by the waters of the San Joaquin River, impounded by Friant Dam. The site of Millerton, originally Rootville and for a time a mining town of some significance, is also covered by Millerton Lake. The streams mentioned between the San Joaquin River and Stockton still carry the same names, though in the case of the Chowchilla and Mariposa with slightly different spellings than those used by Mansfield.

10 Mansfield's digression took him through the southern half of the southern mining region which was still producing some notable gold strikes in 1854. See Hubert Howe Bancroft, *History of California* (XXIII of *Works*), VI, 367–77, especially n. 35 and n. 37.

Gulsh, Quartz Mountain Gulsh, Mockasin Creek, [and] the ferry across Tuolumne River to Sonora. Thence to Columbia and thence by stage via James Town and the ferry of the Stanislaus River to Stockton. Throughout this whole route there is a large American population. The miners are engaged along the rivers and in the gulshes, and in spots the farmer is occupying the ground, and the saw mills and grist mills are supplying rapidly the wants of the people. I saw but few Indians and these very degraded. From Stockton I proceeded to Benicia by steamer, and thence to San Francisco.

From San Francisco[11] we (Lieutenant Mendell and myself) proceeded to Sacramento City by steamer, 130 miles; thence it is 50 miles to Marysville by land or water. Here again I digressed from the direct route to the military posts on my private account and proceeded by stage via Bear Creek and Rough and Ready to Grass Valley and Nevada, the middle mining country, and thence to Marysville at the junction of the Yuba and Feather rivers, whence by stage up the Sacramento Valley to Fort Reading, 125 miles from Marysville.

From Fort Reading[12] we proceeded on mules via Shasta City, 25 miles; Towers Tavern, 12 miles; Weaversville, 28 miles; Oregon Gulsh, 5 miles; Cañon Creek; Trinity River—Big Flat, 24 miles from Weaversville—Manceneta; Vances Bar where we crossed the ferry; Burnt Ranch, 30 miles from Vances Bar;

[11] Mansfield does not give this portion of his route in much detail. His second digression, which took him into the central mining district, was less extensive than the first in which he engaged. The distance from Nevada City to Marysville by modern highway is only forty-one miles. See *ibid.*, 356–57.

[12] Mansfield's route from Fort Reading to Fort Humbolt is roughly that followed by U. S. Highway 299 from Redding to Blue Lake on the Mad River and thence to Arcata and Eureka. Again he was passing through a gold mining region, though without the necessity of a digression. Most of the places mentioned will be found on present-day maps of the area. Tower's Tavern, if shown, is Tower House; Manceneta is Manzaneta Bar; Big Flat is Big Bar; Union is now called Arcata; and Bucksport has been absorbed by Eureka.

crossed south fork of the Trinity at its junction with that river, 10 miles; Willow Creek, 10 miles; Red Wood Mountain (Durkey's Ranch), 10 miles; Mad River thro' an immense forest of redwood, pine, and spruce to Union at the head of Humbolt Bay; thence by steamer 11 miles to Bucksport (Fort Humbolt), say 175 from Fort Reading.

From Fort Humbolt[13] we proceeded via Union; Mad River; Red Wood River, 25 miles from Union; Klamath River at McDonald's ferry, 20 miles, where we crossed; thence passed up north side of Klamath River 15 miles to Shavoorams (O'Neil and Bryces) Ferry, where we recrossed the Klamath; passed over Salmon Mountain to Salmon River, 17 miles; thence ascended that river to the forks of the Salmon, 21 miles; continued up the north branch of the Salmon to Bessville, 18 miles; the foot of Scotts Mountain, 13 miles; top of Scotts Mountain, 3 miles; Saw Mill Creek, 9 miles (in Scotts Valley); and Fort Jones, 12 miles on Scotts River. Throughout this whole distance, say 138 miles from Fort Humbolt, the mountains and ravines are heavily wooded with redwood, pine, fur &c &c, and the mule trail over the mountains extremely bad and dangerous.

From Fort Jones[14] we proceeded via Yreka, 15 miles; Shasta

13 Fewer of the places mentioned in this portion of the route appear on present maps but most are locatable. After crossing Redwood Creek, Mansfield went generally north through the Hoopa Valley. As he does not say so, it must be assumed that he did not cross the Trinity River. McDonald's Ferry, then, would be below the mouth of the Trinity, possibly the present Martin's Ferry. Shavoorams must have been in the vicinity of Orleans, then called Orleans Bar, though, with his obvious interest in the gold fields, it is surprising that Mansfield did not mention it. Unless he went some distance out of his way, which the mileage does not suggest, he crossed the Salmon Range north of Orleans Mountain. Bestville, Mansfield's Bessville, no longer exists. It was on the north fork of the Salmon below Sawyer's Bar. His route was up the north fork of Russian Creek, across another range of the Salmon Mountains, to Mill Creek. The Scott Mountains, in which Scott Mountain is a peak, lie south and east of the route followed. Much of this portion of Mansfield's route is still dirt road and trail today.

14 All of the points mentioned on this portion of the route appear on present maps

River, 4 miles; Klamath River (De Witts Ferry), 19 miles—
here we crossed and 34 miles from Fort Jones; Cotton Wood;
crossed the Siskiou Mountain; Bear Creek (Stewarts Creek);
Jacksonville; to Fort Lane on the Rogue River at the mouth of
Stewarts Creek, say 84 miles from Fort Jones over a good wagon
road.

From Fort Lane[15] we proceeded via Evan's Ferry across the
Rogue River, 15 miles below Fort Lane; thence over the military
road 9 miles to Stoney Creek; Grave Creek, 12 miles; Cow
Creek, 10 miles; the Cañon, 8 miles, and 11 miles thro' it, ferry
across the south fork of the Umpqua River, 2 miles; Myrtle
Creek, 6 miles; Deer Creek, 15 miles; Winchester on the north
fork of the Umpqua River, 5 miles; Callapooya Creek, 8 miles;
Pass Creek, 24 miles; across Callapooya Mountain, 8 miles—

except De Witt's Ferry and Cottonwood. De Witt's Ferry was across the Klamath
River seventeen and a half miles from Yreka, according to Second Lieutenant Henry
L. Abbot's report in 33 Cong., 2 sess., *Sen. Exec. Doc. 78*, VI, p. 53. Cottonwood
was on the right side of the Klamath River above the mouth of the Shasta near the
present town of Klamathon. Stuart Creek was named for Second Lieutenant and
Brevet Captain James Stuart, Mounted Riflemen, who died on June 18, 1851, of
wounds received in action with the Rogue River Indians. Stuart Creek as a variant
for Bear Creek seems no longer to be in use.

[15] From Fort Lane, Mansfield followed the south side of the Rogue River to
Evan's Ferry, which was three miles west of the point where Evan's Creek enters
the Rogue River from the north. The military road followed the north bank of
the Rogue and then turned north, approximating the route of the present U.S. Highway 99. The canyon is that through which Canyon Creek flows north to enter the
south fork of the Umpqua River. The place names mentioned north of the Umpqua
to Fort Vancouver are still in use. The construction of a military road from the
mouth of Myrtle Creek, on the Umpqua River, to Camp Stuart in the Rogue River
Valley was authorized by Congress on January 7, 1853. Camp Stuart was a temporary post, established by Captain and Brevet Major Philip Kearny, First Dragoons, in June, 1851, near the spot where Fort Lane was later erected. The road had
not been completed when Mansfield followed it. William Glen Ledbetter, "Military
History of the Oregon Country, 1804–1859," 112–13; 33 Cong., 1st sess., *Sen.
Exec. Doc. 1*, II, pp. 2–3, 67; and 34 Cong., 1 sess., *Sen. Exec. Doc. 1*, II, p.
507–509.

here commences the Willamette Valley—Long Tom Creek; to Corvallis which is 191 miles from Fort Lane and at the junction of Mary's River with the Willamette; thence to Salem, 35 miles; thence to Oregon City, 37 miles; thence to Portland, 13 miles; thence to Fort Vancouver by land, 11 miles. Fort Vancouver is 100 miles up the Columbia River and 290 miles from Fort Lane

From Fort Vancouver[16] we proceeded by steamer up the Columbia River 45 miles to the rapids where the river rushes thro' the Caskade Mountain; thence over a portage of 5 miles; thence by steamer 40 miles to Fort Dalles, another rapids, in all say 90 miles from Fort Vancouver.

From Fort Dalles[17] we descended the Columbia River by steamer and portage to the mouth of the Cowlitz River and ascended that river to Montecello, say 55 miles from Fort Vancouver. Thence we ascended the rapids of the Cowlitz in an Indian canoe for 30 miles to the landing. Thence took horses for 60 miles to Olimpia over a wagon road, and thence 25 miles further to Fort Steilacoom on Puget Sound, 260 miles from Fort Dalles.

[16] Here again the place names are unchanged, even though the face of the Columbia is not. The first steamboat on the lower Columbia was a Hudson's Bay Company boat, the *Beaver*, which reached Fort Vancouver in 1836 but was soon transferred to the Puget Sound service. Regular service was provided on the lower Columbia in 1850 and between the Cascades and the Dalles in 1851. Service above the Dalles did not commence until 1859. Although Mansfield did not avail himself of the facilities, steamboats were operating on the Willamette River above the falls from Oregon City to Salem and, less frequently, as far upstream as Eugene. Oscar O. Winther, *The Old Oregon Country*, 157–64.

[17] Monticello, which no longer exists, was on the right bank of the Cowlitz where Longview, Washington, is today. Monticello had disappeared years before Longview came into being. Mansfield's estimate of fifty-five miles from Fort Vancouver to Monticello is too generous by about ten miles. The trip up the Cowlitz by Indian canoe was not quite the high adventure Mansfield's laconic mention might suggest. Beginning in 1852 regular canoe service was provided for both freight and passengers from Monticello to Cowlitz Landing. Cowlitz Landing was near the present town of Toledo. The road from the landing to Olympia was originally laid out by the Hudson's Bay Company between Cowlitz Farm and Fort Nisqually on Puget Sound. See *ibid.*, 164–65.

From Fort Steilacoom[18] we retraced our route to Portland on the Willamette and took steamer down the Columbia River and along the coast to Port Orford where there is a detachment; thence, touching at Crescent City and Trinidad, reached San Francisco again which closed our tour. And I returned to New York via the Panama route.

« *Climate, Harbours, Rivers, Country and Productions, Resources and Necessity of Military Posts, Indians &c* »

The Pacific Department extends from the latitude of about $32\frac{1}{2}°$ to $49°$, say 16 degrees along the Pacific Coast, comprising the state of California and the Territories of Oregon and Washington, and throughout its whole extent perfectly healthy with the exception of the Sacramento Valley, where the ague and fever prevails. This is undoubtedly occasioned by the overflowings of the immense bottom lands of the Sacramento in the rainy season and the slow drainage, combined with excessive heat in summer. Along the Coast range of mountains, the temperature is happily tempered by the north west winds in summer throughout its whole extent, so that the debility of excessive heat in low latitudes is not felt, while in the winter the coast is thoroughly drenched under a change of winds southward. It is therefore in San Francisco quite necessary to wear woolen clothes all summer, and not unfrequently at evening find a little fire desirable. To the eastward however of the coast range of mountains, the north west winds of the coast lose their efficacy, and the valleys between the Coast range and the Sierra Nevada and its continuation northward under the name of Caskade Mountains into Washington Territory partake of the temperature common to such latitudes on the eastern coast, with the single exception [that] they are not modified by occasional rains during the summer season. Hence the

---

[18] This portion of the route is given in little detail, most of it, of course, by sea. All of the place names mentioned are still in use.

extremely high state of the thermometer at times in the interior. These valleys are thoroughly drenched in the winter or rainy season. It is this peculiarity of dry summers and wet winters, in connexion with the mountainous character generally of this department, which admits of ready drainage, that renders it so generally healthy. Along the whole coast, fogs are frequent and are serious obstacles to commerce; but they are not of long continuence and come and go continually. Yet they do not extend to the eastward of the coast range of mountains, and here in summer generally is seen the clear sky, the perpetually snow capped Sierra, and the magnificent snow topped mounts, Shasta, Jefferson, Hood, Adams, St. Helens, and Ranier.

Harbours. There is one magnificent harbour on this coast—in addition to the little Bay of San Diego at the southern extremity, the Straits of Juan de Fuca at the northern extremity, and Humbolt's Bay in latitude about 41°—and this is the Bay of San Francisco, which is perfectly landlocked against all winds and capacious enough for any navy and commerce that can possibly be required on this coast, and from its local position seems designed by nature and adapted for the supply of the whole country inland of the state of California. The Bay of San Diego is a very safe anchorage, but it is narrow and not adapted for much shipping, but is ample for all the commerce that will ever be carried on from that point. The Straits de Fuca is the entrance into the deep waters of Puget Sound, and here there is abundant harbour and anchorage for the world. Humbolt Bay is second to San Diego, but of more commerce, yet of difficult entrance over the bar and only suitable for vessels of light draft of water.

There are other points such as San Pedro, Santa Barbara, San Luis Obispo, Monterey, Crescent City, Port Orford, Trinadad —mere localities where landing is effected on the beach.

The mouth of the Umpqua River, however, is a place of safety for small vessels and steamers of 15 to 18 feet water and will be of much commercial importance, as it is navigable about 20 miles up the river to Scottsburg. This river breaks thro' the coast range of mountains, thereby affording a ready communication with the south end of the Willamette Valley, Jackson County in Oregon, and Scott's Valley in northern California.

I hardly need add here that the Columbia River, from the bar to the rapids at the Caskade Mountains, is broad and deep, and capable of floating the largest ships of the navy, and as beautiful as it is grand.

At present very little is known to me of Grey's Harbour and Shoal Water Bay[19] in Washington Territory.

Rivers. The drainage of this immense country west of the Rocky Mountains is effected principally through the rivers Colerado, which empties into the head of the Gulf of California; Sacramento and San Joaquine, which empty into the Bay of San Francisco; and Columbia, which empties into the Pacific. The navigable rivers of the department are the Colorado to the Big Cañon,[20] 150 miles above the mouth of the Gila, by small steam-

---

[19] Shoalwater Bay is the large bay immediately to the north of the mouth of the Columbia River on the Washington coast, with the entrance between Cape Shoalwater and Point Leadbetter. See Jean Hazeltine, "The Discovery and Cartographical Recognition of Shoalwater Bay." *Oregon Historical Quarterly,* Vol. LVIII (September, 1957), 251–63. At present only the extreme southern end of the bay is called Shoalwater Bay, the larger portion being designated Willapa Bay.

[20] The Grand Canyon was frequently called the Big Canyon or the Great Canyon in reports of the period. Mansfield underestimated the head of steam navigation on the Colorado, a matter which had not yet been determined in 1854. Ocean-going steamers could not ascend the river; hence, small, shallow draft steamers were necessary to carry the transshipped cargoes from the mouth of the river to their destination. It was not until December, 1852, that river steamboats inaugurated regular service between the mouth of the Colorado and Fort Yuma. The first steamboat on the river was the little side-wheeler, *Uncle Sam,* which was assembled near the mouth of the river and reached Fort Yuma on December 3, 1852. The *Uncle Sam* sank at her moorings on June 22, 1853. Woodward, ed., *Journal of Lt. Thomas*

ers only; the San Joaquine to Stockton; the Sacramento to Sacramento City, thence to Red Bluff; the Feather to Marysville; the Umpqua to Scottsburg; the Columbia to the Cascades, 140 miles, thence portage 5 miles and steamer 40 miles to the Dalles, and portage again & c; the Willamette, 16 miles to the falls at Oregon City, thence portage two miles, and steamer to Salem; [and] the Chechalis[21] is presumed to be navigable.

The other rivers of the department are nominal, so far as they are capable of navigation, and are useful only for fish and irrigation, and water power for saw and grist mills & c, and to carry off the excessive rains of the winter season, which fill many of them at times to a height of 30 to 60 feet of water.

Soil, productions, timber, minerals, metals and ores. The soil is generally good. The valleys, San José, San Juan, Selinas, Los Angelos, Tulare,[22] San Joaquine, Sacramento, Sonoma, Scotts, Willamette, and others in the neighbourhood of Puget Sound are

---

W. Sweeny, 261–262, n. 110. In 1857 two expeditions, one unofficial and the other an official government exploration, sought to determine the head of navigation for steamboats. The unofficial expedition was in the river steamer *General Jesup*, which reached a point seventy-four miles above Fort Mojave, but on the return trip knocked a hole in her bottom some thirty miles above Fort Yuma and sank. The official expedition was in the *Explorer*, a vessel especially constructed for the task and much too small to serve any practical commercial purpose. It ascended the river to within an estimated day's journey of the mouth of the Virgin River and returned successfully to Fort Yuma. Both of these expeditions went more than twice the one hundred fifty miles fixed by Mansfield as the head of steam navigation. Both Fort Yuma and Fort Mojave, more than one hundred fifty miles above Fort Yuma, were successfully served by steamboat for more than twenty years. Arthur Woodward, *Feud on the Colorado*, 31–68, 79–119; and Francis Hale Leavitt, "Steam Navigation on the Colorado River," *California Historical Society Quarterly*, Vol. XXII (March, 1943), 1–25; (June, 1943), 151–74.

21 The Chehalis River, which empties into Gray's Harbor.

22 Mansfield makes the distinction between the Tulare and San Joaquin Valleys which was commonly made at that time. By Tulare Valley he has reference to that portion of the San Joaquin Valley south of the San Joaquin River and including Tulare Lake.

all productive, but not equally so.[23] As a general thing wheat, barley, oats, potatoes, and other roots, and spring vegetables can be raised all over this country in great perfection. But Indian corn does not thrive in this department except in such places as afford a ready irregation in California, and are moist in Oregon Territory, and I will add that irregation seems essential to an abundant harvest in the country south of Monterey. It is owing to this cause that vegetation is so rank and beautiful in the Valley of Los Angeles and the Terjon Reservation. The sweet potatoe thrives best in Southern California and the Irish potatoe in Washington Territory. Although the extent of productive soil is comparatively limited, yet the produce of only the best part of it is, and will be, more than sufficient for the supply of all the population that will occupy this department.

The fruits of the department are of almost every variety. The orange, lemon, fig, pear, apple, peach, plum, quince, current, grape, strawberry, raspberry, blackberry, salmon berry &c &c, grow in great luxuriance, although at this time quite limited as to quantity, yet in a state of cultivation that will in two or three years make the fruits one of the best and cheapest articles of consumption. At Los Angeles the grape, fig, orange, pear and olive grow luxuriently, and in the Willamette Valley the pear, peach, [and] apple are not to be surpassed, and the strawberry literally covers the ground by the acre. Timber of particular kinds abounds throughout the department. The pine, fur, redwood, and cedar, afford abundance of lumber for the whole department, and for exportation; but the oak, although it exists in most of its varieties in this country, is not of a suitable quality for the arts and ship-building, and it is believed to be generally only fit for firewood.

---

[23] Mansfield mentions only those valleys through which his inspection trip took him, hence his list of productive valleys is far from complete. Although he crossed a portion of the Imperial Valley he was not, understandably, impressed by its potential productivity.

It partakes of an unhealthy growth in the southern part of California and limited in quantity; but at the four creeks it seems to be abundant, and of large and healthy growth.[24] There are many other descriptions of trees, such as sycamore, willow, poplar, cottonwood & c, of no very great importance except for firewood, and wild fruits, and nuts. Coal abounds on the coast in Coose Bay, Billingham Bay, and on the Dwamish River, which empties into Puget Sound, yet [is] variable as to quality, that of Billingham Bay [being] the best. I doubt not abundant coal in other places will soon be discovered to equal the demand for steamers on this coast. Ordinary building stone and lime and marble are abundant, but altho' granite abounds, it has not yet been found to equal in quality and durability the granite of the Atlantic States —almost the entire mineral kingdom shows the marks of great heat and volcanic action. Fish of many kinds are found in the waters, but the salmon in the northern rivers and Puget Sound and the cod in Puget Sound are abundant, and the craw fish in Southern California [are] abundant on the coast. Gold is found from the extreme south to the extreme north of this department in the ore and native state. The rich localities, however, where the mining is carried on with the greatest success are the southern mines about Mariposa and Sonora, the middle mines about Nevada, and the northern about Shasta City and Yreka, and Jacksonville in Oregon Territory. Quicksilver ore is also found in great richness near San José, at Almadine[25] and extracted readily. Ice has become a very common article of consumption, and cer-

[24] There are seventeen species of native oaks in California, some live and some deciduous. The live oak, which is the more common, is a hardwood, evergreen tree of limited commercial use. In the descriptions of the period the wood of the various oaks was often described as brittle and sometimes as porous. See the botanical report prepared by J. S. Newberry in 33 Cong., 2 sess., *Sen. Exec. Doc. 78*, VI, pp. 27–33.

[25] Almaden, named for the famous mercury mines of Spain, was the site of the New Almaden mercury mine. For a description of the mine at about the time of Mansfield's inspection see Bartlett, *Personal Narrative*, II, 53–70.

tainly in summer a very desirable one, is had from Oregon for the supply of the sea-board and from the snow topped mountains in the interior for towns and mining regions.

Population. The population of this department may be divided into the following classes: 1t, the Indians or aboriginals, and these may now be subdivided into the partly civilized or friendly and the uncivilized or unfriendly; 2d, the native Californians, descendents of the Spanish and a cross with the Spanish and Indian; 3rd, the Canadian (Oregon Trapper) and the cross with the Indian; 4h, the Chinese; and 5h, the American or Anglo Saxon race so called.

The friendly Indians live along the coast, and between the Sierra Nevada and Cascade range of mountains, and the Coast range and in the mountains among the miners; and some of them have permanent little villages and plant the soil and live by industry. These are not at all troublesome. Others are extremely degraded and lazy and live on roots, grass seed, grasshoppers, fish and game, and are generally found gleaning the fields of the Americans. This whole race are fast disappearing before the white man by disease and other causes. Many of them in Southern California are the remnants of the Spanish missions which were established by the Franciscan monks from the year 1769 to 1839 to the number of 20 to 25,[26] all of which have been broken up, and nothing remains of them but the ruins of buildings inhabited by the owl and the martin, and which in those days in that country were magnificent, but to the eyes of Americans are merely walls of adobes, erected under a primitive state of the arts. If any success ever attended these efforts at the civilization of the Indians, but few traces remain at this day. The number of In-

[26] Actually there were twenty-one missions from San Diego in the south to San Francisco Solano, north of San Francisco Bay, plus the two short-lived missions for the Yuma Indians on the California side of the Colorado River. Mansfield obviously had little appreciation of mission architecture.

[97]

dians I should estimate from all I have seen and learned of them to be as follows. 1t, south of Los Angeles, say 2,500 souls or 500 warriors mostly in little settlements and localities scattered among the mountains, where they labour more or less at the cultivation of the soil. These Indians do not desire to move into the Indian Reservation of Tejon, but prefer to bury their bones where they have always lived. The land they occupy too is of very little value, and they are so situated that a combination among them, or a union of them with the wild Indians farther east, for war purposes, is not at all to be apprehended. 2d, at the southern extremity of the San Joaquin Valley south of Kern River and to the eastward of Kern Lake[27] is the Indian Reservation of California. Here may be 2,000 souls, and between this reservation and so far north as Stockton there may be 2,000 souls more, say 4,000 souls or 800 warriors. From these Indians very little damage is to be apprehended. They are generally disposed to labour some, and those on the Tejon Reservation are industrious, and their fields exhibited, where they were harvesting, excellent wheat and corn in addition to other vegetables. The Indian Agent, Mr. E. F. Beale,[28] had made much progress in turning their attention to agricultural pursuits. He had in charge 9 (nine) small "rancherias" within a few miles for each particular tribe or gang where they were hutted and managed their own fields. And in addition he had two large fields in common at which all the Indians contributed labour, the object of which was to have bread

[27] Kern Lake no longer exists. It was south of the present Bakersfield and east of Buena Vista Lake in the area labeled Kern Island on present Geological Survey maps.

[28] Edward F. Beale, a former lieutenant in the United States Navy, was appointed Superintendent of Indian Affairs for California in 1851. He held the position until 1854 when he was dismissed as a result of attacks by political opponents. In June, 1854, Beale reported that there were twenty-five hundred Indians on the Tejon Reservation. The first harvest produced forty-two thousand bushels of wheat and ten thousand bushels of barley. John W. Caughey, *California*, 387–89. According to Bishop William Ingraham Kip there were fewer than three hundred Indians on the reservation when he visited it in 1855. *A California Pilgrimage*, 43.

[98]

stuffs in one common granary to aid the incoming Indians till they could prepare the ground and plant for themselves, and to prevent famine. 3rd, north of Stockton to Oregon Territory, these Indians may be said to number about 8,000 souls, say 1,600 warriors. But they are scattered over a great extent of country, and in small bands, and can never act in concert, even if so disposed, to carry on war against the whites, and as they subsist on fish (principally salmon), roots, berries, nuts, and are in many localities much diseased, very little is to be apprehended from them in future. It is true however the miners in this northern part of California necessarily injure the salmon fishery by the disturbance of the waters of the rivers, and deprive them of a subsistence thereby, and oblige them to resort sometimes to murders and depredations for a livlihood; and on this account the Indians of the Trinity and Klamath rivers and Yreka are most to be feared and are the most numerous relatively. 4h, from the northern boundary (the Ciskiou Mountains) of California to the Callapooya Mountains (the southern extremity of the Willamette Valley), there are about 3,000 souls and say 600 warriors; about 1,000 of them are in and about the Indian Reservation on the north side of the Rogue River at Fort Lane, under the direction of Mr. S. H. Culver,[29] the able Indian Agent, and are particularly disposed to be friendly if they meet with no abuses from the whites. They are active and intelligent, and the agent is endeavoring to get them into the cultivation of the soil. The residue of these Indians are scattered along west of the Cascade Mountains, some planting little patches for themselves and fishing & c & c, and others working for the whites. These Indians are not at all likely to make war on the whites as this section of the coun-

---

[29] Samuel H. Culver had been sub-agent at Port Orford and became agent for the newly established Rogue River Reservation in 1853. C. F. Coan, "The Adoption of the Reservation Policy in the Pacific Northwest, 1853–1855," *Quarterly of the Oregon Historical Society*, Vol. XXIII (March, 1922), 33–34.

try is well settled and filling up fast. 5h, from the Callapooya Mountains to the Columbia River, the Indians are not numerous. There may be 1,000 souls scattered along the coast and thro' the Willamette Valley subsisting on fish, nuts, gleanings &c &c. Little or nothing is to be apprehended from these Indians, and the population here too is numerous and able to resist them successfully. They are degraded like most of the coast Indians. 6h, from Fort Dalles, 90 miles above Fort Vancouver, to the mouth of the Columbia River, and thence northwardly to Fort Steilacoom and west of the Cascade Mountain, there are 1,500 friendly Indians or 500 warriors scattered from whom there is not much to be feared on the score of war against the whites. 7h, in and about Puget Sound there are about 4,500 Indians or 900 warriors, about one half of whom are dangerous and require careful supervision, and here as in other parts their progress in civilization is very slow.[30]

[30] Mansfield's estimates of the number of Indians in any given area are not entirely reliable. The widespread outbreak of Indian hostilities in both Oregon and Washington in 1855–56 also belies his belief that not much was to be feared of the Indians residing west of the Cascades. Brigadier General Stephen Watts Kearny, in 1847, estimated the number of Indians in California as 15,000, about one-third being mission Indians. Kearny to Brigadier General Roger Jones, March 15, 1847, in 31 Cong., 1 sess., *House Exec. Doc.* 17, p. 285. Kearny's figure apparently did not include the desert dwelling Indians, but is obviously too small. More recent estimates place the number of California Indians considerably higher, though by 1854 they were well below their peak. See A. L. Kroeber, "The Native Population of California," in *The California Indians* (R. F. Heizer and M. A. Whipple, eds.), 68–81. Governor Isaac Stevens, in his report of 1854 (33 Cong., 1 sess., *House Exec. Doc. 129*, I, p. 94), estimated the number of Indians in Washington Territory west of the Cascade Mountains as 6,903. A second estimate, more detailed, being broken down into tribes and bands, for the western district of Washington Territory, places the number at 7,559. *Ibid.*, 464–65. For the Indians east of the Cascade Mountains in Washington Territory, all classified by Mansfield as wild Indians, there were several estimates: for 1851, 7,103 (incomplete); for 1853, 7,006; and for 1854, 7,356. *Ibid.*, 94, 441. In 1857, Colonel and Brevet Brigadier General Newman S. Clarke, Sixth U. S. Infantry, commanding the Department of the Pacific, estimated that there were 10,444 Indians along the shores and tributaries of Puget

The wild or unfriendly Indians occupy the country to the eastward of the Sierra Nevada and Cascade range of mountains and commit their depredations on the Americans by attacking weak parties crossing the Rocky Mountains and making incursions into the civilized parts occupied by the Americans, and murder the border inhabitants and drive off their live stock & c. These Indians it is difficult to enumerate with much accuracy. There are probably 1,000 warriors in the regions about Fort Yuma, occupying both California and New Mexico, and are not to be trusted. About 1,000 more warriors may be said to occupy the country east of the Sierra Nevada range of mountains along by Owen's Lake, Mono Lake & c to the northern boundary of California. About 1,000 more warriors in Oregon Territory east of the Cascade Mountains, and about 100 more warriors east of the Cascade Mountains in Washington Territory. Thus showing in this department about 4,000 warriors or 16,000 wild Indians who live on hunting, rooting, fishing, nuts, seeds & c & c. Of course a very dangerous class of the human family when in want of food, they

Sound alone. Clarke to Lorenzo Thomas (assistant adjutant general), September 14, 1857, in 35 Cong., 1 sess., *Sen. Exec. Doc. 11*, II, p. 133. Governor Stevens, also in 1857, placed the number of Indians east of the Cascade Mountains at 12,000 and west of the mountains at 9,712, giving a total of 21,712 for Washington Territory. Hazard Stevens, *The Life of Isaac Ingalls Stevens*, II, 504. Governor Joseph Lane gave the total Indian population of Oregon Territory in 1852 as 23,078. Leslie M. Scott, "Indian Diseases as Aids to Pacific Northwest Settlement," *Oregon Historical Quarterly*, Vol. XXIX (June, 1928), 157. The estimated Indian population of California in 1853 is also given at 100,000 and that of Oregon Territory as 23,000, this last obviously being the figure provided by Governor Lane the previous year. DeBow, *Statistical Review of the United States*, 191. Secretary of War Jefferson Davis gave a figure of 134,000 Indians for the Department of the Pacific in 1854. By his definition the department included the Territory of Utah and part of the Territory of New Mexico. *Report of the Secretary of War, 1854*, in 33 Cong., 2 sess., *House Exec. Doc. 1*, II, p. 6. The census of 1860 placed the Indian population not enumerated in the census and retaining tribal characteristics at: California, 13,540; Oregon Territory, 7,000; Washington Territory, 31,000. Kennedy, *Preliminary Report*, in 37 Cong., 2 sess., *Sen. Doc.*, 136.

are tempted to attack weak parties of emigrants from east of the Rocky Mountains which afford rich plunder in cattle, horses, mules, and other supplies. More will be said of these Indians as well as the freindly Indians on reference to the military posts.

The native Californians occupy that part of California south of San Francisco, and are most numerous at San José, Monterey, San Juan de Capitano, Los Angeles, and Old San Diego, but are quite limited as to numbers and seem to be generally contented with the raising of stock and a few vegetables.[31]

The Canadian and cross with the Indians are found generally in Oregon and Washington Territories, having been introduced into the country by the Hudson Bay Company, and are least numerous of all.

The Chinese are quite numerous in California and are scattered over the whole trading and mining country except Oregon and Washington Territories where they seem not to have penetrated as yet. Their object seems to be the finding of gold and not permanent settlement particularly. Still they have stores and trading houses in the cities of California. This class, next to the Americans, are decidedly the most numerous and probably will increase faster than the Americans by immigration hereafter.[32]

[31] Estimates of the number of native Californians at the time of the United States occupation vary from seven thousand to ten thousand. The census of 1850 does not distinguish between this element of the population and other citizens of European extraction. Reasonably exact estimates are available for the number of native Californians in various towns and districts but for the area as a whole the figures are usually generalized. The term "native Californian" was used to designate those of mixed Indian and European blood as well as those of pure European strain.

[32] The census of 1850 gives a Chinese population for California of 660 and for Oregon Territory of 2. A decade later there were almost 35,000 Chinese in California but none listed for either Oregon or Washington Territory. On September 30, 1854, it was announced that during the preceding nine months, 26,744 more persons had arrived in California than had left the state. Of this number, 13,255 were Chinese. Throughout 1854 the San Francisco press reported the arrival of ships from the Orient with large numbers of Chinese immigrants. By the autumn of 1855 this trend had been reversed. On October 15 the clipper ship *Sea Serpent* was reported

The Americans are the most numerous in this department and rule the country without opposition by their superiority in every respect. They are found all over it where land is valuable for any purpose and where gold is found or trade lucrative. They are settled among the native Californians in Southern California and intermarry with them and are engaged in the valleys in agricultural pursuits and, in the regions only fit for grazing, are raising stock. They are very numerous in the gold regions, and are building up fine cities and give tone and character to the whole country. The school house and church and academy and college are rising up as if by magic, and the country, by its grist mills and saw mills and stage lines, is fast assuming a permanent character. The civilized population of Oregon and Washington Territory are almost entirely American. The Valley of the Willamette is occupied by the American farmer throughout its whole extent; and Washington Territory is fast filling up along the Columbia River west of the Cascade Mountains and from the mouth of the Cowlitz River to Puget Sound whereever land is found good. Thus the Americans occupy and control all that part of the department west of the Sierra Nevada and Cascade Mountains, notwithstanding the heterogeneous population scattered among them.[33]

loading 420 Chinese passengers for Hong Kong. On November 1 the clipper *Chalenger* sailed for Hong Kong with more than 400 Chinese. On November 20 the clipper *Galatea* sailed with the incredible number of "between two and three thousand Chinese passengers, all from the mines." The exodus was blamed upon the increasing tax levied upon foreign miners. Dorothy H. Huggins, comp., *Continuation of the Annals of San Francisco*, Part 1, *From June 1, 1854 to December 31, 1855*, pp. 14–15, 67, 75, 85.

[33] In 1847, General Kearny estimated the population of California as "probably not exceeding 12,000, of which about one-fifth are emigrants." Kearny to Jones, March 15, 1847, in 31 Cong., 1 sess., *House Exec. Doc. 17*, p. 285. The census of 1850 showed a population of 92,597 for California, reflecting only the initial impact of the gold rush. A decade later, in 1860, California had a population of 379,994. Oregon Territory, which until 1853 included all of the area north of California and

Necessity of military posts and their location. The foregoing brief illustration of the country and resources and population has been given to judge with reason as to the system and propriety of the different military posts as now established and as to the necessity of others.

It is apparent from the view we have taken of the population, and particularly the Indians, that the line of demarkation between the wild or unfriendly Indians and the partly civilized or friendly Indians and other population of this department is along the Sierra Nevada from the Gulf of California northward, and along its continuation under the name of Cascade Mountains thro' Oregon and Washington Territories, and that the emigrant trails from the Atlantic States into the department are thro' the wild Indian territory east of the mountains. One crossing [is] from El Paso in New Mexico via the Gila River and across the Colerado at the junction of the Gila, thence over a desert of 112 miles to the mountains and over the mountains to San Diego and Los Angeles; two [others are] via Fremont's routes in 1844 and 1845 by which California is entered at the south near Los Angeles and at the north near Nevada and Shasta Mount,[34] one [is] called the Columbia Route by which Oregon and Washington Territories are entered.

Troops therefore at suitable stations along this line and on

west of the continental divide, had a population of 13,294 in 1850. Of this number only 1,049 lived north of the Columbia River and almost no one east of the Cascade Mountains. See Carey, *A General History of Oregon*, II, 482–83.

[34] In 1844, Frémont entered California from Nevada by way of Carson Pass. Leaving, he probably crossed the Tehachapi Mountains by way of Oak Creek Pass and moved on out of California along the Spanish Trail. See Henry Warren Johnson, "Where Did Frémont Cross the Tehachapi Mountains in 1844?" *Publications of the Historical Society of Southern California*, Vol. XIII (1924), 365–73. In 1845, he divided his party at Walker's Lake in Nevada, leading one division by way of the Truckee River, crossing the Sierras approximately by the later regular emigrant route; and on to Sutter's Fort. The other division, headed by Joseph R. Walker, crossed the Sierras by way of Walker's Pass.

the emigrant trails would be well placed as depots and rallying points to the population in case a war should break out, or incursions be made by the Indians. And such stations on the frontier would be suitable as a base line of operation in case it should be determined to advance into the Indian country. With these views let us examine the stations as alr[eady] established, as to their adaptation to this object, commencing at [the] southern boundary.

1t, *New San Diego.*[35] Here is simply a sub depot of supplies of quartermaster and commissary stores, and no troops nor population. It was intended for the supply of posts in this quarter. It is three miles south of Old San Diego and placed here in preference to Old San Diego simply because the channel approaches nearer the shore. It is without drinkable water which has to be brought from San Diego River at Old San Diego, but it is possible water may be had after another trial at boring for an artesian well. There is no grazing here nor tillable land. But as the store house is a remarkably good two story building (frame), it would be well to keep it up until the depot can be dispensed with altogether by a successful supply of Fort Yuma by water, as has already been commenced, when that place will become the best locality for a sub depot for the supply of a line of posts along Cooks

[35] New San Diego, or New Town as its founders called it, was established in 1850 by William Heath Davis, Andrew B. Gray, José Antonio Aguirre, Miguel de Pedrorena, and William C. Ferrell as a speculative venture. Davis built the wharf to which Mansfield refers at an estimated cost of sixty thousand dollars. The army originally intended to build the depot at La Playa, across the bay from New San Diego, but Second Lieutenant Thomas D. Johns, Second U.S. Infantry, in charge of the materials for the post, was persuaded to erect the depot at the new town site in return for a share in the venture. Land was given to the government by the town promoters and a corral and two-story building erected. The post thus established was later designated San Diego Barracks. Though not garrisoned continuously, it was not abandoned until 1921. Andrew F. Rolle, "William Heath Davis and the Founding of American San Diego," *California Historical Society Quarterly,* Vol. XXXI (March, 1952), 34–35, 37.

Route[36] to El Paso, and then this building could be taken down and removed to the mission for a large supply at that post to meet contingencies. It is nine miles from the mission and about seven from the Playa. See sketch B hereunto appended [No. 16, Plans and Sketches section].

2d, *Mission of San Diego*.[37] This post is well selected, being six miles from Old San Diego on San Diego River, and about 9 miles from New San Diego and 10 miles from the Playa (landing). It is thus convenient to water transportation for the embarkation or disembarkation of troops. It is 220 miles from, and auxiliary to, Fort Yuma. It is a good grazing region for animals and has abundance of tillable land. It is on our extreme southern boun-

[36] Cooke's route was laid out by Lieutenant Colonel Philip St. George Cooke in 1846. Cooke led the Mormon Battalion from Santa Fe to San Diego, following a route much of which lay within the later Gadsden Purchase Territory. He left the Rio Grande at the point known as San Diego, moved in a southwest direction, and descended into the San Bernardino Valley through Guadalupe Pass. He followed the valley of the San Pedro River, turning west to Tucson then northwest to the Gila. The remainder of the route was that already taken by Kearny and much the same as the later emigrant route. Cooke's trip was notable in that he took wagons over the entire distance, which necessitated the improvement of the road to make it passable by wheeled vehicles in many places. The route was later used by many emigrants in its entirety. See "Report of Lieutenant Colonel P. St. George Cooke," in 30 Cong., 1 sess., *House Exec. Doc. 41*, pp. 552–62.

[37] The Mission of San Diego was first occupied by troops in 1849. The mission buildings and property deteriorated rapidly under the care of the military, virtually everything movable disappearing, while the vineyards and olive grove went uncared for. Woodward, ed., *Journal of Lt. Thomas W. Sweeny*, 249–50, n. 71. In order to discourage the desertion of the troops to the gold fields, Brevet Brigadier General Bennet Riley's command, when it arrived from the east coast early in 1849, was disembarked at San Diego. Most of the troops were quartered at the Mission San Luis Rey but a small force was left at San Diego. Colonel Richard B. Mason to Second Lieutenant Alfred Gibbs, February 27, 1849, in 31 Cong., 1 sess., *House Exec. Doc. 17*, pp. 891–92. The mission, the mission garden, and the olive grove were restored to the church on December 18, 1855, as a result of the land claim filed by Joseph Sadoc Alemany, Bishop of Monterey, in 1851. The land was surveyed in 1860 and the restoration finalized on May 23, 1862. Englehardt, *San Diego Mission*, 344–48. Troops continued to occupy the mission until 1858.

dary, and with all is well located to overawe the Indians and protect the white population in this quarter, which are quite limited,
being confined to Old San Diego and a few scattering ranches.
Very little reliance can be placed on the white population about
here. There are a few traders and a large proportion of native
Californians.

The Indians within one hundred miles of this post number
about 350 warriors, scattered into little localities among the
mountains and some planting, and in the Jacum[38] Valley of Lower California there are about as many more. This post is the
proper place to store all supplies for the interior, as the troops
here are at hand to guard them; whereas, New San Diego seems
to have no merit—except the supplies are intended to be reshipped, which would be a remarkable proceeding, as all the supplies in this quarter come shipped from the Atlantic States direct,
or from San Francisco, with the exception of fresh beef and a few
garden vegetables. For a sketch of this locality and position see
B and C hereunto appended [Nos. 16 and 17, Plans and Sketches
section].

3rd, *Fort Yuma*[39] is beautifully situated on an eminence about
80 feet high directly opposite the junction of the Gila with the

[38] The Jacum, or Jacumba, Valley lies in both the United States and Mexico.
The United States portion is in southeastern San Diego County. The present town of
Jacumba is just north of the Mexican border. The spring which exists at this place
is called Jacum and a Diegueño Indian village of the same name once occupied the
site. A military pack train route was laid out in 1851 by Captain Nathaniel Lyon,
running almost along the Mexican border from San Diego to Fort Yuma, in an
effort to speed the movement of supplies to the fort. The route crossed the Jacumba
Mountains, which rise immediately east of the Jacumba Valley, by way of Jacum
Pass. See Woodward, ed., *Journal of Lt. Thomas W. Sweeny*, 266, n. 124.

[39] Fort Yuma was established on November 27, 1850. It was originally located
on the river bottom opposite and about a mile below the mouth of the Gila River.
In March, 1851, it was moved to the site which it occupied at the time of Mansfield's
inspection and where it remained until it was abandoned in 1890. Not until the
spring of 1855 was the work of erecting permanent quarters at Fort Yuma, except
for the commanding officer, commenced.

Colerado, and at the crossing of the Colerado by the emigrant trail from El Paso on the Rio Grande, and among the wild Indians, and is a very important position, and affords protection to emigrants, and is one link in a chain of posts that should be established on the route to El Paso. It is well selected and should be maintained. It is 220 miles from San Diego, 275 miles from Los Angeles, and 600 miles on Cooks Route to El Paso via the Pimos Villages, which are 185 miles distant. It is 150 miles from the mouth of the Colerado, about 150 miles below the big Cañon, which is supposed to extend from 200 to 300 miles, a few hundred yards from the boundary line and one of its monuments on the opposite side of the Colerado, in latitude 32° 43' 31.58" and longitude 7^h 38^m 12.37^s. It has a commanding and extensive view, with Pilot Knob in the distance lifting its head above the horizon for a beacon. It was once a mission station but destroyed by the Indians.[40] The water of the Colerado, a very rapid stream, is good for drinking, and it is navigable for small steamers to the Gulf of California, and supplies are being furnished that way direct from San Francisco which no doubt will result in a great saving of expense over the transportation across the desert 100 miles with bad water and no grass, and 120 miles over steep mountains and bad roads in wagons exposed to the hazard and suffering consequent to such trips. This mode of supplying will undoubtedly eventuate in making this post a sub depot for the supply of such posts as will probably be established on the route to El Paso. And here I would remark I shall again refer to this subject under the head of posts recommended and endeavour to designate localities, sites, or positions which would open this

[40] The Mission of Puerto de la Purísima Concepción was established on the site in 1780 by Father Francisco Garcés. A second mission, San Pedro y San Pablo de Bicuñer, was established a short distance downstream at the same time. Both missions were attacked and destroyed by the Yuma Indians in July, 1781. Elliott Coues, trans. and ed., *On the Trail of a Spanish Pioneer: The Diary and Itinerary of Francisco Garcés*, I, 19–23.

route to a monthly mail and stage across the country to San Diego or Los Angeles. The Gila is not at all seasons a running stream, and the water is not good, and stands at times in pools in its bed. There are two ferries, one just below the fort and the other at the point of rocks within six miles of this post[41] and a trading house kept by G. F. Hooper, the sutler of the post, at Algodones, about 11 miles further down the river. The whole white population within 100 miles are confined to the ferries and store above mentioned, and probably never exceed 15 men. There is good grazing, abundance of wood, and a garden for vegetables no doubt can be established here by irregation.

The Yuma Indians in this vicinity number about 300 warriors armed with bows and arrows and are of a sulky and uncertain character and not to be trusted. There are other Indians in this quarter—say within 150 miles—which, combined with these,

[41] Apparently the first regular ferry service on the lower Colorado was provided by the Yuma Indians in 1848. The business, proving profitable, was seized by a party of adventurers from the United States, financed by a wealthy merchant of Hermosillo, Mexico. This ferry crossed the Colorado about six and one-half miles below the mouth of the Gila in the vinicity of Pilot Knob, at the base of which the adventurers erected a stronghold which they called Fort Defiance. In the spring of 1850 the Yuma Indians fell on the party, the members of which were purportedly incautious as the result of too much drink, and killed all but three. The Indians then resumed operation of the ferry. For a time in the autumn and early winter of 1849, United States troops were encamped opposite the mouth of the Gila. Their camp, called Camp Calhoun, was established by First Lieutenant Cave J. Couts, First Dragoons, who commanded the military escort for the boundary survey party headed by First Lieutenant Amiel W. Whipple. A ferry was maintained by the soldiers for the convenience of the survey party, and emigrants were also accommodated. Wagons were ferried across the river for fifty cents a piece and cattle for ten cents a head, less than was charged by the Indians or the later ferry companies. A more permanent service was established in August, 1850, by a company which included Louis J. F. Jaeger, who was to maintain the ferry for many years. The ferry, at first, crossed the Colorado about a mile below the mouth of the Gila. See Bartlett, *Personal Narrative*, II, 174–76; Conkling, *Butterfield Overland Mail*, II, 200–204; Charles Pancoast, *A Quaker Forty-Niner*, 254; Grant Foreman, *Marcy and the Gold Seekers*, 305, 315; and Woodward, *Feud on the Colorado*, 20–40.

might raise the number to 1,000 warriors. For a sketch of this position see D hereunto appended [No. 18, Plans and Sketches section].

4h, *Fort Miller.*[42] This post is at the foot of the Sierra Nevada Mountain and on the south bank of the San Joaquin River and well located for the present to overawe and restrain the Indians and protect the white settler, and should be retained some years. It is 286 miles from Los Angeles, and 583 from Fort Yuma, and 505 from San Diego, and 160 from Benicia via Stockton on the San Joaquine River. To all these places there is a passable road for wagons except from Stockton to Benecia where there are good steamers. There is good grazing and abundance of wood and hay and some tillable land for a garden. The supplies must all come from San Francisco via Stockton except fresh beef and barley and flour. The Indians in this quarter number within 75 miles about 500 warriors who are under different local names and armed with bows and arrows, and are disposed to work for miners and others by the day, but do not wish to remove to the reservation. The American population at Millerton and this immediate vicinity may number 500, and this country is filling up with miners and the good lands being taken up. A post office should be established at Millerton where there is a ferry across the San Joaquin. [See No. 19, Plans and Sketches section].

5h, *Fort Reading.*[43] This post is on Cow Creek, an eastern tributary of Sacramento River, and 25 miles above Red Bluff, the head of navigation of that river in the Sacramento Valley. It is 25 miles by good wagon road south of Shasta City. It is 185

[42] Fort Miller was established on May 26, 1851, and abandoned on October 1, 1864. It was located on the south bank of the San Joaquin River, about 150 miles above Stockton.

[43] Fort Reading was established on May 26, 1852. The garrison was withdrawn on April 1, 1856, though the post was occasionally occupied thereafter. It was located on the right bank of Cow Creek, a mile and one-half above its junction with the Sacramento River, at the present town of Redding.

miles by mule trail over mountains from Fort Humbolt on Humbolt Bay, 120 miles by mule trail over mountains from Fort Jones, 115 miles by wagon road from Marysville. There is abundant of grazing, wood, water, and facilities for a good garden. All other supplies except fresh beef must come from San Francisco via the Sacramento River and [are] landed either at Colusa, 120 miles off, at the low stage of the water, or at Red Bluff, 25 miles off, at the high stage. Thence to be transported in wagons.

The Indians in this vicinity within seventy-five miles number about 400 warriors, armed with bows and arrows, known under different local names, but are disposed to work for the whites in many instances. The Americans within the same distance are, inclusive of Shasta City, scattered as miners and farmers, and may be said to number at least 2,000 souls.

It appears to me, however, that this post is not at this time properly located, however suitable it might have been when established in 1852. I would therefore recommend this post should be removed further eastward towards the emigrant trail at the mountains, after a suitable reconnaisance, as a post in that quarter seems necessary.[44] Another objection to this post is its decidedly sickly locality (the Sacramento Valley) where the ague and fever prevails and the officers and men are kept constantly sick and unfit for duty in the field. Further it is exposed to overflows in the rainy season, and a bridge has been actually constructed to communicate with the soldiers kitchens on such occasions. For a sketch of this position see F hereunto appended [No. 20, Plans and Sketches section].

6h, *Fort Jones*[45] is well located in Scotts Valley on a reserva-

[44] Fort Crook was established on July 1, 1857, on the west side of the Fall River, a confluent of the Pit River, in Shasta County. Though this was not the direct result of Mansfield's recommendations, it was in line with them.

[45] Fort Jones was established on October 16, 1852, and abandoned on June 25, 1858. Its location was the same as that of the present town of Fort Jones.

tion of 640 acres on Scotts River, in latitude 41° 35′ 56″ and longitude of 122° 52′, and 18 miles from the junction with the Klamath. It is 120 miles from Fort Reading over a mule trail, 150 miles over a mule trail to Fort Humbolt, 15 miles from the town of Yreka, [and] 84 miles from Fort Lane over a good wagon road. There is abundant grazing, wood, water, tillable land for gardens, oats, barley, wheat, and vegetables in the immediate vicinity, and grist mill and saw mill convenient. All other supplies have been heretofore received via Shasta City and Fort Reading, but in my opinion should hereafter come from San Francisco, over the wagon road thro' Fort Lane to Scottsburg, 224 miles.

This is an important post from its vicinity to the Trinity and Klamath rivers, and the number of Indians on and about them, and should be maintained till the population becomes sufficient to protect themselves beyond doubt and be secure against massacre. The Indians within 30 miles number about 100 warriors, and are armed with good rifles and guns; and this post, in conjunction with Fort Lane on the Rogue River, exercises a constraining influence over say 1,000 warriors within 250 miles. The American population within 30 miles, including the town of Yreka, may be put down at 2,000, scattered as miners and traders and farmers.

This is a beautiful valley about 30 miles long and about 10 broad and is fast filling up with American farmers. The small grains grow extremely well here, and the mountains afford abundant timber for lumber. There is a semi-weekly stage line from this valley to Jacksonville in Oregon over the Siskiou Mountains. [See No. 21, Plans and Sketches section].

7h, *Fort Lane*[46] is extremely well located on a reservation of

---

[46] Fort Lane was established on September 28, 1853, and abandoned on September 17, 1856. It was located south of the Rogue River a few miles northwest of the present town of Medford and opposite Lower Table Rock.

Mansfield's
SKETCHES AND PLANS
of Forts and Locations

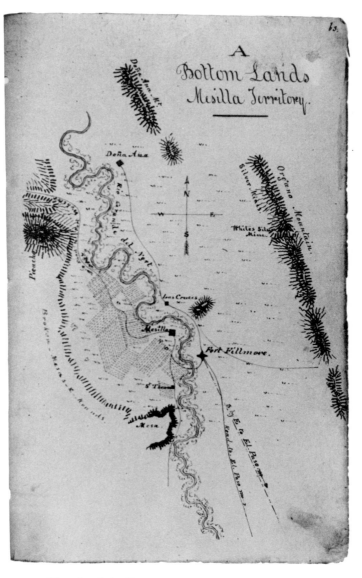

A

Bottom Lands
Mesilla Territory.

1. Sketch of the Bottom Lands, Mesilla Territory

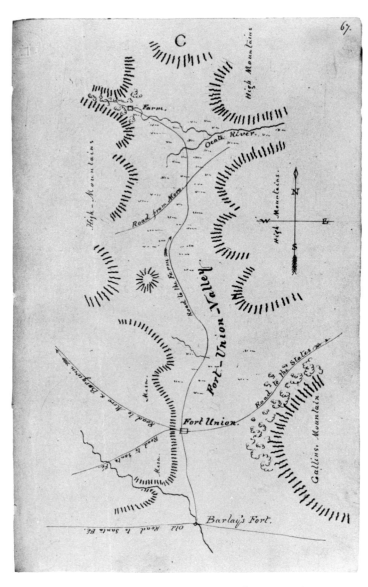

C

High Mountains

High Mountains

Farm.

High Mountains

Ocate River

High Mountains

N

W E

Road from Mora

S

Road to the Farm

Fort Union Valley

Road to the States

Road to Mora & Taplanes

Mora

Mora

Road to Santa Fe

Mora

Gallines Mountain

Fort Union.

Old Road to Santa Fe

Barlay's Fort.

2. Sketch Showing the Location of Fort Union

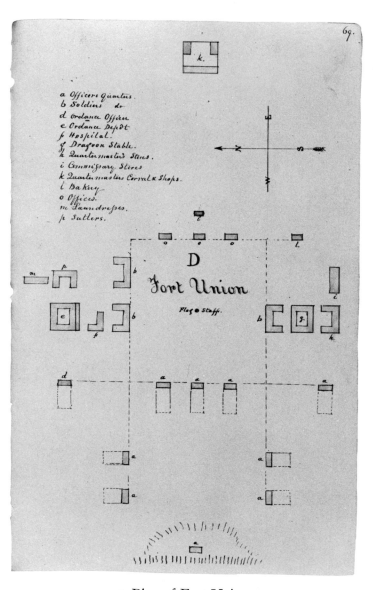

a Officers Quarters.
b Soldiers do
d Ordnance Officer
e Ordnance Depot
f Hospital.
g Dragoon Stable.
h Quartermasters Stores.
i Commissary Stores
k Quartermasters Corral & Shops.
l Bakery
o Offices.
m Laundresses.
p Sutlers.

D
Fort Union
Flag Staff.

3. Plan of Fort Union

E

Cantonment Burgwin

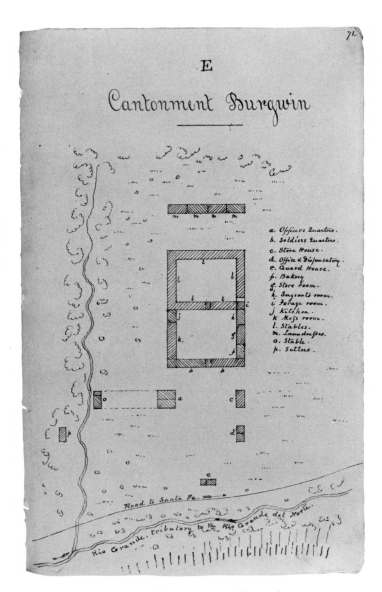

a. Officers Quarters.
b. Soldiers Quarters.
c. Store House.
d. Office & Dispensatory.
e. Guard House.
f. Bakery.
g. Store room.
h. Sergeants room.
i. Forage room.
j. Kitchen.
k. Mess room.
l. Stables.
m. Laundresses.
o. Stable.
p. Sutlers.

Road to Santa Fe.

Rio Grande, tributary to the Rio Grande del Norte.

4. Plan of Cantonment Burgwin

F

Fort Massachusetts

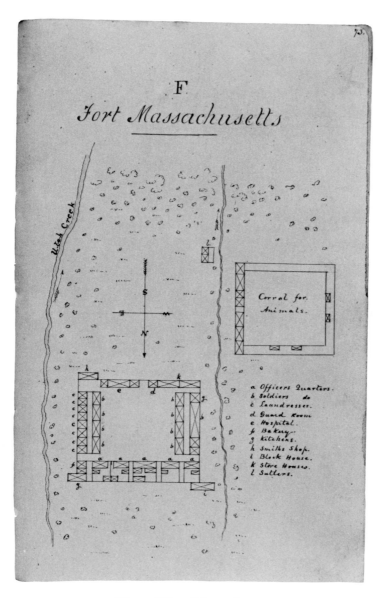

Utah Creek

Corral for Animals.

a Officers Quarters.
b Soldiers   do
c Laundresses.
d Guard Room
e Hospital.
f Bakery.
g Kitchens.
h Smiths Shop.
i Block House.
k Store Houses.
l Sutlers.

5. Plan of Fort Massachusetts

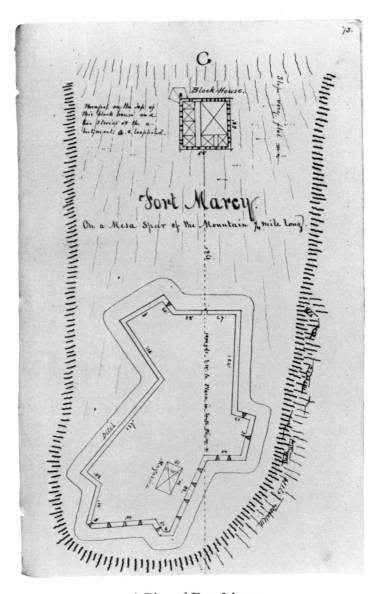

6. Plan of Fort Marcy

H.

Locality of Fort Defiance.

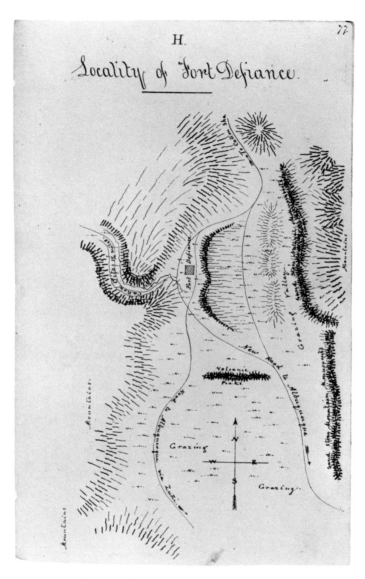

7. Sketch of the Locality of Fort Defiance

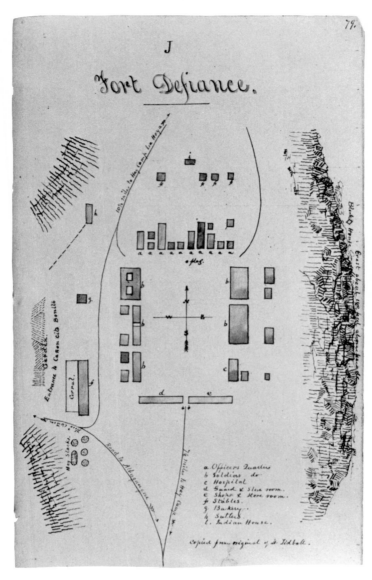

8. Plan of Fort Defiance

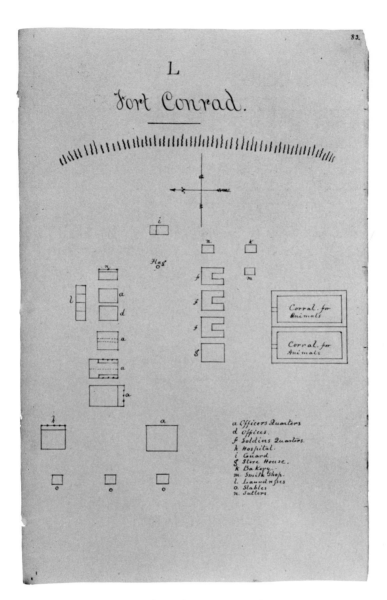

9. Plan of Fort Conrad

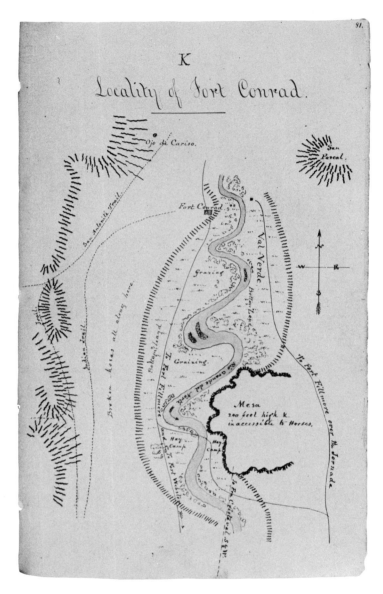

K

Locality of Fort Conrad.

10. Sketch of the Locality of Fort Conrad

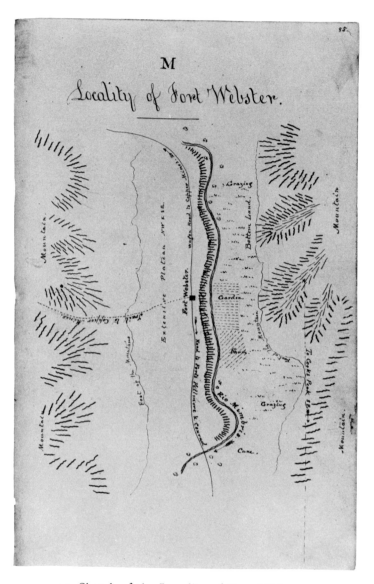

11. Sketch of the Locality of Fort Webster

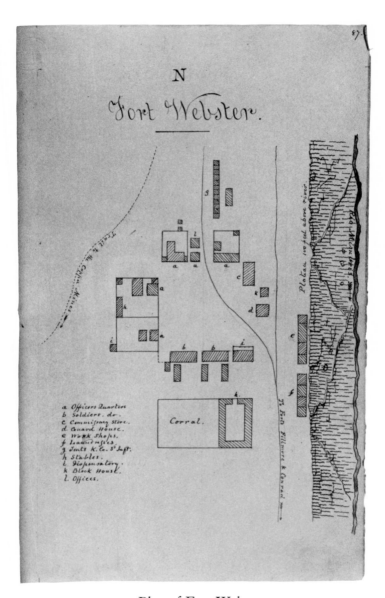

N

Fort Webster.

a. Officers Quarters
b. Soldiers. dr.
c. Commissary Store.
d. Guard House.
e. Work Shops.
f. Laundresses.
g. Tents K. Co. 3ᵈ Inft.
h. Stables.
i. Dispensatory.
k. Block House.
l. Offices.

Corral.

12. Plan of Fort Webster

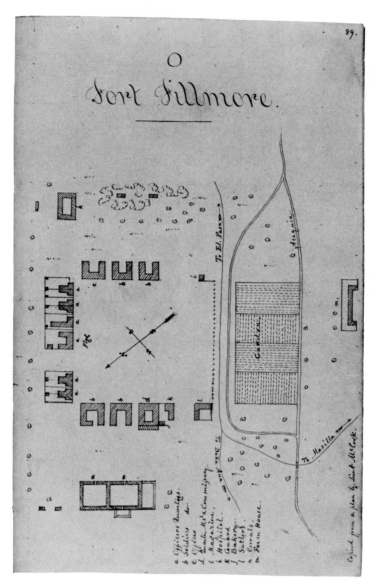

13. Plan of Fort Fillmore

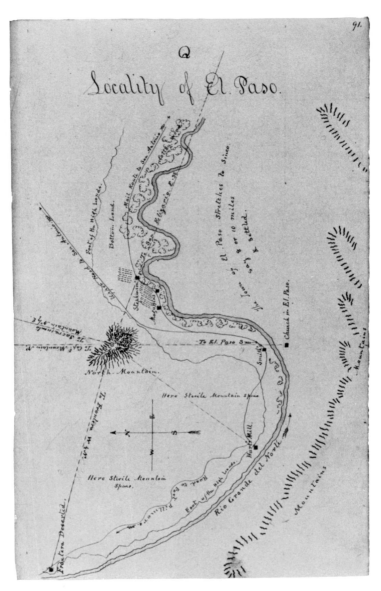

14. Sketch of the Locality of El Paso

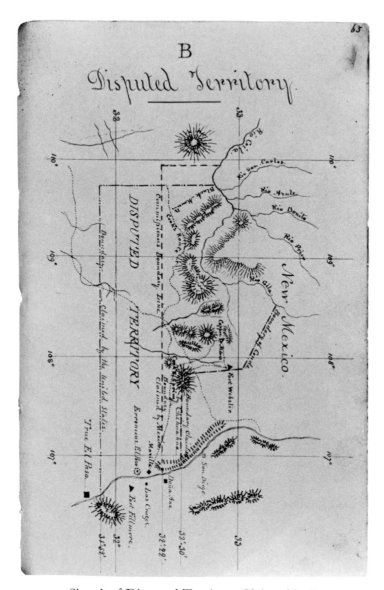

15. Sketch of Disputed Territory Claimed by Both
the United States and Mexico

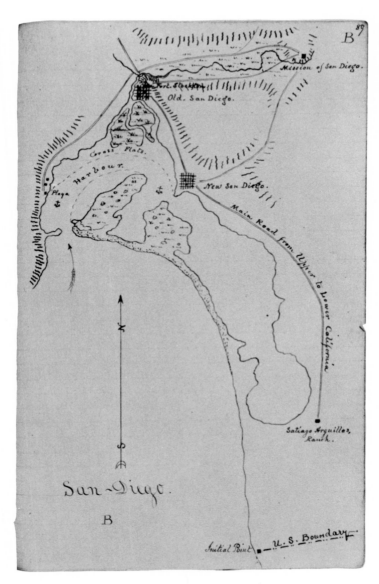

16. Sketch Showing the Location of San Diego

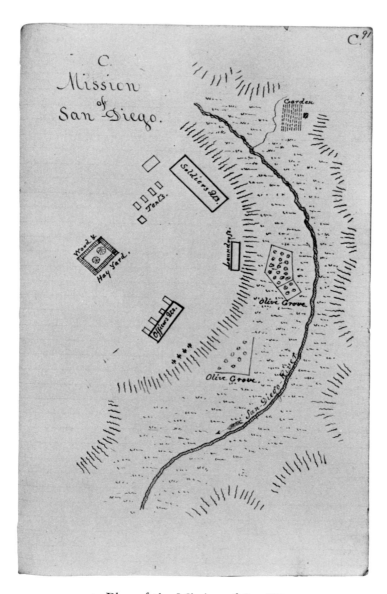

17. Plan of the Mission of San Diego

D.

Fort Yuma.

N — S

Colorado - River.

Gila River.

Monarch

Old fields.

Fort

Boundary Line

Banks: mud: Same as gra.. line.

Colorado River.

Old Garden.

Road.

Slough filled by freshet in June.

Road.

18. Sketch Showing the Position of Fort Yuma

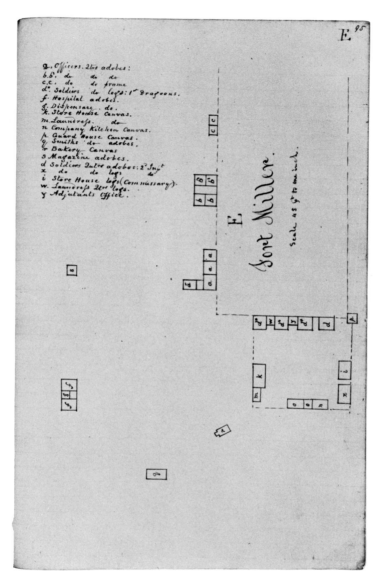

a, Officers. 2br adobes:
b.b. do do do
c.c. do do frame
d. Soldiers do logs: 1st Dragoons.
f. Hospital adobes.
g. Dispensary. do.
k. Store House Canvas.
m Laundress. do
n Company Kitchen Canvas.
p. Guard House Canvas
q Smiths do adobes
r Bakery Canvas
s Magazine adobes.
d Soldiers 2ntre adobes: 2d Inft
x do do logs do
i Store House logs (Commissary).
w. Laundress 2nt logs.
y Adjutants Office.

Fort Miller.

Scale 45 yts to an inch.

19. Plan of Fort Miller

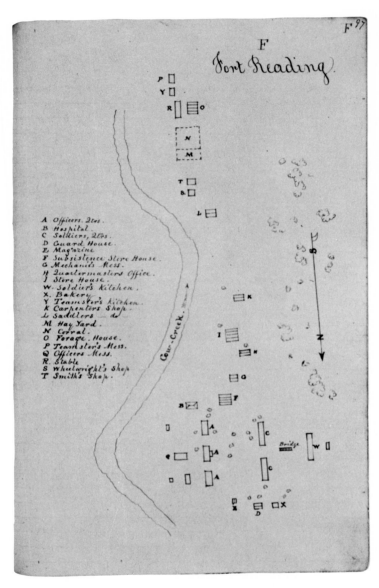

20. Plan of Fort Reading

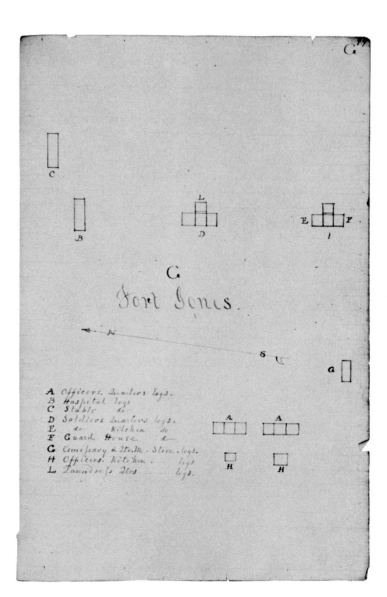

21. Plan of Fort Jones

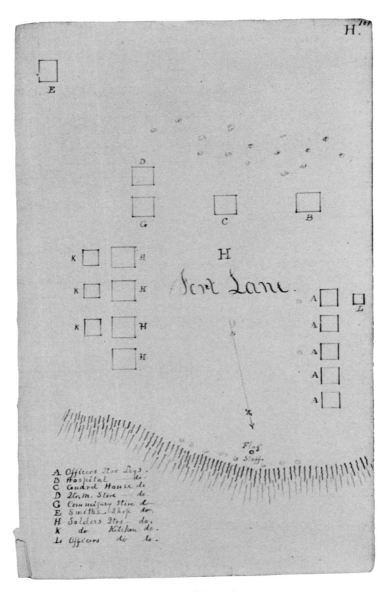

E

D

G

C

B

K   H

K   H   H   Fort Lane   A   L

K   H   A

H   A

A

A

Flag
Staff

A Officers New Logs.
B Hospital   do.
C Guard House do.
D Qu. M. Store   do.
G Commissary Store do.
E Smiths Shop do.
H Soldiers Qtrs. do.
K   do   Kitchen do.
L Officers   do   do.

22. Plan of Fort Lane

I

Fort Vancouver.

A Officers. 2tro Legs
C Soldiers " "
D do Kitchens do
H Hospital frame.
E Magazine Legs.
G Guard House Legs
K Corral.
J Quarter Ms't frame
L Store frame.
N Sold'rs Garden
■ Hudson Bay
Buildings.
O Sutler

Oat. Field

Garden.

Catholic Church

water line

Columbia = River.

23. Plan of Fort Vancouver

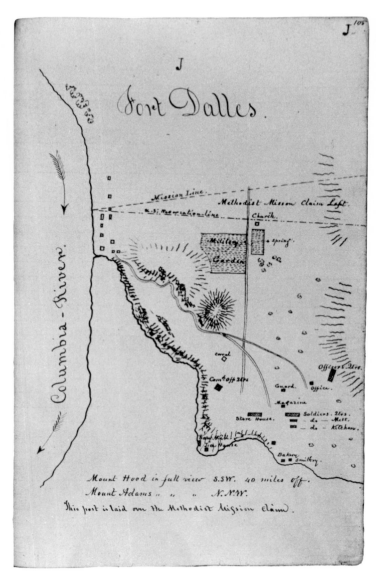

24. Sketch of the Locality of Fort Dalles

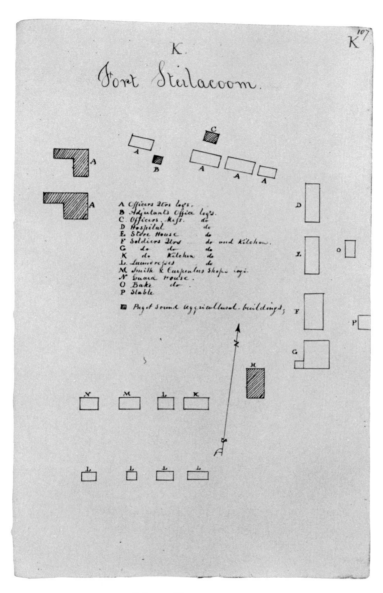

K.

Fort Steilacoom.

A Officers 2tro logs.
B Adjutants Office log's.
C Officers Mess do
D Hospital do
E Store House do
F Soldiers 2tro do and Kitchen.
G do do do
K do Kitchen do
L Laundresses do
M Smith & Carpenters Shops logs.
N Guard House.
O Bake do.
P Stable

■ Puget Sound Agricultural buildings;

25. Plan of Fort Steilacoom

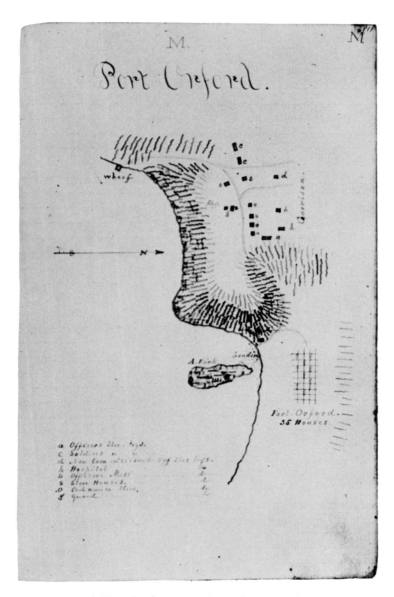

26. Sketch of the Locality of Port Orford

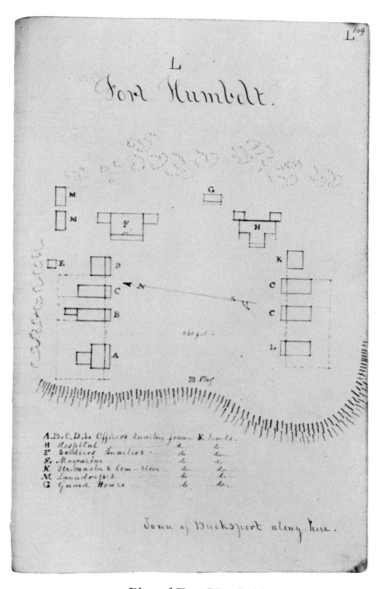

27. Plan of Fort Humboldt

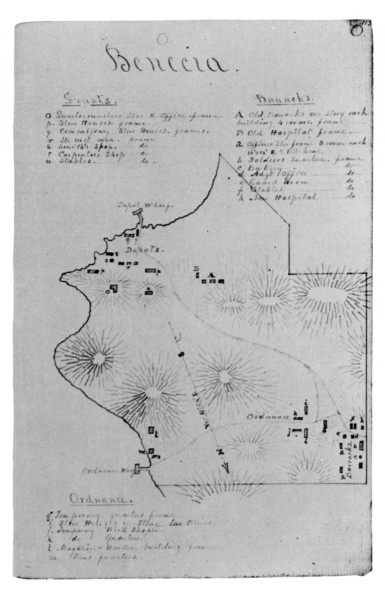

Benecia.

Depots.

o Quartermasters Stos & Office frame.
p. Store Houses frame.
q Commissary Store Houses. frame.
r 2te most men. frame
s Smith's Shop. do
t Carpenters Shop do
u Stables. do.

Barracks.

A Old Barracks one Story each
   building 4 rooms. frame
B Old Hospital frame.
a Officers Stos frame 3 room each
   16'x14' & 2 Kitchens.
b Soldiers Quarters. frame
C Bakery do
d Adgt Office do
e Guard Room do
f Stables do
h New Hospital do

Ordnance.

g Temporary quarters frame
i Store Houses of Stone two stories.
j Temporary Work Shops.
k do Quarters.
l Magazine Wooden building frame
m Mens quarters.

28. Sketch of the Locality of Benecia (Benicia)

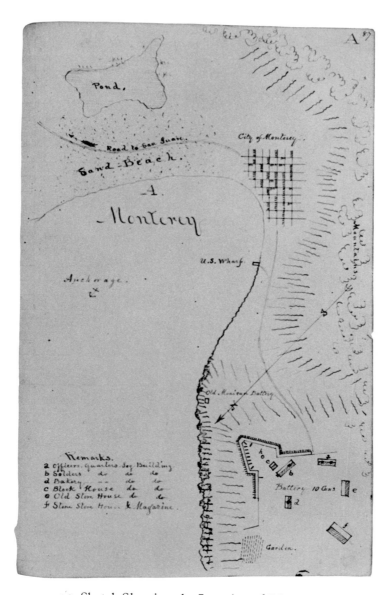

Pond.

Road to San Juan.

Sand Beach.

City of Monterey

-A-

Monterey

Anchorage.

U.S. Wharf.

Old Mexican Battery

Battery 10 Guns

Garden.

Remarks.
a Officers. quarters. log Building
b Soldiers   do   do   do
d Bakery ---   do   do
c Block House   do   do
o Old Store House   do   do
f Stone Store House. k Magazine.

29. Sketch Showing the Location of Monterey

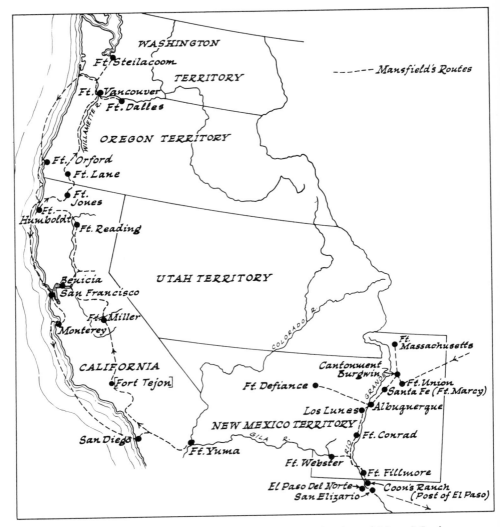

Map of the State of California and the Territories of New Mexico, Utah, Oregon, and Washington Showing Mansfield's Routes

640 acres (which lays over a claim of a Mr. Jennison from which he had to flee during the Rogue River war. This, of course, it would be just and correct under the law of Congress to compensate him for. See my report to General Wool on the subject hereunto appended [see page 193])[47] in Jackson County in Oregon Territory, and on the south side of Rogue River in latitude 42° 30′ where Stewarts Creek (Bear Creek) enters that river, and fronting Table Rock; and thus is situated between the white population and the Indian reservation on the north side of Rogue River. It is 84 miles from Fort Jones over a good wagon road; 140 miles over a wagon road to Scottsburg, which is 25 miles from the mouth of the Umpqua River and in direct communication by water with San Francisco; 8 miles north of the town of Jacksonville; 290 miles to Fort Vancouver over a wagon road thro' the Valley of the Willamette which is fast filling up with an excellent agricultural and mining population. It is 110 miles from Crescent City and 100 miles from Port Orford over the mountains and along mule trails. It has abundant grazing, wood, water, and tillable land for garden. The supplies of oats, barley, flour and fresh beef are had in this immediate vicinity and other supplies from San Francisco via Crescent City. Here, I will remark, there are now two small steamers on the Umpqua River which connect with an ocean steamer to San Francisco; and as this is the only place on the coast in this quarter that communicates by wagon road with Forts Lane and Jones, it is undoubtedly the port thro' which the supplies of these forts must come, as well as the supplies of southern Oregon and northern California. Fort Lane has been supplied by packing from Crescent City at a great expense. The military road from Rogue River (Fort Lane) to

[47] A commission was appointed in 1854 to settle the claims of settlers arising from the Rogue River War. Among the claimants was Albert B. Jennison. They were eventually paid 34.77 cents on the dollar of their claims. Hubert Howe Bancroft, *Oregon* (XXX of *Works*), II, 320–21.

Myrtle Creek was opened under an appropriation by Congress; but a portion of it, built by contract on the north side of Grave Creek Hill, is badly done, and more expenditure should be made on the Cañon of 11 miles, and I would accordingly here recommend an appropriation of 5,000 dollars. Another appropriation of 20,000 dollars has been made to continue this road from Myrtle Creek to Scottsburg. It is thus apparent that Scottsburg is the place thro' which the supplies of this post should come. [See No. 22, Plans and Sketches section.]

This fort and Fort Jones in conjunction with Fort Humbolt watch over the Indians of the Klamath, Rogue River &c &c to the number probably of 1,000 warriors, although the number of warriors within 30 miles of this post probably does not exceed 180, who are all armed with rifles and guns. But those more remote as in the Pitt River and parts of the Klamath and Trinity &c are armed with bows and arrows.

The American population within 30 miles of this post, inclusive of the town of Jacksonville, may number 1,500, engaged in trading, mining, and farming.

8h, *Fort Vancouver*[48] is a beautiful site on the north bank of the Columbia River, in latitude 45° 36′ 56″ and longitude 122° 4′, six miles above the mouth of the Willamette and one hundred miles above the mouth of the river, on a reservation of 640 acres, which lays over land claimed, and in part occupied by, the Hudson Bay Company, in full view of Mounts Hood and Jefferson (see sketch I hereunto appended [No. 23, Plans and Sketches section]). This post is essential and important for a depot for the supply of the posts in this quarter up [the] Columbia River and in parts of Washington Territory, but it would have

[48] Fort Vancouver, originally a Hudson's Bay Company post, became a United States military post in 1849, although the company did not entirely withdraw until 1860. Originally called Columbia Barracks, the military post was officially designated Fort Vancouver on July 13, 1853, and Vancouver Barracks on April 5, 1879.

been better located below the mouth of the Willamette, if a suitable site had been found, as in that case, it would be on the river route of the steamers bound up the Willamette, as well as those bound above the Willamette, and would not have laid over land claimed by the Hudson Bay Company and could better control the navigation. It is in direct communication by water with San Franscisco, whence it receives its supplies, except flour, beef, and lumber; and with Puget Sound and Fort Dalles, 95 miles up the river; and with Portland, 6 miles up the Willamette. It is 290 miles from Fort Lane via Portland, Oregon City, Salem, Corvallis & c over a wagon road—but [there is] no road to Fort Dalles, and when the river is closed [it is] difficult of access—170 miles from Fort Steilacoom on Puget Sound as follows, down the Columbia River 50 miles and 5 miles up the Cowlitz River to Montecello, thence 60 miles by wagon road to Olimpia, and thence 25 miles [by] wagon road to Steilacoom. A direct wagon road should be opened from this post through the country to Fort Steilacoom and another direct along the Columbia River to Fort Dalles, and I would here recommend an appropriation for both these objects. A practicable wagon road of 10 miles has already been opened to Portland.

There are no Indians near this post of consequence in a military point of view. Yet as a depot and reserve station, it cannot be dispensed with at present. In due time a fortification at the mouth of the river will supply the place of this post. And here I will remark that the fortifications for the protection of this river (a great arm of the sea for 140 miles inland), cannot be commenced too soon.[49] There is a large American population at Portland and at other places within 50 miles.

[49] Mansfield's recommendations in this respect were not followed until the time of the Civil War. Construction of fortifications on both sides of the mouth of the Columbia was commenced in 1863. Fort Canby, originally Fort Cape Disappointment, on the Washington side, was first garrisoned on April 5, 1864. Fort Stevens,

9h, *Fort Dalles* [50] is on a reservation of 640 acres laid over the Methodist Mission Claim. It is on the south bank of the Columbia River at the Dalles, in full view of Mount Hood and Mount Adams. The former bears about south west and the latter north west from this post. It is 40 miles down the river by steamer to the rapids thro' the Cascade Mountains, 5 miles portage past the rapids, and 50 miles further down the river by steamer to Fort Vancouver, whence it receives all its supplies except wood and a very few vegetables obtained on the spot, before the river closes with ice. There is grazing here, but little soil for planting purposes in consequence of the want of seasonable rains and the difficulty of irregation. A spring however waters a small garden. On this side of the Cascade Mountains, the change in the face of the country and mountains is in strong contrast with the heavily timbered country on the west side. Here the mountains are shorn of timber as far as the eye can see, and the only relief from this sublime barrenness is the snow topped mountains above mentioned. It is 100 miles by wagon road to Oregon City, which is impassible in winter on account of snows.

This post is important as a link in the chain of posts that should be established to keep up the line of communication across the mountains and is the first east of the Cascade Mountains on the emigrant trail and bordering on the wild Indians. The warriors immediately about this post within 50 miles number 160, armed with rifles and guns. The wild Indians east of the Cascade Mountains in Oregon and Washington Territories, under different local names, number about 2,500 warriors, and many of them armed with the Hudson Bay guns. Of course this post is liable to

---

on the Oregon side, was first garrisoned on April 25, 1865. Neither post is active at present, but both military reservations are retained by the government.

[50] Fort Dalles was established on May 21, 1850. It was not regularly garrisoned after 1861, although it was maintained as a quartermaster's depot. It was transferred to the Interior Department on March 28, 1877.

serious attacks, and as the white population within 50 miles are quite limited, say 100 Americans, no succor can be expected from any point short of Fort Vancouver and Oregon City and Portland.

This has been a mission station of the Methodists and Roman Catholics for many years; but I have very little faith in the efficacy of their work at civilizing the Indians in a locality like this, where vegetation thrives only by irregation.[51] For a sketch of this post see J hereunto appended [No. 24, Plans and Sketches section].

10h, *Fort Steilacoom*[52] is in latitude 47° 10' 57" and longitude 122° 33', occupying ground and some buildings of the Hudson Bay Company, and is 6 miles north of Fort Nisqually of that company and two miles from the shore of Puget Sound and the town of Steilacoom where there may be 100 American population. It is 170 miles from Fort Vancouver via the Cowlitz River and 25 miles from Olimpia where there may be a population of 500 Americans. Its supplies, excepting fresh beef, are received thro' Fort Vancouver and direct from San Francisco. There is abundant wood and grazing here. No reservation has been made, but one is in contemplation about 5 miles to the north east of the

[51] The Methodist mission at the Dalles was established in March, 1834, by Jason Lee and H. W. K. Perkins. It was maintained until August, 1847, when the Methodists decided to abandon it. The buildings and improvements were offered to Marcus Whitman without charge, and he agreed to purchase the moveable property for $721.13. His young nephew, Perrin B. Whitman, was sent to occupy the mission, which he did until shortly after the Whitman massacre. Neither the Methodists nor the Presbyterians made any effort to reopen the mission. Nevertheless, both lodged claims with the government. William I. Marshall, *Acquisition of Oregon*, II, 51–52. The Catholics did not have any mission activity at the Dalles at this time, though they later established a church and school there.

[52] Fort Steilacoom was established on August 28, 1849, and abandoned on July 22, 1884. Congress, on January 7, 1853, authorized the construction of a military road from Fort Walla Walla, a Hudson's Bay Company post, to Fort Steilacoom. At the time of Mansfield's inspection, the route had been surveyed but no significant construction undertaken. Ledbetter, "Military History of the Oregon Country," 112–13.

present site, where the garrison has an excellent garden, the nearest point capable of cultivation to the present site, and on the emigrant trail from Wallah Wallah thro' the Nahchess Pass[53] of the Cascade Mountains. This is the only post in this quarter. It should be preserved as indispensable as a depot and rallying point for the inhabitants in case of outbreak. The Indians about here number about 900 warriors but [are] very much scattered on the shores and islands of Puget Sound. [See No. 25, Plans and Sketches section.]

From Steilacoom there is a direct water communication to Olimpia and other parts on Puget Sound. A military road of about 100 miles should be opened direct to Fort Vancouver and another to Fort Dalles, which would increase the safety of each post, as well as the population, by a communication at all times not interrupted by ice of the rivers & c, and would open the country to the control of the Americans. The magnificent Mount Ranier covered with its snowy mantle is in full view, bearing about south east, and just to the northward of it is the Nahchess Pass. Port Townsend is about 100 miles and Billingham Bay, 150 miles by water. Coal has been discovered in large quantities at the latter place and on the Dwamish River. Lumber is abundant as there are two saw mills in this vicinity and several at Olimpia, and salmon, herring, clams, and oysters [are] abundant.

11h, *Port Orford*[54] is a mere locality on the coast and a lieutenant's command and has no harbour. Its supplies come direct from San Francisco except fresh beef. A small American settle-

[53] Naches Pass, elevation 4,833 feet, leads through the Cascade Mountains between the headwaters of the Naches and Greenwater Rivers. It is today traversed only by a trail. A crude road was opened across the pass by settlers of the Puget Sound area and paid for with funds raised by subscription. The road was poorly constructed, and the route did not prove popular. See Ezra Meeker, *Pioneer Reminiscences of Puget Sound*, 140–57.

[54] The post called Port Orford by Mansfield was officially designated Fort Orford. It was established on September 14, 1851, and abandoned on July 10, 1856.

ment exists here of 35 houses or 100 souls. This post was designed to protect the inhabitants and preserve peace with the Indians, who are scattered about here in the interior and along the coast. In a short time it may be proper to abandon it. It has no military merit. It is 100 miles by mule trail over the mountains to Fort Lane. For a sketch of this position see **M** hereunto appended [No. 26, Plans and Sketches section].

12h, *Fort Humbolt*[55] is in latitude 40° 46′ 38″ and longitude 124° 9′ 01″ at Bucksport, on Humbolt Bay, on a reservation of 640 acres, of 700 yards front (on the water and town) by 4,444 yards deep; thus securing wood land, and gardens and keeping off grogeries. It is well selected in rear of the town, on the high ground, and commands a good view of the harbour and its entrance. There are four little settlements on this bay. At the northern extremity is the town of Union; 7 miles south of it is the town of Eureka; 3 miles further south is Bucksport; and 4 miles further, opposite the entrance of the harbour, is the town of Humbolt.[56] Thus there is quite an American population on this bay, with a good steam tug to bring in vessels and a small steamer to communicate daily with the different places. The Indians in this quarter number about 250 warriors and are much degraded. On the Mad River and Eel River they are armed with bows and arrows. Fifty miles from this post is the junction of the Trinity River with the Klamath; and this post undoubtedly exercises an important influence over the Indians on these rivers, in conjunction with Fort Jones in Scotts Valley, which is 150 miles distant over a bad and dangerous trail. There are constant trains of pack mules between Union and the mining villages on the Klamath, Trinity, and Salmon rivers; and there is a large amount invested

[55] Fort Humboldt was established on January 30, 1853, and abandoned in September, 1867.

[56] The town of Humboldt City, established in April, 1850, was the first town on Humboldt Bay. It existed for a few years only.

in saw mills at Eureka and Bucksport which should be protected against any combination of Indians who could concentrate on either of the three posts, Fort Lane, Fort Jones, or Fort Humbolt. This post is important now and should be maintained for some time yet to come, if not always, for the defence of this bay— particularly as the troops here on an emergency may be regarded as a reserve that a steamer could transport to any point along the coast. The American population within 50 miles may be 600 or more. There is abundant lumber, wood, grazing, fresh beef, potatoes, and barley here. All other supplies come from San Francisco. [See L for a plan of the post.][57]

13h, *Benecia*.[58] This post is of great importance as a depot of supplies generally and arsenal, and is particularly well selected for the latter, being about 30 miles from San Francisco on the water communication between that city and the interior of the country up the San Joaquin and Sacramento valleys, and secure against direct attacks by sea. It is also a good post for supernumerary troops and recruits for instruction and should be maintained permanently. There is nothing to be apprehended from Indians in this quarter, surrounded as it is by the American population far into the interior. The Indians however from Clear Lake along the Valley of Sonoma and on Russian River may number 400 warriors. For a sketch of this position see O hereunto appended [No. 28, Plans and Sketches section].

14h, *Monterey*[59] has been a post and is now occupied by a mili-

[57] The brackets are in the original manuscript; No. 27, Plans and Sketches.

[58] Benicia was chosen in 1849 as the site for a storage depot by Brevet Major General Persifor F. Smith and Commodore Thomas ap Catesby Jones. It replaced facilities previously maintained in San Francisco which were considered unsatisfactory. The site was occupied on April 30, 1849, by two companies of infantry. Benicia Barracks and Benicia Arsenal were added later. Benicia is located on the north side of Carquinez Strait between San Pablo and Suisun Bays.

[59] The post of Monterey was not the old Spanish presidio but the redoubt and accompanying quarters erected by order of Colonel Richard Barnes Mason, First

tary store keeper and magazine with arms, ammunition, and some heavy guns. It contains about 1,400 population, but [is] a place of no military importance in time of peace and really no harbour at all for shipping. The most an enemy in time of war could obtain here would be some fresh provisions. I would recommend the guns and stores &c [be] withdrawn to the arsenal at Benecia and the public land preserved for ulterior purposes. For a sketch of this place see A hereunto appended [No. 29, Plans and Sketches section]. There are no Indians of consequence about here.

15h, *San Francisco*.[60] This is a very important point and should be permanently and strongly fortified against any attempt on the part of an enemy in command of the sea entering this harbour. At least two hundred guns should occupy Fort Point. The Gov-

Dragoons, in 1847. Mason was commander of the department and military governor of California. Monterey, at the time, was both the capital of California and the headquarters of the military department.

[60] The fortification of San Francisco Bay dates from the establishment of the presidio on September 17, 1776. In 1794 the construction of the Castillo de San Joaquín on the south side of the Golden Gate was commenced. It was from the presence of the *castillo* that the name Fort Point was derived. Both the presidio and the *castillo* had deteriorated considerably by the close of the Mexican period, though both were still maintained. The presidio became a United States military post in 1847. It was officially designated "the Presidio" in 1850 and "the Presidio of San Francisco" in 1938. It is, counting the Spanish and Mexican periods, the oldest operative military post in the trans-Mississippi West by half a century. The *castillo* was completely effaced in 1854 when Fort Point was graded to the water's edge and a fort, similar to Fort Sumter in construction, commenced on the site. This fort was known simply as Fort Point until 1883 when it was designated Fort Winfield Scott. Alcatraz Island was set aside as a military reservation in 1850 and the construction of fortifications, both permanent and temporary, started shortly thereafter. The military reservation of Point San José, or Black Point, was also declared in 1850. It was first occupied by troops in 1863 and was designated Fort Mason in 1882. Angel Island was declared a military reservation in 1850 and first occupied by troops in 1863. Yerba Buena Island became a military reservation in 1868. On the north side of the Golden Gate, a series of military reservations were set aside, but the development of permanent posts in that area was a post-Civil War undertaking.

ernment reservation for this purpose consists of that point of land to the northward called Fort Point extending southward about three miles to include the presidio. This is all sufficient and none too much, as it comprises those heights necessary to be occupied by strong redoubts to protect the batteries on the water, and [is] a very suitable place for barracks for troops at the presidio, so essential for manning the batteries and occupying the redoubts & c. In addition there is reserved the whole of Alcatrazes Island, a highly important point in the water defences, where two hundred guns more should be mounted. Further on the opposite shore to Fort Point, which is one mile across the Golden Gate channel, an additional powerful battery should be erected.

I will here remark that it just so happens that this reservation at Fort Point & c is no obstacle to the growth of this beautiful city, nor is it a safe part of the bay for shipping to lay at the wharfs secure against the prevailing winds. Further this bay is so extensive that the city can advance for miles southward to satisfy all the demands of commerce. I look upon this point as the key to the whole Pacific Coast in a military point of view, and it should receive untiring exertions.

« *Posts Recommended and Steamer Revenue Cutters* »

In addition to the posts already established, other small posts seem necessary at this time to encourage and strengthen a population, necessarily very much scattered and exposed to Indian depredations, and to complete the chain of defence and security. Here I must remark that the friendly Indians have great respect for Government officers and soldiers, however few in number they may be; for they seem to understand that there is a power behind, more than sufficient to make up for any present weakness, in case they commit depredations. And in addition, these posts are always a nucleus for the scattered population to rally around in case of threatened troubles. With such views, I recommended

to General Wool, agreeably to his request of me, the establishment of a one-company dragoon post at the Tejon Indian Reservation, heretofore spoken of, where there is every facility for
such a post as to grazing, water, gardening, fuel &c &c. Here
there are many trails where the wild Indians from Owen's Lake
come over the Sierra and commit depredations on the inhabitants of this valley and on the friendly Indians and on the people
of the coast range at Santa Barbara, San Luis Obispo &c. This
point, as I observed before, is in direct wagon road communication with Los Angeles, where there is a population of 2,100, and
in Los Angeles County, a population including the city of 7,000
souls—about one-third American, and about 130 miles distant.
An express from Los Angeles to this post, would enable the troops
to cross the mountains eastward and cut off any party of wild Indians from Owens Lake that may have been committing depredations in that quarter. This post would complete the chain west of
the Sierra and be 156 miles from Fort Miller and 385 from San
Diego and afford the needful protection in this quarter, and I
presume, at this time, is already established, as orders had been
issued by General Wool to that effect before I left California.[61]

I also recommended to General Wool the establishment of a
post about 350 miles eastward of Fort Dalles, on Snake River,
near Boissé River, in the neighbourhood of the late emigrant
massacre, which I presume will have to be supplied from the
region of the Great Salt Lake. This would be only a link in a
chain of posts that seem indispensable to keep up a proper communication with the western coast.[62] I likewise recommended the

[61] Fort Tejon was established on August 10, 1854. It was located in the Cañada
de las Uvas, about fifteen miles southwest of the Tejon Indian Reservation, near
the present town of Castaic. It was abandoned on September 11, 1864. For a brief
history and description of the post see Clarence Cullimore, *Old Adobes of Forgotten
Fort Tejon.*

[62] Fort Boise was established near the site recommended by Mansfield, but not
until July 4, 1863.

establishment of a one-company post at Billingham Bay, near our northern boundary and the coal beds, to protect the scattered and defenceless population there against Indians, who approach in boats. This post could be supplied directly by water from San Francisco, or thro' Port Townsend.[63] And here I must remark that a proper defence of the Sound can only be had by steamers, in addition to these posts, to watch over the waters, and keep up a communication with the mouth of [the] Columbia River. A steamer revenue cutter of the propeller model is required. A vessel dependent on sails alone, can do nothing in this quarter of consequence, either for revenue or other purposes, such are the prevailing winds and counter currents. With such a cutter, the mail could be regularly brought, twice or thrice a month, from Astoria in connexion with the Pacific Mail Steamers, and the coast thoroughly guarded in this quarter against smuggling.

I would here suggest the propriety of a chain of posts across from Fort Yuma on Cooks Route to El Paso on the Rio Grande, a distance of 600 miles. Such a line would more effectually control the wild Indians, as well as afford protection to the emigrant and trader in live stock, and finally end in the establishment of a mail across the country. The supplies could readily come from Fort Yuma and El Paso for these posts. The precise locality for these posts, it is not practicable for me to name. A reconnaissance for that object would certainly be necessary.[64]

While at Fort Yuma, I met Mr. A. B. Gray,[65] a distinguished

[63] Fort Bellingham was established on August 26, 1856, more as a result of the appeal of the settlers of the area for protection against Indian hostilities than because of Mansfield's recommendations.

[64] A series of posts, not unlike that proposed by Mansfield, was established over a period of years, but only two, Fort Buchanan (1856) and Fort Breckenridge (1860), prior to the Civil War. Both were in the present Arizona.

[65] Andrew B. Gray, who previously had served as United States Surveyor for the linear survey of the United States-Mexican boundary under the provisions of the Treaty of Guadalupe Hidalgo. See also note 35 on page 105. Gray later served as a Major General in the Confederate Army.

civil engineer in the employ of a New York company, with his party, who had been exploring the practicability of a rail road route, and was very familiar with this region. He remarked one station of two companies would be well located either on the San Pedro River, near the destroyed Ranch of Babocomeri,[66] or the head springs of the Jonoita,[67] where wood, water, grazing, tillable land, & c & c, are abundant; with a healthy and good climate. This position would be about half way between Yuma and El Paso, and within the limits of the U. S. and via a good wagon road over the whole way, and the best and shortest line. I would respectfully refer to him for additional particulars.

(The Boundary survey and the explorations of Lieutenant Parke give full information in regard to this section.)[68]

« *Command of the Department, Troops, &c &c* »

San Francisco, 4h to 15h May. This department was under the command of Brevet Major General John E. Wool, who succeeded Brevet Brigadier General E. A. Hitchcock. His head quarters I found at San Francisco on my arrival in that city on the 4h May. It has been subsequently removed to Benecia, and was there when I left San Francisco on the 16h September. General Wool's staff consisted of Brevet Major E. D. Townsend in

[66] The rancho of San Ignacio de Babacomeri was a Mexican grant of December 25, 1832, made to Ignacio Eulalia Elías. The ranch headquarters were located on Babocomari Creek in the present Cochise County, Arizona. The ranch was abandoned because of Apache depredations. Will C. Barnes, *Arizona Place Names*, 29.

[67] The Sonoita River, a confluent of the Santa Cruz, entering it from the east.

[68] This material was inserted later and is not in Mansfield's writing. Second Lieutenant John G. Parke was assistant topographical engineer for the survey of the Pacific Railway in California in 1853 and topographical engineer in charge of the survey of the Pacific Railway along the portion of the route near the thirty-second parallel from the Rio Grande to the Gila, 1854–56. For Lieutenant Parke's report see 33 Cong., 1 sess., *House Exec. Doc. 129*, III; and 33 Cong., 2 sess., *House Exec. Doc. 91*, II. Secretary of War Jefferson Davis' instructions to Lieutenant Parke, November 18, 1853, are in 33 Cong., 1 sess., *House Exec. Doc. 1*, II, 61–63.

chief assisted by Brevet Captain D. E. Jones, assistant adjutant generals; Major Osborne Cross, chief quartermaster; Brevet Major Amos B. Eaton, chief of the Subsistence Department; Surgeon Charles S. Trippler [Tripler], chief of the Medical Department; Major Hiram Leonard, chief of the Pay Department, with 1t Lieutenant J. A. Hardie and 1t Lieutenant T. Moore, 2d Infantry, his aides; and Brevet 2d Lieutenant G. H. Mendell of the Topographical Engineers, who I subsequently found at Benecia attached to head quarters.

Adjutant Generals Department. This office as well as all other staff offices at head quarters, as well as the office of General Wool were in one building on Montgomery Street at a monthly rent of 600 dollars, or 7,200 dollars per annum. Here the records of the department were neatly and handsomely kept and systematized and the public papers filed away in a manner very creditable to Major Townsend, the chief of this department. There were in this office Brevet Captain D. E. Jones, assistant, and two sergeants of the army in the capacity of clerks.

Quartermaster's Department. Major Osborne Cross, the chief of this department, has been in charge since April, 1852, and controls the operations of the officers of this particular branch of the service. There are twelve posts to be supplied, towit, the Mission of San Diego, Fort Yuma, Fort Miller, Benecia, Fort Reading, Fort Jones, Fort Lane, Fort Vancouver, Fort Dalles, Fort Steilacoom, Port Orford, Presidio of San Francisco, and, in addition, the Depot of Benecia and the Sub Depot of New San Diego. There are seven assistant quartermasters in this department, towit, Brevet Major Allen, Captains Gordon [Jordan], Clary, Brent, Folsom, [and] Miller, and Brevet Major McKinstry. Of these, at the time of my inspection, there were at San Francisco besides Major Cross, Brevet Major Allen in the city and Captain Folsom at the presidio. But subsequently, by direction of the Secretary of War, only Captain Allen performs the quarter-master's duty in this city and at the presidio.

Funds are obtained from Washington by drafts and on estimates by him and all funds of the different posts in this department are supplied by Major Cross on estimates approved by the commanding general of the department. The supplies, also shipped from the Atlantic States direct to him, are on estimates approved in like manner. The balance of funds in his hands on the 30h April last was 76,608 78/100 dollars, which was deposited in the banking house of Palmer, Cook, & Co.[69] previous to the regulations of the 7h March[70] and which he had not yet deposited with the assistant treasurer, owing to arrangement as to checking not having been completed with the treasurer. These funds were presumed to be safe for the present. The average quarterly amount of funds that passes thro' this officer's hands is 164,763 dollars, of which 114,056 dollars is in advances in cash to subordinate officers and 50,717 dollars, expended by himself. No doubt hereafter the expenditures would be reduced for the same number of troops 35 per cent if it were not for the circum-

---

[69] Palmer, Cook, & Company was a San Francisco banking house. It weathered the panic of 1855, but was involved in the legal battles following the collapse of Adams & Company. See Huggins, comp., *Continuation of the Annals of San Francisco*, scattered references, 46, 79, 84–92, 94–96, 100, 102–103.

[70] Secretary of War Jefferson Davis stated in his report for 1854:

> The arrangement made by the Treasury Department, by which disbursing officers are enabled to keep funds on deposit with the assistant treasurers of the United States, proves to be of great advantage to the service, and promises, when more perfectly understood and carried into full effect, to obviate most of the inconveniences heretofore experienced in transmitting funds and making disbursements in remote parts of the country. It preserves the control of the department over the public moneys till the moment of their expenditure, and enables it, in the event of the death of an officer, to reclaim its funds without waiting for the appointment of an administrator or the settlement of his accounts. It also removes, in a great measure, those temptations which the possession of large sums of ready money, in times of active speculative excitement, cannot fail to present.

33 Cong., 2 sess., *Sen. Exec. Doc. 1*, II, p. 22.

stance that the log buildings now occupied by troops must be gradually renewed by substituting good plank houses, the cheapest kind under the present abundance of lumber all over this department. Labour has hitherto been very high, but is now moderate, and lumber is quite low, and oats and barley are low, and a contract has been made to supply Fort Yuma by water up the Gulf of California at a great saving, undoubtedly. And here I would recommend a public steamer in preference to a reliance on a contractor, who is liable to fail and leave the post without supplies. Further, a public steamer could be used for the transportation of troops &c in other quarters on the coast. And the time saved in making the trips would more than compensate for the difference in expense, on such a coast as this, between a steamer and sail vessel. Less expense will attend the supply of Forts Jones, Lane &c, and much of their supplies will hereafter be had on the localities, such as barley, flour, lumber, fresh beef—all which are already greatly reduced below the prices of a year ago.

Three citizens are employed in this office, one clerk at 200 dollars and one at 150 dollars and one porter at 75 dollars per month.

The public records books and returns of Major Cross' office are well kept and the duties performed to the interest of the Government.

Brevet Major Allen, the post quartermaster of San Francisco, performs his duty in a distinct office, and they are those of an ordinary assistant quartermaster. He pays transportation of troops, purchases and receives and ships supplies to the different posts, under the direction of Major Cross &c &c. For his office he pays 100 dollars per month for three rooms and has two clerks at 150 dollars per month each, and a messenger at 60 dollars per month. He has only performed this duty since the 1t April, and in that month he expended 10,742^{29}/100 dollars and had on hand 13h May, 4,225^{33}/100 dollars, of which 4,125^{33}/100 dollars was in the private banking house of Lucas Turner & Co.[71] which he had not yet, for reasons given in the case of Major Cross, deposited with the sub treasurer.

Subsistence Department. Brevet Major Amos B. Eaton, the chief of this department, has been on this station since the 4 March, 1851, and has the general charge and direction of the subsistence of the troops. There is no other officer of the Subsistence Department on this coast. There is a principal depot at Benecia and a sub depot at San Diego and another at Fort Vancouver, and he has twelve posts to supply. The supplies from the Atlantic States are received on yearly estimates, approved by the commanding general of the department and shipped for six months at a time. The subordinate officers of this department receive their funds and supplies thro' Major Eaton on estimates approved by the commanding officers of the posts. The amount of funds in his hands on the 8h May was 43,583 0⅗/100 dollars, deposited in a private banking house subject to his checks for specie. Here the regulation of the 7h March, for the reasons given in the case of Major Cross, had not yet been carried into effect. The funds however were presumed to be safe for the present.

The supplies of flour, beans, and fresh beef, I presume, will hereafter be had in this department, and convenient to the respective posts, at greatly reduced prices, and of the best quality.

The duties of Major Eaton are satisfactorily performed and the books and public records well kept. He has in his employ two citizens, one clerk and one porter.

There is considerable inconvenience attending the necessity of the acting assistant commissaries on this coast, obtaining certificates from Washington before they can draw their pay, and I would here call attention to this point.

[71] Lucas, Turner & Company was a banking house that was located in San Francisco.

Pay Department. Major Hiram Leonard is chief of this department. There are two subordinate paymasters under him, Major N. W. Brown and Major A. J. Smith, who receive their funds thro' major Leonard. Major Leonard, being at head quarters, pays the posts of the Presidio, Benecia, Forts Miller, Readings, Jones, and Lane. Major Brown is stationed at New San Diego and pays the posts at the Mission of San Diego and Fort Yuma. Major Smith is also stationed at San Francisco and pays the posts of Fort Humbolt, Vancouver, Steilacoom, Dalles, and Port Orford. I would recommend however that this officer be stationed at Fort Vancouver, as decidedly more suitable and convenient to both officers and soldiers. The discharged soldier would find it very inconvenient to go as far as San Francisco for his pay.

The troops are payed as promptly as the difficulty of travel in certain localities will admit. There is no complaint on this score, and the department is judiciously managed with the single exception of two paymasters stationed at San Francisco, which can only be justified on the grounds the funds must come from that city to pay the troops stationed at the northern posts. To this point I alluded in my report to the commanding general of the department.

Major Leonard had on hand on the 8h May 111,442⁷⁴⁄₁₀₀ dollars deposited as follows: in the sub treasury, 100,000 dollars; in the private banking house of Page Bacon & Co.,[72] 10,090⁶⁴⁄₁₀₀

[72] The banking house of Page, Bacon, & Company was a branch of Page & Bacon Company of St. Louis. The failure of the parent house led to a run on the San Francisco bank as soon as the news reached the coast. Page, Bacon, & Company was forced to suspend business on February 22, 1855, at both its San Francisco and its Sacramento office. As a result of the closing of Page, Bacon, & Company, runs on the other banks of the city developed on February 23. None of the others in which United States Army funds had been on deposit were forced to close. Lucas, Turner, & Company was placed under considerable pressure but survived. Palmer, Cook, & Company and Sanders & Brenham were less seriously affected and continued their ordinary business. Huggins, comp., *Continuation of the Annals of San Francisco*, 36. Page,

dollars; and in his own hands, 1,352¹⁰⁄₁₀₀ dollars (as follows—
at Fort Miller, 1,093⁰¹⁄₁₀₀ dollars, Fort Reading, 252³³⁄₁₀₀ dollars, Fort Jones, 67⁶⁄₁₀₀ dollars). Here again the regulation of
the 7h March had not yet been carried fully into effect, but would
be as soon as arrangements for checking on the sub treasurer were
made. The funds in the private banking house were presumed to
be safe for the present. His funds are obtained by estimates and
drafts from Washington.

Major Smith had on hand 1,754⁰¹⁄₁₀₀ dollars on the 8h May,
of which 1,354⁰¹⁄₁₀₀ dollars were deposited in the private banking house of Lucas Turner & Co, and 400 at Fort Steilacoom in
the quartermaster's safe. Here the regulation of the 7h March
had not yet been carried into effect, for reasons heretofore given,
but would be soon. His funds for the present were presumed to
be safe.

Medical Department. Surgeon Charles L. Tripler, chief of
this department, has under his orders one surgeon and thirteen
assistant surgeons distributed at the different stations. Dr. Tripler has been in this department since August, 1852. He obtains
his annual supplies on estimates, and this branch of the public
service is also well managed. Up to this time his private quarters
has been used as an office in San Francisco.

Topographical Engineer. I found in this city Lieutenant R. S.
Williamson, who had been engaged in the survey of the passes
out of the San Joaquin Valley to the Gila with a view to a rail road
under instructions from the Secretary of War dated 6h May,
1853.[73] He had completed his field work about the 1t January

Bacon, & Company soon arranged with its creditors to resume business, but again,
on May 2, 1855, was forced to suspend business, this time permanently. *Ibid.*, 42.
Sanders & Brenham closed their doors on November 7, 1855. *Ibid.*, 77. Adams &
Company, which had not been a depository for army funds, closed on February 23,
1855, and did not reopen. See note 97 on page 177.
[73] For Lieutenant Williamson's reports of the railroad surveys in California see

and was completing his report. He had expended on the 11h
May, 28,331^{43}/100 dollars, and had a balance in his hands of
1,668^{57}/100 dollars in the private banking house of Sands and
Brenham.[74] For reasons heretofore given in like cases, the regulation of the 7h March had not yet been carried into effect. Lieutenant Williamson was sick at the time I inspected his office but
was notwithstanding present.

« *Fort Point—5h and 6h May* »

The charge of erecting the fortifications on this point is in the
hands of Brevet Major J. G. Barnard of the Corps of Engineers,
who assumed command on the 1t January, 1854, assisted by 1t
Lieutenant W. H. C. Whiting and Brevet 2d Lieutenant N. F.
Alexander, both of the Corps of Engineers. The superintendence
of this work was originally assigned to Brevet Lieutenant Colonel
J. L. Mason, who arrived here on the 7h July and died on the 5h
September.[75] During the interval between the death of Colonel
Mason and the arrival of Major Barnard, Lieutenant Whiting
proceeded with the operations and commenced the construction
of temporary quarters for workmen which were about one-third
finished. Since the arrival of Major Barnard, these quarters have

---

33 Cong., 1 sess., *House Exec. Doc. 129*, III; and 33 Cong., 2 sess., *Sen. Exec. Doc.
78*, V. Secretary of War Davis' instructions are in 33 Cong., 1 sess., *House Exec.
Doc. 1*, II, 60–61.

[74] The San Francisco banking house of Sanders & Brenham. C. J. Brenham, one
of the partners, was the second mayor of San Francisco, elected in April, 1851. See
note 72 on page 130.

[75] Captain James L. Mason, Corps of Engineers, had contracted a fever while
crossing the Isthmus of Panama. "In his zeal in the discharge of the important duties
confided in him, he was led to neglect his enfeebled health, and was soon prostrated
by a return of the isthmus fever. Under the pressure of his extreme anxiety for the
rapid prosecution of his work, he grew gradually worse, until his life became the
sacrifice to his unremitted efforts." Report of the Chief Engineer (Colonel Joseph
G. Totten), November 30, 1853, in 33 Cong., 1 sess., *House Exec. Doc. 1*, II, p. 173.

been completed and a wharf commenced and nearly finished and some excavations made preparatory to superstructure. The plans however of this battery were not yet settled and as this is a matter of much importance, it should be well studied by the Board of Engineers. My own impressions are that 200 guns at least should be the armament of a suitable and efficient battery for so important a defence. The reservation for this battery and the necessary redoubts to occupy the commanding ground and for quarters, which will include the presidio, is all sufficient; and as there are no squatters on it at present, great care should be taken to keep them off.

The force employed here are of course citizens who are readily had at this time, but at high rates compared with the Atlantic States. Labourers get 3 dollars per day, carpenters, 7 to 8 dollars per day & c. But labour as well as materials for building are gradually taking a lower rate, as competition increases in business of all kinds. Major Barnard had in his hands, unexpended, [on] 5h May, 19,576^{04}/100 dollars on account of Fort Point as follows: 10,000 dollars in a treasury draft and 9,576^{04}/100 dollars deposited in the private banking house of Lucas Turner & Co. He had also in that same house 4,388 dollars, an amount due Major Fraser, U.S. Agent at New York, and 2,477^{87}/100 dollars on account of light house on Alcatrazes Island, and 463^{71}/100 dollars in cash in safe on same account. The regulation 7h March as to deposits with sub treasurer, for reasons heretofore given in like cases, had not been yet carried into effect but would be soon. These funds were presumed to be safe for the present.

There is some difficulty in obtaining suitable building stone, but it is presumed [that] after further search, there will be found a good article, and in due time a good brick will be manufactured in this neighbourhood fit for arching.

This work progresses systematically and well and the books and records suitable and the officers well qualified for the duties in all respects. They quarter in the city, as there are no other quarters for them.

« *Alcatrazes Island—5h and 6h May* »

This is a very important position for the defence of San Francisco and is only second to Fort Point. The batteries here are being constructed under the supervision of Brevet Major Z. B. Tower who reached here on the 5h August, 1853. He is assisted by 2d Lieutenant F. E. Prime and both of the Corps of Engineers. Temporary buildings for the accommodation of workmen have been erected, excavations made, [and] masonry commenced. Here, as at Fort Point, labour & c are high, and there is difficulty in obtaining a good material of granite and brick. If funds could be obtained, the batteries on this island might be completed in about one year. The plans I did not look into as they were presumed to be the work of the Board of Engineers appointed for that purpose by the War Department. No particular objection to them was brought to my notice.

Major Tower had in his hands on the 5h May, 35,324$^{99}/_{100}$ dollars. Of this, 20,000 dollars was in a treasury draft and 15,324$^{99}/_{100}$ dollars deposited in the private banking house of Lucas Turner & Co. The recent regulation of the 7h March as to deposits with the sub treasurer had not yet been carried into effect for reasons given heretofore in like cases, but would be soon. Major Tower had also in his hands several small amounts received for the sale of treasury drafts which will appear on his quarterly accounts current as they occur. He also had on account of the Board of Engineers 2,127$^{67}/_{100}$ dollars deposited with Major Fraser, U.S. Agent in New York. These funds are all presumed to be safe for the present. This work, too, progresses systematically and creditably and proper books and records kept, and both these officers are well qualified for their positions. They quarter in the city of San Francisco as there are no quarters for them on the island.

« *Presidio of San Francisco—10h May* »

This post was under the command of 1t Lieutenant and Brevet Captain J. H. Lendrum of the 3rd Artillery since the 1t February, 1854. The command consisted of Company M (Captain E. D. Keys [Keyes] absent with leave), 1t Lieutenant J. H. Lendrum commanding company and 2d Lieutenant Richard Arnold absent on detached service, 3 sergeants, one corporal, 29 privates for duty—8 privates sick, 9 privates on extra duty, one corporal and 4 privates confined. Aggregate present: one commissioned officer and 55 privates. Absent on detached service: one commissioned, one corporal. Absent with leave: 1 commissioned officer and 7 privates. Absent sick: one private. Total present and absent: 67. Attached to this post was Assistant Surgeon J. F. Hammond and Assistant Quartermaster Captain J. L. Folsom.

The discipline of this command was good, but the company was not well instructed in the infantry drill and not at all as skirmishers. This is in consequence of many recruits having recently joined. A squad was selected of the old soldiers who were carried, by Captain Lendrum, through the artillery drill with two pieces handsomely.

The arms and equipments of this company were in good serviceable condition for the field. The quarters for the soldiers were miserable adoby buildings, the leavings of the Mexican Government, but were kept in good police and order. And the quarters for the officers [were] not much better. A temporary barrack for the soldiers has been subsequently erected by order of General Wool. A remodelling and rebuilding of this post and quarters will be necessary at a future day when they will be required for troops to man the fortifications & c & c. The store houses for arms and clothing badly ventilated and not suitable—and there is no musician at this post.

The Medical Department, in the charge of Dr. Hammond, who had been here but a short time, was in good order, but there was a deficiency of bunks, and the hospital building [was] a poor structure, and it should be levelled as it occupies the ground suitable for drills, parades, &c.

The Quartermaster's Department was in the hands of Captain Folsom, who had been here since the 1t April, and the supplies suitable, but all the buildings for stores &c &c worthless. He had expended 3,496^{47}/100 dollars, and had on hand 885^{03}/100 dollars, deposited in the private banking house of Lucas Turner & Co. which, for reasons heretofore given in like cases, had not yet been deposited with the sub treasurer. He had in his employ one citizen clerk.

The Commissary Department was in charge of Captain Lendrum and the supplies good and accounted for. He had in his hands 854^{62}/100 dollars, of which 813^{7}/100 dollars was in the private banking house of Lucas Turner & Co. and, for reasons heretofore given in like cases, had not yet been deposited with the sub treasurer. These funds are all presumed to be safe for the present.

There were here ten long 32-pounders which required overhauling, and the carriages cleaned up, and there is a large supply of balls here; and the post battery of four 6-pounder field pieces required painting. A garden existed here, but it was in very bad order and not, in my opinion, sufficiently large, yet there is land enough.

This post is three miles by land and about the same by water from San Francisco and about one mile by land or water from Fort Point, and is on the leward side of the heights which shelter it from the prevailing northwest winds, and is in full view of Alcatrazes Island, about one and a half miles off, and the only spot about here suitable for a command of troops, either for the forts or for instruction, and is ample and convenient.

Brevet Captain Lendrum is an ambitious and meritorious young officer, but the duty of commander of post and of company and acting commissary, and the instruction of troops cannot be performed by one officer to the advantage of the service.

I found, at this post, Company L, 3rd Artillery, commanded by Lieutenant J. Kellogg, temporarily attached to it, and 2d Lieutenant E. H. Day. The men were all recruits, and just landed from the Alantic States, and did not know the manuel of the musket and had not got cleaned up, and were occupying tents for want of quarters. As I found this company subsequently at Fort Vancouver in a very different condition and highly creditable to the young officers in charge, I shall not further notice it here.

This post was last inspected by Colonel McCall, late inspector general.[76] There are no Indians about here.

« *Monterey—18h to 21t May*[77] »

This post is 120 miles by land from San Francisco [by] stage route, and less by water. There are no troops here. A military store keeper, B. G. Baldwin, resides here and takes the charge of the public property and endeavours to keep off squatters from the reserve, which should be definitively marked out, and on which

[76] Colonel McCall's report of the inspection of the presidio, dated May 26, 1852, is in "McCall's Inspection Report, Department of the Pacific, 1852." As did Mansfield, McCall complained of the lack of instruction in drill and of the condition of the buildings at the post.

[77] For McCall's inspection report of the Redoubt of Monterey, dated July 9, 1852, see *ibid.* Monterey was an active post at the time of McCall's inspection, garrisoned by Company F, Third U. S. Artillery, commanded by Captain Henry S. Burton. McCall expressed the opinion that, "unless the force at present in California shall be very considerably increased, it appears to me that the troops now at the *Redoubt of Monterey* might be advantageously posted elsewhere. . . ."

is the remains of a battery, a block house, and four old log houses for quarters and a stone ordnance store house used for powder also. The U.S. quarters for soldiers within the city has been turned over to the Monterey Library Association for their use and safe keeping, a very good arrangement. There is no necessity for a garrison here. The population do not fear the Indians. There is a colector and deputy collector here but only a U.S. wharf and that of very little value. The place possesses no military merit, and I would recommend that all the stores and supplies now here, in a precarious state as to safety, be shipped to Benecia by one of the quartermaster's vessels, and the post left in the hands of the collector. Mr. Baldwin had in his hands 177⁴¹⁄₁₀₀ dollars on account of Ordnance Department. Among the ordnance here are 10 iron twenty-four-pounder guns mounted, 3,411 twenty-four-pounder balls, and 1,109 shells for eight-inch mortars and in store 2,440 bright flint lock muskets and 903 flint lock pistols, and a large quantity of powder in barrels and fixed ammunition.

It would be a small matter at a future day on the verge of war to ship a battery from Benecia of the largest caliber and range, should it be at that time desirable to establish one here. The battery above mentioned of twenty-four-pounders is not heavy enough for such a locality, where an enemy has so much sea room.

For a sketch of this post see A hereunto appended [No. 29, Plans and Sketches section].

« *Sub Depot of New San Diego—25h to 28h May* »

This Station was under the command of Brevet Major J. Mc-Kinstry, assistant quartermaster, the ranking staff officer here. Here was stationed Major N. W. Brown, paymaster, and 1t Lieutenant A. R. Eddy, 1t Artillery, acting commissary of subsistence, in charge of that department as a sub depot. There were no soldiers at this station, nor nearer than nine miles, the Mission of San Diego, but one sergeant here on detached duty from that post. The water for this station is hauled three miles from San Diego River at a cost of 12 dollars per day. An attempt was made to bore for an artesian well, but the contractor, after reaching one hundred feet without success, absconded. Wood is brought here twenty miles at 25 dollars the cord. There is no grass at this place, nor near here for several miles, for animals of the Quartermaster's Department, and these animals have to be sent off sixty miles to graze, and the only advantage it has over Old San Diego is a greater depth of water near shore and a good wharf which is private property built on speculation. There is a good quartermaster's two-story frame building store house. And all the supplies of quartermaster and commissary are well cared for. Each department at this post was in excellent order and condition as to offices, records, work shops, &c.

Major McKinstry was relieved from his duties at this post by order of Brevet Brigadier General Hitchcock on the 1t March, when the U.S. owed him according to his accounts 59^{2}%$_{100}$ dollars. He resumed his duties here again, by order of Brevet Major General Wool, on the 23rd May, and had no funds in hand at date. Lieutenant Eddy had about 200 dollars of quartermaster's funds in his hands at date not yet turned over. There are in the quartermaster's employ 23 citizens, towit, 2 agents, 90 dollars per month; 11 teamsters at 50 dollars; 3 herdsmen at 50 dollars; 2 express riders at 80 dollars; one smith at 5 dollars per day; one clerk at 150 dollars; one carpenter at 5 dollars per day; one wheelwright at 5 dollars per day; one harness maker at 5 dollars per day. The mules of this department were in good order: all the supernumeraries were grazing at San Isabel, about sixty miles on the road towards Fort Yuma and the only suitable place, and very convenient to obtain fresh animals as the trains passed along. Hay is had at 30 dollars the ton, and barley at 3 cents the pound, and corn not to be had at all. The supplies of this depot generally come from San Francisco.

Subsistence Department. Lieutenant Eddy controls this department, and it is well administered, and supplies well stored. Flour frequently spoils before it reaches here from the Atlantic States, and pork does not keep well: 691 barrels flour and 93 barrels of pork have been condemned since the 1t January, 1852. Hereafter, it is presumed, flour will be supplied from California and Oregon, where there is abundance of the best manufactured. There is no bacon on hand, and this is believed to be better than pork, and not so easily spoiled. Fresh beef is 12 cents the pound. This depot supplies Fort Yuma and the Mission of San Diego. But recently the supply of Fort Yuma has been undertaken by water direct from San Francisco. Still it will not do to break up this depot till other means of supply have been fully tested. Lieutenant Eddy has been in charge since November, 1851. He has in his employ one clerk at 125 dollars, and one store keeper at 70 dollars per month and one ration. He had in his hands at date 3,589$\frac{12}{100}$ dollars as follows: 1,507$\frac{12}{100}$ in iron safe, and the balance in the private banking house of Page Bacon & Co. & John Perry.[78] For reasons herefore given in like cases, the recent regulation of the 7h March as to deposits with sub treasurer had not yet been carried into effect.

Pay Department is in the hands of Major N. W. Brown. This officer pays the troops in Southern California, which at present comprises the posts of the Mission of San Diego and Fort Yuma. It is well conducted, and the Mission of San Diego is paid punctually once in two months and Fort Yuma, once in four months.

[78] John Perry was prominent in San Francisco affairs in this period. He served as assistant alderman and, in October, 1854, was appointed to the board of education. There is no indication that he maintained a public banking house. See Huggins, comp., *Continuation of the Annals of San Francisco*, 18, 36.

The distance, danger, and difficulty of reaching Fort Yuma is sufficient reason why the troops cannot be paid oftener. There is no complaint on this score. He had on hand at date 15,994⁵⁴⁄₁₀₀ dollars as follows: in safe in his office, 14,282⁵⁴⁄₁₀₀ dollars; in National Bank, New York, 1,066⁰⁰⁄₁₀₀ dollars; in private banking house of Page Bacon & Co., San Francisco, 646 dollars. For reasons heretofore given in like cases, the recent regulation as to deposits with sub treasurer had not yet been carried into effect. Major Brown keeps no clerk, as one cannot be had for the legal compensation. It is my impression this paymaster should be stationed at the mission, where there are troops and where his safe, with the funds that he must necessarily have at all times, might be guarded.

New San Diego has been laid out into a city, but there is nothing to build it up. No back country of value, and the private property put into the wharf and several buildings is probably a total loss. For a sketch of this locality see B hereunto appended [No. 16, Plans and Sketches section].[79]

« *Old San Diego—27h May* »

At this place has been stationed 2d Lieutenant G. H. Derby of the Topographical Department. He has been engaged in turn-

[79] McCall's report of the inspection of the Depot at New San Diego, dated June 3, 1852, is in "McCall's Inspection Report, Department of the Pacific, 1852." McCall strongly recommended the supplying of Fort Yuma by water rather than from New San Diego. He reported that the post was not garrisoned and was only a depot of supplies for the southern district of California and the station for a paymaster. In regard to the store house which Mansfield praised so highly, he wrote:

But the storehouse (the only one belonging to the Government at this place) in which the supplies of both Departments are stored, is not of sufficient capacity for the purpose; nor is the building in its present condition of sufficient strength to sustain the weight (either on the 2nd or on the 1st floor) of the stores which, in respect to build alone, it would contain. This building was framed in the Atlantic States, & sent out ready to be put up; the timbers being too slight for the support of heavy weights have given way; & it has become necessary, to save the building, to remove a portion of the heaviest articles.

ing the San Diego River into False Bay,[80] which seems to have been well accomplished; but perhaps not yet permanently. A further appropriation will probably be made. Lieutenant Derby was not here, but in San Francisco, when I examined his work. He wrote to me however subsequently that he had expended all his funds and wanted more.

« *Mission of San Diego—26h and 27h May* »

This post was under the command of Captain H. S. Burton, 3rd Artillery, who has been in California since March, 1847, and in command of this post since June, 1853. It is properly a two-company post. Attached to this post is Assistant Surgeon C. C. Keeney and Chaplin Reverend John Reynolds and Ordnance Sergeant Richard Kerren. The force consists of Company I, 1t Artillery, 86 in the aggregate (Captain and Brevet Lieutenant Colonel J. B. Magruder ordered to Washington 31t May, 1853, and on leave of absence since 27h December, 1853, in Europe), 1t Lieutenant A. R. Eddy on detached duty at New San Diego acting commissary since 17 October, 1851; 2d Lieutenant A. J. Slemmer on detached duty at Fort Yuma with one sergeant and 15 privates since 3rd December, 1853; one sergeant, one corporal, [and] 15 privates on detached service since 24h January, 1854, as escort to 2d Lieutenant J. G. Park, Topographical Engineer, for a rail road route to the Atlantic States; one sergeant and 7 privates on detached service at Jacum, an express route to Fort Yuma; 3 privates in charge of mission of San Luis Rey; one private on detached service at head quarters, Pacific Department; one private in San Francisco confined for desertion. Thus shewing on detached service and on leave and absent confined an aggregate of 49 and present for duty 37, of which 5 privates were sick and 2 confined and one non commissioned officer and 14 privates on

[80] False Bay is now called Mission Bay and it is into this that the San Diego river debouches.

extra daily duty, and 1t Lieutenant F. E. Patterson in command of company and acting commissary and quartermaster—one sergeant, one musician, 2 artificers, and 10 privates for ordinary duty.

—And Company F, 3rd Artillery, 89 in the aggregate, Captain H. S. Burton in command of post; 1t Lieutenant J. Hamilton on detached duty acting commissary of subsistence at Depot of Benecia since 9h July, 1853; 1t Lieutenant J. S. Mason on detached duty at Fort Yuma with one corporal and 49 privates since 3rd December, 1853; 2d Lieutenant B. Dubarry on duty at the Military Academy; one sergeant on detached duty at quartermaster's depot, New San Diego; 6 privates at Jacum on the express route to Fort Yuma. Thus shewing on detached service 60, leaving present for duty 29, of which 14 were on extra daily duty—10 privates, one artificer for ordinary duty, and 3 confined and no musician. Thus shewing an aggregate available force at this post of 2 officers of the line and 67 rank and file.

There were also at this post, temporarily, one private of Company K of the Mounted Rifles in confinement for desertion and one Private of Company A, 3rd Infantry.

The discipline of this command is good, and their arms and equipments in good serviceable order. There is however but a limited supply of ammunition on hand, 500 rifles and 5,000 musket ball cartridges in addition to the supply of Company I, consisting of 1,399 six-pounder cartridge bags and 500 pounds [of] powder.

The quarters of the soldiers at present are worthless: Company I occupies some miserably old adobe buildings, and Company F are in tents. The quarters of the officers are quite indifferent and not suitable. They will answer for offices when new quarters can be put up. Captain Burton with his men is converting the old church of this mission into an excellent barrack for the soldiers, two stories high, the walls being thick and firm. But most of the other buildings, except the officers quarters, being merely ruins, should be leveled, and other buildings prepared and erected for store houses, laundresses &c. This is a beautiful locality on an eminence above the bottom lands of the river, is healthy, and there is a fine garden and olive grove attached to it, with abundant water in the bed of the river.

The Medical Department is in excellent hands, Dr. Keeney's. The north end of the old church has already been fitted for that purpose—dispensary below, and a fine airy wardroom above. The sick are well provided for.

At present all supplies of ammunition &c are very badly stored, but as well as the means at command would allow. Great credit is due to Captain Burton for his efforts to make his command comfortable, and I doubt not he will succeed perfectly.

The chaplin of the post has a small school, but is not at all popular, and no doubt the officers would be glad to get rid of him.

Detachments from this post are stationed at Jacum and at San Luis Rey. The former is on the express trail route to Fort Yuma, where there is a change of mules for the express rider who passes only twice a month. One sergeant and thirteen men are here stationed for this object only and must necessarily have supplies sent to them. This trail only shortens the distance, and it appears to me it would be better for the express rider to keep the wagon road and dispense with this detachment, which is not strong enough to defend themselves if attacked by the Indians. The latter is an old mission forty miles to the northward that has been reserved, but is of no use, except to turn over to the Indians as a reservation. It has no military merit at all.[81]

81 The Mission San Luis Rey de Francia, which had been secularized in 1834, was first occupied by troops in 1847 and irregularly thereafter. Beginning in 1851, it was treated as a sub-post of the Mission San Diego. Except for a detachment to guard the property, the mission was not occupied after July, 1852. Although Mansfield was of the opinion that the Mission San Luis Rey was without military merit, Major Osborne Cross, two years earlier, had reported, "I know of no place so well calcu-

ıt Lieutenant F. E. Patterson has in his hands as assistant quartermaster, 381 dollars; as assistant commissary, 451 $^{35}/_{100}$, and as recruiting officer 112 dollars—all of which is kept in an iron safe. There is no post fund here but a balance on that account due Lieutenant Patterson of 2 $^{90}/_{100}$ dollars. All supplies come from New San Diego and are good.

There is at this post belonging to Company I two brass 6-pounder guns and two brass 12-pounder howitzers for the field.

For a sketch of this position see C hereunto appended [No. 17, Plans and Sketches section].

The previous commanders of this post were Brevet Major S. P. Heintzelman and Brevet Lieutenant Colonel J. B. Magruder, and it was last inspected by Colonel McCall, late inspector general.[82] The American population within fifty miles capable of bearing arms might number one hundred.

lated as this for mounted troops, in consequence of fine grass throughout the valley, as well as a plenteous supply of water." Cross to Thomas S. Jesup, August 31, 1852, in 32 Cong., 2 sess., *House Exec. Doc. 1*, II, p. 85. See also Zephyrin Engelhardt, *San Luis Rey Mission*, 138–42, 145–47, 155–60.

[82] McCall's report of the inspection of the Mission San Diego, dated June 4, 1852, is in "McCall's Inspection Report, Department of the Pacific, 1852." At the time of McCall's inspection the mission buildings had not yet been occupied as a barrack. He wrote:

The only building erected here by the troops is a frame one, containing ten small rooms, intended for Officers quarters. This affords sufficient quarters for the officers of one company of Artillery & the Military Staff of the Post. But there are no quarters for enlisted men—and the latter are consequently still in tents. These tents are shedded so as to afford shelter from the sun; but not so as to give any protection from wet & cold during the rains of winter.

There are no storehouses at the post; and the Government stores of all descriptions are now thrown together in the old building, where they are secure neither from the weather nor from theft.

If the troops are to remain here—the necessity for which, however, is not altogether apparent to me—the requisite buildings should be erected without delay. There would be required, Quarters for the enlisted men; a Hospital; and storehouses for the Quarter Master, & subsistence stores. These are absolutely necessary in winter, during which season the rains prevail.

« *Fort Yuma—4h to 7h June* »

This post is under the command of Brevet Major S. P. Heintzelman of the 2d Infantry. It was established by him in 1850, and was abandoned by Captain D. Davidson of the 2d Infantry without authority[83] and again reoccupied by Major Heintzelman in February, 1852. Attached to this post is Assistant Surgeon R. O. Abbott. The force consists of Company D, 2d Infantry, 41 in the aggregate, Captain and Brevet Major S. P. Heintzelman; 1t Lieutenant N. H. McLean acting adjutant of the post; 3 sergeants, 2 corporals, 20 privates present for duty, 4 privates sick, 2d Lieutenant J. D. OConnell and 8 privates on extra daily duty, and one private in confinement.—A detachment of Company I, 1t Artillery, from the Mission in San Diego, 17 in the aggregate, commanded by 2d Lieutenant A. J. Slemmer, who is also acting commissary of subsistence and assistant quartermaster; one sergeant, one corporal, 10 privates for duty, 2 privates on extra daily duty, 2 privates in confinement.—A detachment of Company F, 3rd Artillery, from the Mission of San Diego, 51 in the aggregate, commanded by 1t Lieutenant J. S. Mason; 2 sergeants, 2 corporals, 37 privates for duty, 2 privates sick, 7 privates on extra daily duty. No musicians at this post.

Thus shewing an aggregate available force of 5 officers and 106 men. Also at this post one private, 1t Dragoons, Company H, in confinement for desertion. The discipline of this post is good, and the troops have been instructed—their arms and equipments in good serviceable order. Major Heintzelman gave a very

[83] Because of the difficulty in supplying the post, all of the troops except a small detachment, which was left as a guard, were withdrawn to Santa Isabel in June, 1851. In November, 1851, the guard was reinforced by a detachment of the Second U.S. Infantry under the command of Captain Delozier Davidson. On December 6, 1851, Davidson abandoned the post entirely because of threatened Indian hostilities, scurvy, and the exhaustion of supplies. Lieutenant Sweeny said that all of the officers present agreed to the abandonment as there "was no alternative but starvation." Woodward, ed., *Journal of Lt. Thomas W. Sweeny*, 139.

handsome battalion drill and some target firing. There are two 12-pounder mountain howitzers in good serviceable order and a suitable supply of ammunition for all arms of the service, but no magazine, and the powder is piled in the centre of the parade and covered with a tarpaulin and secure against the weather. The quarters of the men and Officers and store houses and hospital, being constructed of willows, with the single exception of the commanding officer's quarters just erected of adobes, are worthless. General Wool has subsequently directed that good temporary quarters be erected here for at least two companies on a plan of Major Heintzelman, approved by the quartermaster and recommended by myself, which were well adapted to the locality.

The Medical Department is well managed by Dr. Abbott, and the sick are as well cared for as the hospital would admit.

Lieutenant Slemmer has in his hands, as commissary of subsistence, 1,468^{27}/100 dollars and as assistant quartermaster, 150 dollars kept in an iron safe. Major Heintzelman, as recruiting officer, has in his hands 52 dollars. The post fund is in debt 17^{84}/100 dollars. George F. Hooper is sutler and gives satisfaction.

The supplies of this post are good and obtained from San Francisco either direct by water, or via the sub depots at New San Diego by land, with the exception of hay and wood which are had by cutting from two to ten miles off. A garden has been established here, but owing to the saline soil and want of suitable moisture, has been a failure. It will however be undertaken again. As before observed, the water of the Gila is brackish, but that of the Colorado is good and permanent. Major Heintzelman is entitled to great credit for the improvements in the roads and for the manner he has supplied the post with water. By a force pump and mule power, seated on the bank of the river, he raises the water into a reservoir about eighty feet high, and above the level of the parade, and conducts the water, after it has settled, by pipes into a reservoir near the parade, where the garrison get an abundant supply.

The ration of coffee and sugar at this post is not enough, and a complaint was made of too much salt meat and too few vegetables.

A small steamer[84] now plies between this post and the mouth of the Colerado, a distance of about 150 miles, and has a contract for the transportation of supplies. The present road to San Diego is in places very bad, particularly over the steep mountains and thro' the narrow Cañon. An appropriation of 10,000 dollars on this road judiciously expended would be very advantageous, not only to the Government, but for emigrants.

It seldom rains here, and the sand storms from the desert, at times, fill the whole atmosphere and shut out the rays of the sun.

There was great harmony among the officers here, and they all mess together.

This post was inspected by Colonel McCall in 1852.[85]

[84] This was the side-wheeler, *General Jesup*. See note 20 on page 93. Major Osborne Cross, in 1852, made a contract for supplying Fort Yuma by water from Benicia. The cost involved was one hundred twenty dollars a ton for transportation from Benicia to the mouth of the Colorado, plus fifty dollars a ton additional for delivery to Ford Yuma. Cross wrote:

> This contract was received after advertising in the public prints for nearly four weeks; and I was in hope that some one having sufficient capital would undertake it, but no one seemed disposed to make the experiment; and I am fearful that this will also prove as much a failure as the one entered into last winter by my predecessor.

Cross to Jesup, August 31, 1852, in 32 Cong., 2 sess., *House Exec. Doc. 1*, II, p. 85. The service proved successful despite Cross's trepidations.

[85] McCall's inspection report of what was then Camp Yuma, dated June 14, 1852, is in "McCall's Inspection Report, Department of the Pacific, 1852." McCall stated:

> With respect to the best means of furnishing this post with Subsistence, there can be, I think, no question. The last supply brought by water from San Francisco, cost $75.00 per ton. The next should not probably, exceed $40.00. Whereas, the supply now crossing by a wagon train which I passed a few days since upon the desert, will not be delivered here at a cost short of $333.00, per ton. This estimate is thus arrived at.
>
> It is assumed that a wagon train would make twelve trips between San Diego

Since I left, I understand Brevet Major G. H. Thomas, 3rd Artillery, with his command, has relieved Major Heintzelman, and the detachments of Companies I and F from the Mission of San Diego.

« *Tejon Reservation—22d to 24h June* »

At this post I found a detachment of one sergeant, one corporal, [and] 10 privates—mostly recruits—stationed here temporarily with the Indian Agent, F. E. Beal. They were from Company A, 1t Dragoons, temporarily commanded by Lieutenant Thomas F. Castor, and which was designed by General Wool to establish a post here. The men were in the old uniform and with swords and musketoons, but no pistols. They were in good discipline, and their arms and equipments in good serviceable condition, and their horses and horse equipments in good order. But they had not been instructed and could not go thro' the broad sword exercise, not even the sergeant, who was an excellent noncommissioned officer, but had been transferred from the 3rd Infantry, Company B, Captain Shepherd, and came over from New Mexico with 25 men under Lieutenant Tidball, as an escort to Lieutenant Whipple of the Topographical Engineers.[86]

& Camp Yuma per year—each wagon carrying 2000 lbs. The Government is then charged with the interest on the outlay, the wear & tear, the wages of wagon masters & teamsters, cost of forage, in fine all the expenses of maintaing [*sic*] the necessary train for twelve months, & it appears that the cost of the transport of each ton of subsistence would not fall short of the sum above stated. This, too, is a liberal estimate for I have not included losses by accident. Moreover, instead of twelve trips with 2000 lbs each, I do not believe a train would make more than eleven trips, (altho' 30 days is the time usually occupied in a trip,) with 1800 lbs each.

McCall added that the loss of subsistence stores transported overland, because of the excessive heat, was 10 per cent.

[86] First Lieutenant Amiel W. Whipple was in command of the Pacific Railroad survey along the thirty-fifth parallel in 1853–54. First Lieutenant John C. Tidball had been adjutant at Fort Defiance before joining the survey. See p. 46. For Whipple's official report, see 33 Cong., 1 sess, *House Exec. Doc. 129*, II; and 33

There were about 1,500 Indians here with the agent, and no American population but employees.

« *Fort Miller—28h to 30h June* »

This post was established by 1t Lieutenant T. Moore, 2d Infantry, in 1851. Captain N. Lyon, 2d Infantry, assumed command 7h February, 1852. Brevet Major G. W. Patten, 2d Infantry, relieved Captain Lyon 17h July, 1852. Brevet Major H. W. Wessells, 2d Infantry, relieved Major Patten 21t May, 1853, and left the command to 2d Lieutenant T. Wright, 2d Infantry, 6h April, 1854, and 1t Lieutenant T. F. Castor, 1t Dragoons, assumed command 21t June, 1854, who with Company A, 1t Dragoons, was temporarily here expecting to move to establish a post at the Terjon Reservation.

Attached to this post is Assistant Surgeon John Campbell and Captain Thomas Jordon, assistant quartermaster.

The force consists of Company A, 1t Dragoons (Captain J. W. Gardner [Gardiner] absent sick and not at his company since promoted), 63 in the aggregate, commanded by 1t Lieutenant T. F. Castor, 2 sergeants, 2 corporals, one musician, 22 privates for duty, 6 rank and file sick, 7 rank and file on extra daily duty, one private in confinement, in all 42 present; Brevet 2d Lieutenant J. E. Latimer, 4h Infantry, temporarily on duty with this since 11h April, 1854; 2d Lieutenant George F. Evans on sick leave since 30h October, 1850; 16 rank and file on detached service; 2 rank and file on furlough; one non commissioned officer absent sick—in all 21 absent and   horses.—Company G, 2d Infantry (Captain and Brevet Major H. W. Wessells on recruiting service 6h April, 1854), 35 in the aggregate, commanded by 2d Lieutenant Thomas Wright, who is also acting

---

Cong., 2 sess., *House Exec. Doc. 91*, III and IV. Secretary of War Davis' instructions to Lieutenant Whipple, May 14, 1853, are in 33 Cong., 1 sess., *House Exec. Doc. 1*, II, 58–60.

commissary of subsistence; 2d Lieutenant John Nugen, 4h Infantry, temporarily attached to this company; 2 sergeants, 4 corporals, 2 musicians, 11 privates for duty; 4 privates sick, 7 on extra daily duty, 2 in arrest; in all, 33 present. 1t Lieutenant G. H. Paige absent as regimental quartermaster. Thus shewing a total force of 75 in the aggregate for duty at this post.

The command as a whole was in a good state of discipline, but Company A was not instructed properly and they were mostly recruits and could not drill mounted, and had but a few horses. They marched indifferently and drilled as skirmishers and were armed with musketoon and sabre. There were but three pistols to this company. Their arms were in good and efficient order and the men in the old uniform. The horses were old and generally worn out and but few (and here I regret I have omitted to note the exact number) and not properly shod. I condemned six California horses and one sore-backed American horse, and recommended they be turned into the Quartermaster's Department. The horse equipments such as bits, breastplates, and stirrup irons were dirty. Much allowance however should be made for the fact this company had recently marched from Benecia and had had but little time to clean up, and they were under orders for the Terjon Reservation. There were two laundresses to this company and the quarters were neat and comfortable altho' quite contracted.

Company G was in the old uniform with arms and equipments in good serviceable order, drilled well at infantry and as skirmishers, but the musicians were indifferent and wanted instruction. One laundress attached to this company, and the quarters were neat and comfortable although contracted.

The Medical Department was under the direction of Dr. Campbell. Hospital good, a small kitchen only wanted to complete the necessaries for the sick. The post healthy.

There is a good bakery and a magazine built of adobes, which answers a good purpose, and there are quarters sufficient for one company—all that is necessary here, and store houses of canvas, which of course are not suitable for the supplies. A good garden is had in a small valley about one-half mile off, where irrigation and suitable soil is found, and wood and grazing and hay abundant, within reasonable limits.

At this post are two 12-pounder field howitzers which require painting, but a limited supply of fixed ammunition for them, say 130 rounds, of all kinds. There is also about 18,600 ball cartridges at the post all told.

The Quartermaster's Department is under the charge of Captain Jordon, who was absent on duty. It is in good condition and the records and accounts well kept, and supplies as well stored as the buildings made of cloth would admit, but it is apparent that supplies are not safe in such buildings. There is, in the employ of the quartermaster, 17 citizens as follows: one clerk at 150 dollars per month; 2 carpenters, 150 dollars each per month and one ration; one smith at 150 dollars and one ration; one assistant forage master at 70 dollars and one ration; one acting wagon master at 100 dollars and one ration; 7 teamsters at 70 dollars and one ration; one herdsman and harness maker; two labourers at 75 dollars and one ration each; and one messenger, 20 dollars per month. Barley is had at 4 cents the pound and hay at 7 dollars the ton and hauled by the department. Other supplies [are] furnished thro' Stockton, 130 miles off over land, and it takes 12 days to make a trip with U.S. teams. The supplies are sent to Stockton by steamer and otherwise are there stored on an old U.S. vessel with a man in charge. The average quarterly expenditures in this department amounts to about 9,000 dollars for the last four quarters. Captain Jordon has at this time in his hands 7,642 $^{46}/_{100}$ dollars, which are deposited in the private banking house of Lucas Turner & Co. of San Francisco and not yet with the treasurer under recent regulations for reasons heretofore given in like cases.

The duty of commissary of subsistence is performed by 2d Lieutenant Thomas Wright. The supplies, generally good; the ration of coffee and sugar, too small; fresh meat, antelope and beef, the former at 12 to 15 cents and the latter 20 to 25 cents the pound, is had here: other supplies come from Benecia. No doubt a great reduction in prices will soon take place. The records and accounts are properly kept, and Lieutenant Wright has in his hands 553⁴⁹⁄₁₀₀ dollars which is deposited with the assistant quartermaster for safe keeping. There is no post fund here.

The American population is so numerous within 100 miles in a northerly direction that any outbreak of Indians would be severely punished. In the mining towns there are uniform companies of militia, and every white man in this quarter is completely armed with a revolver and knife at least.

This post was last inspected by Colonel McCall in August, 1852.[87] For a plan of the post see E hereunto appended [No. 19, Plans and Sketches section].

« *Benecia Barracks—8h July* »

This post was under the command of Major and Brevet Lieu-

---

[87] McCall's inspection report of Fort Miller, dated July 29, 1852, is in "McCall's Inspection Report, Department of the Pacific, 1852." McCall said of Fort Miller:

> I consider the maintenance of a Military post in this section of country very important, & that the garrison should consist of two or three Companies. But I think the site of Fort Miller is ill-chosen: it is in a *cul-de-sac*, formed by a deep curve in the mountain-range, the river passing through it near the apex of the curve. Just below this point Fort Miller is situated, at about 200 yards from the river bank. It is, therefore, shut out from a free circulation of air, as necessary to health in the interior vallies of California, where the heat is *extreme* during the summer months. And it possesses no advantage in a Military point of view to counter-balance this serious objection of unhealthiness, which the Medical Officer ascribes to the position of the Post.

McCall recommended that the post be moved some six hundred to eight hundred yards to a more elevated point where there would be a free circulation of air and that the log buildings be replaced with buildings of adobe.

tenant Colonel G. Nawman [Nauman], 3rd Artillery, and is the headquarters of that regiment. His field and staff are as follows: 1t Lieutenant C. Winder, regimental adjutant; Assistant Surgeon C. H. Laub attached to the post; sergeant major; quartermaster sergeant; one corporal and 11 privates (the band); aggregate present, 17; absent—1t Lieutenant John S. Mason, regimental quartermaster, in route to join, and one private sick —total 19.

One Company B only of this regiment was at this post (Captain E. O. C. Ord absent detached since 4h June, 1853) commanded by 1t Lieutenant R. B. Ayres, 2d Lieutenant J. Edwards; 2 sergeants, 2 corporals, one musician, one artificer, 15 privates for duty, 4 rank and file sick, 10 rank and file on extra daily duty, 6 rank and file in confinement; aggregate present, 43. 1t Lieutenant J. Kellogg detached in command of Company L, 3rd Artillery, since 5h May, 1854, and 23 rank and file on detached service to Port Orford since 22d May, 1854—total absent, 25. Total present and absent 68.

Thus the whole force present for duty is 59. In addition to the above, there are temporarily two privates of Company M, 3rd Artillery, as cook and steward in hospital and 2 privates sick of Company A, 1t Dragoons, and K, 3rd Artillery.

This command was in a good state of discipline. The books of the regiment new and in excellent order. The troops in the old uniform, but their arms and equipments in good serviceable condition. They were all well quartered, a good hospital and bakery. Lieutenant Winder was acting commissary of subsistence, and the supplies were good and obtained at the depot here. And all public property in a good state of preservation.

Assistant Surgeon Laub, in addition to attendance on this garrison, performed the duty of purveyor in this department, and the supplies were in a good state of preservation. His quarterly expenditures on this account have been about 200 dollars for the past year. He had on hand on the 8h July, 1,323 ^{43}/100 dollars as follows: in cash, 1,100 dollars, and deposited in the private banking house of Lucas Turner & Co. of San Francisco, 222 ^{64}/100 dollars. The recent regulation as to funds here too had not been carried into effect for the reasons before given in like cases.

A garden is attached to this garrison.

The Government reservation here is ample for all purposes of troops, arsenal and depots that will be required in this quarter of this department. There are about 200 population in the town of Benecia capable of bearing arms, but the Town can never be of importance as a commercial city.[88]

For a plan of this position see O hereunto appended [No. 28, Plans and Sketches section].

« *Benecia Arsenal—7h July* »

This Arsenal was established by Lieutenant and Brevet Captain C. P. Stone, chief of the Ordnance Department, in this department in July, 1851, and has been under his command ever since. He was assisted by 2d Lieutenant W. T. Welcker [Welker] of the Ordnance Corps. The discipline and arrangements of the post are good, and Captain Stone is entitled to great credit for his untiring efforts. He has under his command 44 enlisted men and stands his own guard, which requires three men daily, and they are armed and equipped with the musketoon and were in very good order. He also has in his employ four citizens, as follows: one clerk at 3 ^{50}/100 dollars and one ration per day; one master armourer at 5 dollars and one ration per day; one armourer at 4 dollars and one ration per day; and one labourer at

[88] At the time of McCall's inspection the headquarters of the department were located at Benicia and the military installations consisted of Benicia Barracks, or the Post of Benicia, and Benicia Arsenal. His inspection reports concerning Benicia Arsenal, dated August 6, 1852; staff departments at the headquarters of the Pacific Division, dated June to September [1852]; and the Post of Benicia, dated August 5, 1852, are in "McCall's Inspection Report, Departmnt of the Pacific, 1852."

2 dollars and one ration per day. These armourers were employed, he states, because the enlisted men were not qualified for the best work, and not enough of them. This force were comfortably quartered altho' cramped. The enlisted men were engaged at building an additional stone store house, in addition to refitting arms & c, and making up ammunition. General Wool on the 10h March ordered an additional permanent store house, the one now being erected 100 feet long, 40 feet broad, and two stories high, the stone for which is quarried on the U.S. land and was not to cost over 12,000 dollars, and was absolutely necessary, yet it was ascertained after it was in part contracted for and constructed that the funds could not be applied to it, and accordingly the drafts of Captain Stone on Washington City were protested, and he has had to pay the costs of protests and interest on the money he had used. The contractor preferred to proceed with his work and complete it before the wet season, after having already received on account 3,602 dollars, and to wait the result of the action of Congress in preference to losing money by suspending it. I presume in due time the Ordnance Department will make up this loss to Captain Stone.

The building now used as a magazine is wooden and breaking down under the weight therein. A stone magazine about 105 feet by 36 feet on the general plan recommended by Captain Stone would be suitable for this post and hold all the powder required for this department. As it is, the powder is now very unsafe. Most of the work of the buildings required can be executed by the enlisted men of the Ordnance Corps, and a very good quarry is at hand on U.S. land.

With the completion of the new store house and the construction of a new magazine and some additional canvas coverings, the public property can be properly preserved.

There was due Captain Stone by the Government on the 30h June, 9,044 $^{06}/_{100}$ dollars, the result of the non payment of the two drafts of 6,000 dollars, each on account of the new store house.

I was obliged to condemn 30 barrels of cannon powder caked, 3 barrels [of] rifle powder, one barrel [of] musket powder—also to be broken up, 71,760 musket buck and ball cartridges, 1,500 rifle ball cartridges, and sundry other articles to be broken up, dropped, and sold. Captain Stone remarked that the powder marked Loomis, Swift & Masters of Schaghticocke [Schaghticoke], New York, invariably deteriorated very much in a few years, cakes and loses strength.

The duties of this station are well performed by Captain Stone, and he is entitled to the confidence of the department.

A good garden is attached to this arsenal.

For a sketch of this post see O hereunto appended [No. 28, Plans and Sketches section].

« *Benecia Subsistence Depot—8h July* »

This Depot has been under the immediate charge of 1t Lieutenant John Hamilton, 3rd Artillery, since 1t August, 1853. He has in his employ one clerk at 150 dollars and one ration per month, [and] one issuer at 100 dollars and one cooper at 100 dollars per month each and a ration. The supplies here are well stored and abundant and the duties and records properly performed and kept, and the buildings good. There has been condemned, since Lieutenant Hamilton has been in charge, 3 barrels [of] pork, 301 barrels [of] flour, 373¾ bushels [of] beans, and 118 kegs [of] pickles. Hereafter it will be advantageous to obtain all the flour and beans required for the service in the Pacific Department, where they are had to any desirable extent and where they can no doubt be had at a less price. Fresh beef at present is 19 cents the pound here.

The average expenditure here for the past year by the quarter is about 2,225 dollars. Lieutenant Hamilton had in hands on the 30h June, 2,472$\frac{95}{100}$ dollars as follows: in safe, 1,446$\frac{15}{100}$ dollars; and on deposit in San Francisco with Page Bacon & Co., 1,026$\frac{80}{100}$ dollars. These funds had not yet been deposited with the sub treasurer for reasons heretofore given in like cases. All his funds are obtained from Major Eaton, chief of subsistence, at head quarters of the department.

« *Benecia Quartermaster's Depot—7h July* »

This depot has been under the immediate charge of Captain R. E. Clary since June, 1852, who has all the stores, supplies, books, records &c &c in excellent order. He has built a wharf and made many improvements. The buildings are ample and good, and there is no essential deficiency. He has in his employ 26 citizens as follow: 2 clerks at 150 and 125 dollars per month and a ration each; one store keeper at 125 dollars per month and one ration; one smith; one wheelright and one carpenter at 6 dollars per day each and one ration; one ship captain at 5 dollars per day and one ration; one saddler at 100 dollars per month and a ration; one clothing store keeper at 90 dollars per month and a ration; one cook at 70 dollars per month, 4 teamsters at 65 and 70 dollars per month, one striker at 70 dollars, one watchman at 70 dollars per month, 9 labourers at 65 and 70 dollars per month each and all a ration.

This department keep one brig, the *Patterson*, at a monthly expenditure of 544 dollars; one schooner, the *Monterey*, at a monthly expenditure of 525 dollars; and one sloop, the *Maria*, at a monthly expenditure of 260 dollars. The brig and schooner are constantly employed along the coast north and south in transporting supplies to the posts from San Diego to Puget Sound, &c; and the sloop, between here and San Francisco and to Stockton.

The average quarterly expenditure at this post for the past year is about 22,750 dollars inclusive of all accounts. Captain Clary had in his hands but 429$\frac{95}{100}$ dollars deposited in a substantial vault in his own office and quarters. He obtains his funds thro' Major Cross, chief of this department, at head quarters.

For a sketch of this post, see O hereunto appended [No. 28, Plans and Sketches section].

« *Fort Reading—18h to 21t July* »

This post was established by 2d Lieutenant N. H. Davis, 2d Infantry, in 1852, by order of Brevet Brigadier General Hitchcock, and Major and Brevet Lieutenant Colonel George Wright has been in command since September, 1852. His authority extends over northern California and southern Oregon as far west as Weaversville and east to the Sierra Nevada including Pitt River and Rogue River and Shasta and Klamath valleys—say 200 [miles] north and south and 200 east and west, comprising an Indian country of say not over 1,000 warriors very much scattered. Forts Jones and Lane fall within his authority.

Attached to this post is one assistant quartermaster, Captain M. S. Miller, and Assistant Surgeon P. G. S. Ten Broeck. His force consists of Company D, 3rd Artillery (Brevet Major F. O. Wyse Captain in arrest), 51 in the aggregate, commanded by 2d Lieutenant James Van Vost [Van Voast]; 3 sergeants, 2 corporals, one musician, one artificer, [and] 24 privates for duty; one non commissioned officer, 5 privates sick; 10 privates confined; in the aggregate 48 present for duty; 1t Lieutenant J. J. Reynolds on detached duty at Military Academy and not joined his company since promoted to the Regiment 11h May, 1846, a period of eight years; 1t Lieutenant C. C. Churchill sick at New York since 6h April, 1853. Total absent, 3 commissioned officers.

Company D, 4h Infantry (Brevet Lieutenant Colonel Henry L. Scott Captain on detached duty as aid to commanding general of the Army since 1840), 46 in the aggregate, commanded by 1t Lieutenant Edmund Underwood, who is also acting commissary of subsistence; 2d Lieutenant F. H. Bates; Brevet 2d Lieutenant

W. M. E. Dye; 3 sergeants, 3 corporals, 18 privates for duty; one non commissioned officer and 5 privates sick; 9 privates on extra daily duty; 2 rank and file confined; total present for duty, 44. One rank and file on detached service at Fort Humbolt.

Thus shewing an aggregate force present for duty of 93.

In addition to the above there was temporarily at the post one private, 1t Dragoons.

The discipline of this post was good, and the troops well instructed. Colonel Wright gave two handsome battalion drills, and the companies drilled well at infantry and as skirmishers. But there was a great want of musicians, only one drummer boy at the post. They were all in the new uniform, and their arms and equipments, in excellent serviceable order. There were two 12-pounder mountain howitzers and 200 rounds of ammunition for the same, with about 15,000 rounds for small arms in addition to the company supplies, and a suitable magazine. The quarters were in excellent order although unfinished and a little limited as to kitchens for the men. A post bakery and a post fund of $82^{77}/_{100}$ dollars on hand. And two laundresses to each company. And all the books of the post well kept.

The Medical Department was well conducted under Assistant Surgeon Ten Broeck. The dispensary, storeroom, and wardroom too limited for the number of men at the post. Dr. Ten Broeck was himself sick, and in short the post is decidedly sickly, and the doctor made to me an official report to that fact. The prevailing complaint is the intermittent fever. Troops so generally afflicted with it, are powerless in the field, with broken constitutions. Colonel Wright does not himself complain of the sickness, but he tells me he always takes quinine pills when he feels the attack coming on. Other officers complain much, and I doubt not these troops should be advanced more into the Indian country as heretofore recommended, in speaking of this post.

The rain falls here in the months of November, December,

January, February, and March, and the hot season at times is oppressive, say as high as 107° in July, August, and September. Such seasons, combined with general overflow almost into the parade of the post, is no doubt the cause of this prevailing complaint, and it extends all thro' this Sacramento Valley.

The Quartermaster's Department is well conducted under the direction of Captain M. S. Miller, assistant quartermaster, who has been at this post since 27h September, 1852. The storerooms, stables, and work shops [are] ample and the public property and records well managed and conducted. He supplies Fort Jones, 120 miles to the northward and over a mountain trail beyond Shasta City, most of the articles for which go directly on pack mules from the landing at Red Bluff, or Colusa, 120 miles off, according to the stage of the water in the Sacramento River. He keeps in his employ 8 citizens, as follow: one clerk at 150 dollars; one forage master at 100 dollars and a ration; one store keeper; 3 herdsmen; 2 ostlers each at 75 dollars per month and a ration.

His average expenditures for the year 1853, were 44,133 dollars the quarter and for the first and second quarters of 1854, 9,564 dollars. Thus showing a great reduction in 1854, caused by not supplying Fort Lane as heretofore. He has on hand at date 4,628 $\frac{05}{100}$ dollars which he keeps in an iron safe in his quarters. He receives his funds from Major Cross at head quarters. My impressions are that Fort Jones should be supplied via Fort Lane, to which post there is a good wagon road and at a materially less cost. There is a ferry over the Sacramento River eight miles to the northward, belonging to this department, that has been offered for sale, very properly.

Subsistence Department. This duty has been performed by Lieutenant Underwood since 15h November, 1852, and the supplies good and well stored. His expenditures were 77 $\frac{40}{100}$ dollars [in the] first quarter and 625 $\frac{06}{100}$ [in the] second quarter [of] 1854, and he had on hand at date 3,154 $\frac{75}{100}$ dollars, of which 1,803 $^{60}\!/_{100}$ dollars were in sub treasury at San Francisco and 1,351 $^{15}\!/_{100}$ dollars, cash in hand.

There has been condemned from 15h November, 1853, to 19h July, 1854, 392 pounds [of] flour, one barrel [of] pork, 15 bushels [of] beans, 2 half barrels [of] corn meal, and 25 pounds [of] peaches. These articles were probably damaged in the transportation or forwarded in that state, as they were condemned the day after received.

A good garden is attached to this post and a fine stream (the Cow Creek) for the men to bathe in, so desirable in this climate, and abundant shade trees, wood, and grazing. But it is to be regretted so much labour and expense has been put on a post situated as this is, in an unhealthy spot, and at the same time not a particularly good military position in the defense against the Indians.

The American population capable of bearing arms within fifty miles may number 500.

The officers of this post mess together, and there is a great harmony among them.

This post was last inspected in 1852 by Colonel McCall.[89]

For a sketch of this post see F hereunto appended [No. 20, Plans and Sketches section].

« *Fort Humbolt—27h, 28h, and 29h July* »

This post is under the command of Captain and Brevet Lieutenant Colonel R. O. Buchanan, 4h Infantry, who established it 30h January, 1853. Attached to this post is Assistant Surgeon Josiah Simpson. The force consists of Company B, 4h Infantry (Captain R. C. Buchanan), 41 in the aggregate: 2 sergeants, 2

[89] McCall's inspection report of Fort Reading, dated July 20, 1852, is in "McCall's Inspection Report, Department of the Pacific, 1852." At the time McCall inspected Fort Reading, 25 per cent of the garrison, including the assistant surgeon, were sick.

corporals, one musician, 17 privates for duty; 1 rank and file in confinement; 2 rank and file sick; 11 rank and file on extra daily duty; total 37 present for duty. 1t Lieutenant J. B. Collins, 4h Infantry, absent on recruiting service; 2d Lieutenant C. S. Rundell on service in New Mexico, not having joined since promoted 5h August, 1853; one rank and file absent sick; one rank and file on furlough. Total present and absent, 41.

Company F, 4h Infantry (Captain Henry M. Judah), 32 in the aggregate: 1t Lieutenant L. C. Hunt also acting assistant quartermaster and commissary and recruiting officer; 2 sergeants, one corporal, one musician, 15 privates for duty; 3 rank and file sick; 5 rank and file on extra daily duty; total present, 29: 2d Lieutenant John Withers on detached service at Fort Vancouver as regimental quartermaster since 25h October, 1853; Brevet 2d Lieutenant A. E. Latimer on duty at Fort Miller with Company A, 1t Dragoons, not joined since promoted 1t July, 1853; one rank and file absent confined. Total present and absent, 32.

Thus shewing an aggregate force present for duty of 66.

The discipline of this post is good. Both companies were in the old uniform, and their arms and equipments in good serviceable order, and attention paid to the comforts of the men. The quarters however were only sufficient to accommodate one full company. These troops have done a great deal of work, and put up all their quarters, under the direction of Colonel Buchanan, at a small cost in purchasing materials and hiring labour so that all the quarters of this post have cost only 11,664⁹⁹⁄₁₀₀ dollars, and the men have supplied their own wood and made a very valuable garden. In short, great credit is due this command for its industry &c. A good bakery, hospital, store house and magazine have been built, and abundant quarters for officers. The plan adopted by Colonel Buchanan of small, snug plank buildings for each officer is an excellent one and readily executed. There was a post fund on the 30h June of 29⁸⁶⁄₁₀₀ dollars. Colonel Buchanan gave a handsome battalion drill, and Captain Judah, a handsome company drill at infantry. The drill as skirmishers was indifferent. There was a deficiency of music, only one drummer and one bugler. There is at this post one mountain howitzer with 74 rounds of fixed ammunition for it and 12,500 rounds musket ball cartridges. And the post records in good order.

The Medical Department is under the direction of Assistant Surgeon Simpson and the sick well cared for. This is a healthy locality and the greatest heat of temperature in July, 73°, and the changes not great and strongly contrasted with Fort Reading in about the same latitude 175 miles by mule trail eastward over the coast range of mountains and beyond the influence of the north west winds which blow steadily in the dry season.

The Quartermaster's Department is in the hands of Lieutenant L. C. Hunt, whom I found in quite ill health and expecting soon to leave. His average expenditures for the last four quarters was 1,890 dollars, and he had on hand at date 3,284 $^{71}/_{100}$ dollars which is kept in an iron safe in his office. There are no citizens in his employ and all his records in good order, and supplies well stored. His funds on this account come from Major Cross at head quarters.

Lieutenant Hunt also performs the duty of commissary of subsistence and the supplies good and abundant. The price of fresh beef here is 15 cents the pound on the hoof. Other supplies come from San Francisco, and are sometimes shipped beyond this to Crescent City and have to be reshipped back, thereby increasing the time and causing damage. There is no necessity for this as lumber vessels are constantly here direct from San Francisco. Lieutenant Hunt had on hand on this account 995 $^{66}/_{100}$ dollars which is also kept in an iron safe in his office. His funds for subsistence come from Brevet Major Eaton at head quarters. There was condemned in this department this year 20 barrels [of] flour and 185 pounds [of] coffee.

The duty of recruiting officer too is performed by Lieutenant Hunt, and he has in his hands on this account 346 dollars in an iron safe in his office.

My attention was called here to the flannel shirt which is white, and shrinks so badly after washing as to be unfit for service: whereas I was informed the coloured flannel does not shrink.

The American population capable of bearing arms in the four little towns on this bay may be stated at 200.

For a sketch of this post see L hereunto appended [No. 27, Plans and Sketches section].

« *Fort Jones—4h to 8h August* »

This post was established in November, 1852, and has been under the Command of Lieutenant J. C. Bonneycastle, 4h Infantry, since November, 1853. Attached to this post is Assistant Surgeon F. Sorrel. The force consists of Company E, 4h Infantry (Captain   ), 34 in the aggregate: 2d Lieutenant G. Crook, who also acts as assistant quartermaster and commissary; Brevet 2d Lieutenant J. B. Hood; one sergeant, 2 corporals, 11 privates for duty; 2 privates sick; one sergeant, one corporal, 7 privates on extra daily duty, and 2 privates confined—total 30 present. Absent the captain (formerly U. S. Grant), one sergeant clerk at head quarters of the department, one sergeant on furlough till the end of enlistment, and one private sick at Fort Vancouver.

The discipline of this post was good. The troops were in the old uniform, their arms and equipments in good serviceable order. There was no musician at the post. Lieutenant Bonneycastle gave a handsome drill at infantry, but the drill as skirmishers was indifferent. There was about 14,700 musket and rifle ball cartridges at this post.

The officers and soldiers quarters, and store rooms, and hospital, and stable, were of logs, and erected by the men. Of course quite indifferent, but such as other people enjoy and sufficient for the present.

The Medical Department is under Assistant Surgeon Sorrel and well conducted, and the books and records properly kept. This is a healthy locality, and yet during the summer and dry season, the thermometer is as high at times as 101°.

The quartermaster's duty is performed by Lieutenant Crook. There are no citizens in his employ. His expenditures for the quarter ending 30h June were 1,346⁹⁷⁄₁₀₀ dollars, and he had on hand at date 886⁸¹⁄₁₀₀ dollars, kept in his quarters. Barley is had here at 6½ cents, and hay at 20 dollars the ton, and grazing and wood abundant. All supplies will eventually be less as population increases, as wheat and oats grow luxuriently here.

The commissary duty is also performed by Lieutenant Crook. Beef costs here, as required daily, 17 cents the pound; other supplies are brought from San Francisco via Fort Reading and are all good. But a good flouring mill is now probably in operation in this valley, and undoubtedly flour will be had here soon and at a much less cost. The transportation, now being on pack mules and over mountains, is expensive—12 cents the pound from this to Fort Lane. Lieutenant Crook expended in the second quarter of 1854, 533³³⁄₁₀₀ dollars and had on hand at date 2,364³³⁄₁₀₀ dollars which is kept in his quarters.

There is a good bakery and garden. The officers mess together, and harmony exists among them; and there is a post fund of 138⁶⁴⁄₁₀₀ dollars. This post is on a reservation of 640 acres.

The Indian Agent, A. M. Rosborough,[90] resides in this vicinity. There are probably 75 Indian warriors within twenty-five or thirty miles, well armed with rifle and gun. But the American population within the same limit probably exceeds 2,000 souls.

[90] A. M. Rosborough, one of the founders of Crescent City, was appointed special Indian agent for northern California to hear complaints and to adjust difficulties until suitable arrangements could be made to care for the Indians on reservations. Alex. J. Rosborough, "A. M. Rosborough, Special Indian Agent," *California Historical Society Quarterly*, Vol. XXVI (September, 1947), 201.

For a plan of this post see G hereunto appended [No. 21, Plans and Sketches section].

« *Fort Lane—10h to 12h August* »

This post was under the command of Captain A. J. Smith, 1t Dragoons, by whom it was established 25h September, 1852, on a reservation of 640 acres very judiciously. Attached to this post is Assistant Surgeon C. H. Crane. The force here consists of Company C, 1t Dragoons (Captain A. H. Smith); 2 sergeants, one bugler, 9 privates for duty, 4 rank and file sick, 3 privates on extra daily duty. Total present, 20. Absent 1t Lieutenant W. H. Stanton on recruiting service 11h August, 1853; 2d Lieutenant George Stoneman on detached service as escort to Lieutenant J. G. Parke, Topographical Engineers, since 27h November, 1852; one rank and file on detached service: aggregate 23 and 28 horses.—Company E, 1t Dragoons (Capt. and Brevet Major E. H. Fitzgerald, absent on leave, from 22d August, 1853, to 22d May, 1854, but not since joined his company), commanded by 2d Lieutenant C. H. Ogle, who is also acting assistant quartermaster and commissary and adjutant of post; one sergeant, 4 corporals, one bugler, 14 privates for duty, 6 sick, 2 privates on extra daily duty; aggregate present, 29. 1t Lieutenant R. C. W. Bradford [Radford] on recruiting service since 1t July, 1854, 3 rank and file on detached service. Aggregate 34 and 30 horses.

Thus shewing an aggregate force present of 49 and 58 horses.

The command here has suffered much by recent desertions. Company G lost 22 by desertion in July last, and Company E, 12 since last April and all of them recruits but two. There is no reason given for this except the desire to go into the gold diggings and the facility of escape among the gulshes and miners.

The discipline of this post is good and the post with all the departments of it well conducted and creditable to the service. The troops were in the old uniform, and their arms and equipments in good serviceable order. There were, however, but 9 pistols to Company C and 30 to Company E. The horse equipments were all new on inspection. I however condemned 20 saddles, 20 bridles, 40 sursingles, 34 girths, 7 halter head stalls, 41 blankets, and 19 holsters as unfit for service and to be turned over to the Quartermaster's Department. There was a farrier to each of the companies; but that of Company C was not very good, and the horses feet were not in good condition, and some of them wanted shoes and were badly shod. The musketoon here as elsewhere often out of order in the shackle of the ramrod. It is a worthless arm for mounted men, or the service, and has no advocates that I am aware of. Captain Smith gave a handsome drill on horse back, as far as his recruits were instructed, but they had not yet been taught the charge, nor the sword exercise on horse back, nor as skirmishers. They were taken thro' the broad sword and musketoon exercise on foot and marched well. Captain Smith is well qualified for this command.

The quarters of officers, soldiers, hospital, and store rooms &c are all of logs erected by the men, and as comfortable as could be expected, and the public property well cared for. There is abundant grazing for the horses, and hay and wood are had by the cutting. A good garden is attached to the post, but the grasshopper is very destructive and almost destroys it. There is also good bathing for the men in the river.

The Medical Department well conducted by Assistant Surgeon Crane and the sick cared for. This is a healthy locality. The thermometer here rises as high as 100 in summer.

The Quartermaster's Department has been in charge of Lieutenant Ogle since 24h November. There are 3 citizens in his employ, 2 herders and one interpreter at 60 dollars per month each and a ration. And the average expenditure is 3,699 dollars the quarter. He had on hand at date 4,309 $^{71}/_{100}$ dollars which was on deposit in Rhodes & Co. banking house[91] at Jacksonville. His funds are obtained from Major Cross at head quarters. Barley and oats cost 7 cents the pound. Supplies are at present obtained by packing from Crescent City, 110 miles over mountains, at a cost of 13 cents the pound. This post, however, should be supplied by wagon route to Scottsburg as before stated.

The duty of commissary of subsistence is also performed by Lieutenant Ogle. Fresh beef costs 18 cents the pound and flour 16 cents which will soon be reduced in price—other supplies obtained from San Francisco. There are two grist mills within 30 miles and the Valley of Bear Creek (Stewarts Creek) is very productive with corn, wheat, barley, oats, and good grazing. He had on hand at date 1,382 $\frac{98}{100}$ dollars also in the private banking house of Rhodes & Co. This money, I doubt not, as there is no sub treasurer, would be safer in an iron safe which can now be imported via Scottsburg. He obtains his funds from Major Eaton at head quarters.

The duty of recruiting is performed by Captain Smith, and he had on hand on this account 150 dollars in a treasury draft.

At this post there is one 12-pounder brass field howitzer and one 12-pounder mountain howitzer and 144 rounds of fixed ammunition for the same—also 14,000 ball cartridges for small arms. The carriage of the howitzers require painting and one new wheel.

The Indian Agent, Mr. H. S. Culver, resides here and manages the Indians well. He has planted several fields of potatoes on their reservation for them and to encourage them to settle quietly. By treaty[92] the Government agree to put up several

[91] Rhodes & Company has not been further identified.

[92] The treaty provided that a dwelling house should be erected for each of the three principal chiefs at a cost not to exceed five hundred dollars apiece as soon after the ratification of the treaty as possible. The treaty was ratified by the Senate on April 12, 1854; however, it was not proclaimed until February 5, 1855, because of Senate amendments to which the Indians did not agree until November 11, 1854.

buildings for them which has not yet been done. The Indians within 50 miles number about 180 warriors, not more than half the number of last year, but they are intelligent and active and armed with rifles. The whole American population capable of bearing arms within the same limits may be 800 and most of these within 15 miles.

The officers all mess together and are harmonius.

For a sketch of this post see H hereunto appended [No. 22, Plans and Sketches section].

« *Fort Vancouver—21t, 22d and 23rd August* »

This post was established by Brevet Major J. S. Hatheway in 1848, and on a reservation of 640 acres in latitude 45° 36′ 53″ and longitude 122° 39′ 36″, and unfortunately lays over land and buildings claimed by the Hudson Bay Company (see plan I hereunto annexed [No. 23, Plans]). It is now under the command of Lieutenant Colonel L. E. Bonneville, 4h Infantry, who relieved Brevet Major Hatheway in September, 1852. It is the head quarters of the 4h Infantry. His staff as follows: the adjutant, 2d Lieutenant B. D. Forsyth [Forsythe]; sergeant major; 2 principal musicians; 13 privates (the band). Attached to the post, Surgeon R. M. Byrne; Assistant Quartermaster Captain Thomas E. Brent; and Military Store Keeper Thomas J. Eckerson. Total 21 for duty. The Colonel of the regiment, William Whistler, was absent on leave for six months from 1t June, 1854. 2d Lieutenant J. Withers, Company F, 4h Infantry, acting commissary of subsistence, was absent on seven days' leave and one rank and file on furlough. Total present and absent of staff, 24.

The force here consisted of Company L, 3rd Artillery (Captain H. B. Judd absent, as to whereabout, unknown), 69 in the aggregate, commanded by 1t Lieutenant J. Kellogg, 3rd Artil-

"Treaty with the Rogue River [Indians, September 10,] 1853," in Charles J. Kappler, *Indian Affairs, Laws and Treaties*, II, 604.

lery, temporarily attached to this Company; 2d Lieutenant E. H. Day; 3 sergeants; 3 corporals; 2 musicians; 30 privates for duty; 5 rank and file sick; 11 rank and file on extra daily duty; 7 rank and file confined. Total present, 63. Absent 1t Lieutenant J. R. Duncan on Northern Pacific Rail Road survey; 1t Lieutenant C. S. Winder, adjutant at head quarters of regiment; 3 rank and file on furlough; one rank and file sick. Total 7.

Company G, 4h Infantry (Captain C. C. Auger), 29 in the aggregate, one sergeant, 2 corporals, 8 privates for duty, 3 rank and file sick, 5 rank and file on extra daily duty; one private confined. Total 21 for duty. Absent 1t Lieutenant and Brevet Captain Thomas R. McConnell on recruiting service since 20h May, 1854; 2d Lieutenant A. V. Kautz on temporary duty at Port Orford since 17h October, 1853; one rank and file on detached service; one rank and file without leave; 3 rank and file on furlough; one rank and file confined. Total 8.

Company H, 4h Infantry (Captain H. D. Wallen), 41 in the aggregate, one sergeant, 2 corporals, one musician, 6 privates for duty, 3 rank and file sick, 20 rank and file on extra daily duty, and 4 confined; total 38 for duty. Absent 1t Lieutenant Hiram Dryer, 4h Infantry, at the Mission of San Diego for the benefit of his health since 15h July, 1854; 2d Lieutenant H. C. Hodges on seven days leave; one rank and file on furlough; total 3.

Thus shewing an aggregate force of 139 for duty. In addition there were temporarily at this post three rank and file confined and one on extra daily duty besides Lieutenant Kellogg.

The discipline of this post was good. The arms and equipments of these troops in good serviceable order, and all in the new uniform. Colonel Bonneville gave a handsome battalion drill, and the infantry companies drilled well at infantry and as skirmishers, and the artillery company went thro' the artillery drill handsomely. A great change had come over this Company L which were all recruits and just landed when I saw them at the Presidio at San Francisco. It is now in excellent order, to the credit of Lieutenants Kellogg and Day.

The quarters of the men, although limited, were inferior log buildings, but neat and in good order. The quarters of the officers were ample, but of logs and inferior and, like those of the men, difficult to keep warm in winter. A good bakery, guard house, magazine, and garden exists. The Hospital is a very inferior building, hired of the Hudson Bay Company, and store room for ordnance also in the same. Another store room for subsistence supplies, also hired of the Hudson Bay Company.

The Medical Department is under the direction of Surgeon Burns and well managed and the sick as comfortable as the circumstances would allow. The supplies were ample and the post is healthy. In summer the thermometer rises here as high as 96°, and rain falls in every month of the year, but the wet season is in winter.

The Subsistence Department is in the direction of Lieutenant J. Withers and well conducted in every respect and with great neatness. He was absent on my first visit to this post, but on my second visit I inspected his department again on some points. He had in his employ one citizen herder at 40 dollars per month. His expenditures for the last quarter of 1853 was 987 dollars and for the first quarter [of] 1854, 2,680 dollars and for the second quarter [of] 1854, 2,512 dollars. Fresh beef is had here at about 12 cents the pound, and flour is good and abundant in this region. Other supplies come from San Francisco direct by water, and are good. He had on hand 23rd August, 1,516^{13}/100 dollars which is kept in an iron safe. His funds are obtained thro' Brevet Major Eaton, chief at head quarters.

Lieutenant Withers is also recruiting officer at this post.

The Ordnance Department is under the charge of Thomas J. Eckerson, military store keeper. All the ordnance is well stored and in excellent order as to magazine and store room. He had on hand 137⁸⁹⁄₁₀₀ dollars which he keeps in his office, and receives his funds &c from Captain Stone, chief at Benecia. I condemned here sundry articles to be sent to Benecia Arsenal on the return of quartermaster's vessels and some articles to be dropped and all of no particular value. I also condemned 1,388 pounds [of] rifle powder, some six-pounder cartridges, bursters, priming tubes, fuzes, portfires, slow match, and quick match as worthless. 16,150 rifle cartridges, 154 six-pounder strapped fixed shot and 56 six-pounder canister fixed, to be broken up. There are at this post, 2 six-pounder brass guns, one twelve-pounder brass howitzer, 2 six-pounder iron guns, 100 pounds [of] rifle powder, 437 twelve-pounder cartridges, 122 six-pounder cartridges, about 80,000 rounds ball cartridges for small arms, in addition to supplies held by the three companies to the number of 11,000 rounds. The supply of ammunition is ample for the present at this post.

Quartermaster's Department here a sub depot for the supply of places in this vicinity and is under the direction of Captain T. L. Brent, assistant quartermaster, and the supplies sufficient. He has in his employ one clerk at 150 dollars per month, one master carpenter at 90 dollars, one smith at 90 dollars, one teamster and one herdsman at 70 dollars each. He has a suitable smith's and carpenters' shop and stable. He pays for hay from 11½ to 15 dollars the ton and for oats 1¹⁰⁄₁₀₀ dollars the bushel and for ash wood 4 dollars the cord. There is abundant pine wood had by cutting. Lumber is 20 dollars the thousand and abundant. A six-mule team is constantly employed at hauling water for the troops from the river, about one-fourth of a mile off. He hires of the Hudson Bay Company a building for hospital and ordnance store room at 45 dollars per month, or 540 dollars per annum; and the use of a store house for commissary supplies, 75 dollars per month or 900 dollars per annum, thus paying annually 1,440 dollars for the use of buildings. Captain Brent has estimated for a hospital, store house, forage house, hay shed, stable and wharf. But if the Hudson Bay Company is to be bought out, a suspension of these matters might be advisable.

To repair the log houses of officers and soldiers is a waste. The logs are constantly changing by shrinking and expanding and rotting and settling, and it would be better to put up entirely new buildings of plank.

He expended, [in the] fourth quarter of 1853, $38,911\frac{15}{100}$ dollars; first quarter of 1854, $29,089\frac{76}{100}$ dollars; second quarter [of] 1854, $12,413\frac{94}{100}$ dollars; and had on hand at date $12,119\frac{51}{100}$ dollars, of which 11,300 dollars was in New York sub treasury and the balance, $819\frac{51}{100}$ dollars, in an iron safe in his office. His own quarters and office & c is a very good wooden building near the river. His funds are obtained generally from Major Cross, chief at head quarters. His ordinary expenses for this post is about 6,000 dollars per quarter. He had advanced, on account of Governor Steven's expedition for exploration[93] in 1854, $50,897\frac{14}{100}$ dollars; and Captain Grant, his predecessor, had advanced on [the] same account second and third quarters of 1853, $57,534\frac{83}{100}$ dollars. These of course embrace mules, wagons, &c &c, a part of which were probably returned to this department.

The chaplin, Mr. John McCarty, is attached to this post, and seems to give satisfaction.

There was a post fund on the 29h July of $46\frac{13}{100}$ dollars, and a regimental fund of $472\frac{16}{100}$ dollars.

[93] Isaac I. Stevens, first governor of Washington Territory, was in charge of the Pacific Railroad survey near the forty-seventh parallel from the Mississippi River to Puget Sound, 1853–54. Stevens' "Report upon the Northern Pacific Railroad Exploration and Survey," is in 33 Cong., 1 sess., *House Exec. Doc. 129*, I; and 33 Cong., 2 sess., *House Exec. Doc. 91*, I. Supplementary volumes were published later. Secretary of War Davis' instructions to Governor Stevens, April 8, 1853, are in 33 Cong., 1 sess., *Sen. Exec. Doc. 1*, I, pp. 55–57.

Harmony exists among the officers, and there is an officers' mess. And Colonel Bonneville commands the respect of all.

Mr. W. H. Tappan[94] is the Indian Agent in this quarter west of the Cascade Mountains, but there is nothing here to be feared from their warriors.

This post was last inspected by Colonel McCall.[95]

A good regimental band is here and well instructed which contributed much to break the sublime stillness of this beautiful situation.

« *Fort Dalles—26h, 27h, 28h, 29h, 30h, and 31t August* »

This post was established by the Rifles and is on a reservation of 640 acres, but overlays land claimed by the Methodist Mission, and was under the command of Major G. J. Rains, 4h Infantry. Attached to it is Assistant Surgeon J. E. Summers. The force consists of Company K, 4h Infantry (Captain B. Alford [Alvord] on leave of absence since 13h June, 1854), 31 in the aggregate, commanded by 1t Lieutenant T. J. Montgomery, sick; 2 sergeants; 1 corporal; 10 privates for duty; 2 rank and file sick; 2d Lieutenant R. Macfeely on daily duty as post adjutant since 16 July, 1854; 7 rank and file on extra daily duty; total present, 24; absent, 6 rank and file on detached service.

Company J, 4h Infantry (Captain and Brevet Major G. O. Haller, commanding), 30 in the aggregate; 1t Lieutenant and Brevet Captain M. Maloney; 3 sergeants; 2 corporals; 3 privates for duty; one rank and file sick; 6 rank and file on extra daily duty; and 6 rank and file in confinement. Total 23 present.

[94] William H. Tappan was agent for the southwestern Indian tribes in Washington Territory.

[95] McCall's inspection report of Fort Vancouver, then called Columbia Barracks, dated August 26, 1852, and September 26, 1852, is in "McCall's Inspection Report, Department of the Pacific, 1852."

Absent, 2d Lieutenant B. D. Forsyth detached as adjutant of the 4h Infantry since 21t June, 1854; 6 rank and file on detached service.

Thus the whole strength of the post present is 47.

The discipline of this post is good and the arms and equipments in good serviceable order. The troops are as well quartered as practicable under the circumstances, but the buildings were commenced by the Rifles and faulty in arrangement and now difficult to correct. The hospital is miserable, and the officers' quarters bad and all of logs. It is proposed by Major Rains to erect new quarters for the officers and convert their quarters into a hospital. This will afford ample quarters for the men by releasing to them the present hospital. A good magazine, bakery, carpenters, and smith's shop, and store house, and barn exist. And Major Rains has put in operation on a small stream, a good saw mill, and constructed a good ice house, and is indefatigable in his efforts at improvement. But the force is small, and it is a hard country, and difficulties great. There are four laundresses to each company, and a garden.

The Medical Department is under the direction of Assistant Surgeon J. E. Summers and satisfactorily administered. Dr. Summers was about being relieved by Assistant Surgeon George Suckley when an express arrived from the Indian Agent announcing the murder of emigrants near Fort Boissé,[96] and a de-

---

[96] Fort Boise was a Hudson's Bay Company post. The military post of the same name was not established until 1863. A party of twenty-one emigrants, led by Alexander Ward of Kentucky, was attacked by Shoshone Indians near old Fort Boise, and all were killed with the exception of two young boys. Major Haller led his detachment to Fort Boise, but the Indians had retreated to the mountains; and, since it was too late to pursue them, he returned to the Dalles. The next summer Haller was successful in apprehending and hanging three of the Indians involved in the massacre, and a fourth was shot while, purportedly, attempting to escape. General John E. Wool to Colonel Lorenzo Thomas, September 4, 1855, in 34 Cong., 1 sess., *Sen. Exec. Doc. 1*, II, p. 79; and Carey, *A General History of Oregon*, II, 566–67.

tachment immediately left under Brevet Major Haller for the scene, accompanied by Dr. Suckley, to punish the offenders, and thus it was necessary for Major Rains to retain Dr. Summers till he could be relieved. This is a healthy post, and in summer the thermometer rises as high as 100°. It is necessary to irregate here to produce good crops, altho' it may rain a little every month.

The duties of quartermaster, commissary, and recruiting officer were performed by Brevet Captain M. Maloney. All supplies are good and well stored, and they all come from Fort Vancouver, except fresh beef and hay, both of which are had in this quarter. Beef costs 22 cents the pound and hay and wood got by the cutting. There is one citizen employed as a herdsman at 100 dollars per month. His expenditures as quartermaster were as follows: fourth quarter, 1853, 1,764 dollars; first quarter, 1854, 312^{99}/100 dollars; second quarter, 1854, 1,720^{03}/100 dollars; and cash on hand at date, 893^{50}/100 dollars, on deposit in the banking house of Adams & Co.,[97] Portland. His expenditures on subsistant account, fourth quarter, 1853, 2,064^{48}/100; first quarter, 1854, 105^{36}/100 dollars; second quarter, 1854, 298^{76}/100 dollars, and cash on hand at date, 1,627^{35}/100 dollars kept in [an] iron safe. He had on hand as recruiting officer, 50 dollars.

There were condemned within the past year 3,382 pounds

[97] Adams & Company, originally established as an express company to operate between Boston and New York, entered the California field in 1849. Its banking house in San Francisco was opened in November, 1849, and by 1852 its operations were state-wide. In 1854 the company was reorganized and the operations in California passed into the hands of local owners, though the name Adams & Company was retained. All of its banking houses in the state closed their doors on February 23, 1855, and the express portion of the business was suspended on February 28. Oscar O. Winther, *Express and Stagecoach Days in California from the Gold Rush to the Civil War*, 41–50. In Oregon, the banking activities of Adams & Company were handled by Newell & Company after 1852. The headquarters were in Portland, in an office building erected by Adams & Company in 1851–52. Carey, *A General History of Oregon*, II, 754; and Leslie M. Scott, *History of the Oregon Country*, III, p. 183.

[of] fresh beef, 340 pounds [of] coffee, 491 pounds [of] pork, and 5 barrels [of] flour.

There is at this post one six-pounder brass field piece, and 225 rounds of fixed ammunition and 204 six-pounder cartridges for it, and about 20,000 ball cartridges for small arms, in addition to 9,800 ball cartridges with the companies. I condemned as unserviceable one musket of Company I and 3,000 damaged rifle cartridges to be broken up.

There were a large number of mules and horses left here by Governor Steven's party, that were found very serviceable for mounting the infantry and volunteers, and packing, in pursuit of the Indians, on their recent masacre. Major Rains acted very efficiently here. The news came while I was at the post. He started immediately, Major Haller with his company, in pursuit of the Indians. He mounted his men and took also into service about 50 volunteers, under Captain Nathan Olney,[98] whom he armed, equipped, mounted and supplied, and sent immediately after Major Haller to reinforce him. Yet it was late in the season; and the troops would have to march 300 miles at least before reaching the scene of the masacre, and there was but faint hope of punishing the Indians. After the departure of Major Haller, the remaining force here was very small and the daily guard consisted of one man.

At this post was Brevet Lieutenant Montgomery, quite sick and confined to his room. The officers generally messed together. There was a want of harmony between Major Haller and his commanding officer, and their troubles have been laid before the commanding general of the department.

[98] Nathan Olney was Indian agent for the Snake River district. C. F. Coan, "The Adoption of the Reservation Policy in the Pacific Northwest, 1853–1855," *Quarterly of the Oregon Historical Society*, Vol. XXIII (March, 1922), 23. He led a company of thirty-seven volunteers raised in the Willamette Valley. They captured four Indians who were later reported to have been shot while attempting to escape. Carey, *A General History of Oregon*, II, 567.

Dr. Summers has been in this department since 1849, in all five years and five months, and was extremely anxious to be relieved to visit his family.

There are not many citizens in this quarter. The country is not particularly inviting, and I presume not over 75 citizens could be mustered capable of bearing arms within fifty miles. This however is an important point, and here the road leaves the river for Oregon City[99] in the Willamette Valley. There is a post fund of 61³²⁄₁₀₀ dollars.

For a sketch of this post see J hereunto appended [No. 24, Plans and Sketches section].

Military roads to Fort Vancouver and Fort Steilacoom should be opened, in order to strengthen each post and develop the country.

« *Fort Steilacoom—8h to 15h September* »

This post was established, by the orders of Brevet Major Hatheway, by Captain B. H. Hill, 1t Artillery, in August, 1849, on ground claimed by the Hudson Bay Company, but no reservation has been made, and it has been under the command of the following officers since: 2d Lieutenant W. A. Slaughter; 1t Lieutenant D. F. Jones [Floyd-Jones]; Captain and Brevet Major C. H. Larnard [Larned]; and is now under the command of Captain D. A. Russell, 4h Infantry, in command of Company A. Attached to this post is Assistant Surgeon R. Potts. The force consists of Company A, 4h Infantry: 2d Lieutenant John Nugen,

[99] This was the Barlow Road, a toll road opened in 1846 by Samuel K. Barlow and Philip Foster. The road ran south from the Dalles to the Tyghe Valley, then generally northwest, crossing the Cascades south of Mount Hood, then west to the Sandy River and on to Oregon City. The road, which changed hands on several occasions, continued to be operated as a toll road until 1912 but was always difficult and often in poor repair. See Walter Bailey, "The Barlow Road," *Quarterly of the Oregon Historical Society*, Vol. XIII (September, 1912), 287–96; and Winther, *The Old Oregon Country*, 114–15.

6 non commissioned officers, one musician; 14 privates, 2 rank and file sick; aggregate 25 present for duty—one private on furlough and 3 deserters in confinement at Fort Vancouver. Aggregate 29.

Company C, 4h Infantry, commanded by Captain D. L. F. Jones: 1t Lieutenant W. A. Slaughter, also acting assistant quartermaster and commissary; Brevet 2d Lieutenant W. A. Webb, acting adjutant of the post; 8 non commissioned officers; one musician; 15 privates for duty, 2 rank and file sick; aggregate present, 29—on detached service one private and one deserter at Fort Vancouver. Total 31.

Thus the whole force at the post for duty, 56.

There was temporarily here one private, 1t Dragoons, sick.

In confinement here were 8 Indians with fetters for murder until tried and are kept at police work.

The discipline at the post was good. The arms and equipments in good serviceable order, and the troops well instructed at infantry drill and as skirmishers. The quarters were in good order. There was a hospital, store house, barn, workshops, but all with the quarters, inferior log buildings. Four of these miserable buildings were hired of the Hudson Bay, or Puget Sound Agricultural Company, at an annual cost of 600 dollars.

The Medical Department was under the charge of Assistant Surgeon Potts and in good order, and well conducted. This post is healthy.

The Quartermaster's and Commissary's departments were under the direction of 1t Lieutenant Slaughter, and are well conducted. The supplies were all good, and abundant, and received from Fort Vancouver and direct from Benecia Depot. Hay is had here at 25 dollars the ton, lumber at from 20 to 25 dollars the thousand. Fresh beef costs 22 cents the pound and obtained mostly from the Puget Sound Agricultural Company. A smith is sometimes employed at 4 dollars per day. He expended as quartermaster for the last three quarters, about 1,300 dollars each, and had on hand at date 2,633 03/100 dollars which he keeps in a safe. And as acting commissary he expended for the last three quarters about 700 dollars each and had on hand at date 1,363 37/100 dollars which is also kept in a safe. He receives his funds of head quarters of the department from Majors Cross and Eaton.

There are at this post two 12-pounder mountain howitzers and carriages complete, and 262 rounds fixed ammunition for them, and about 7,500 ball cartridges for small arms, in addition to about 1,500 ball cartridges with the companies.

There is an excellent garden five miles off in a north east direction, on the Walla Walla road, the nearest tillable land, and where it is proposed to make a military reservation.

The officers mess together, and there is great harmony among them. There is no post fund here.

The Indian Agent for the Puget Sound Indians, Mr. M. T. Simmons,[100] represents them as very much scattered to the number of say 900 warriors. These Indians are not as friendly, generally, as on the coast farther south.

The American population within 50 miles capable of bearing arms may number 300.[101]

For a sketch of this post see K hereunto appended [No. 25, Plans and Sketches section].

[100] Michael T. Simmons was appointed special Indian agent for the Puget Sound district by Governor Stevens. Simmons established what is now Tumwater, the first American settlement on the sound, in the fall of 1845. Though he is described as being only semiliterate, he became exceedingly proficient in the Chinook jargon. Hubert Howe Bancroft, *History of Washington, Idaho, and Montana* (XXXI of *Works*), 1–5.

[101] McCall's inspection report of Fort Steilacoom, dated September 13, 1852, is in "McCall's Inspection Report, Department of the Pacific, 1852." McCall was of the opinion that Fort Steilacoom served no particular purpose and that it should be replaced by a post one hundred or one hundred and fifty miles down the Sound. He recommended New Dungeness as a suitable location.

« *Port Orford—27h September* »

This command is a mere detachment under 2d Lieutenant A. V. Kautz, 4h Infantry, of one sergeant, one corporal, and 21 privates of Company M, 3rd Artillery, and one ordnance sergeant—all in excellent serviceable condition as to arms and equipments, and in a good state of discipline. There was also at this post a deserter of Company A, 1t Dragoons.

Attached to this post was Assistant Surgeon Milhau. Lieutenant Kautz performs the duty of quartermaster and commissary, and has only 652 $^{48}/_{100}$ dollars on hand of commissary funds, kept in his quarters. The quarters of officers and men and store houses and hospital are all of a character and of logs, but they are comfortable and the place is healthy, and the sick well provided. The supplies are good and abundant and come from Benecia Depot direct.

The population in this immediate neighbourhood is small, say 50 capable of bearing arms. The Indians are not numerous, and the post of doubtful utility—I would recommend it be abandoned as soon as it will be safe to do so.[102]

For a sketch of this position see M hereunto appended [No. 26, Plans and Sketches section].

« *Conclusion* »

Appended to this report is a tabular statement of the number of commissioned officers present for duty in the department and the number of enlisted men and the number of serviceable arms and field and sea coast guns. This shows 22 companies and 1,059 enlisted men, an average of about 48 men to the company, and a deficiency of 36 men to a company, or about 792 recruits required to fill up these companies. In addition to the force above enumerated and inspected by me, there arrived at San Francisco on the

[102] McCall's inspection report of what he too called Port Orford, dated August 22, 1852, is in "McCall's Inspection Report, Department of the Pacific, 1852."

31t May a command of the 3rd Artillery consisting of Companies D, G, I, [and]K, in the aggregate 220 enlisted men and 10 commissioned officers, inclusive of two assistant surgeons, under Brevet Major G. H. Thomas. Company G of this command, one officer and 49 men, reached the Mission of San Diego after I had inspected it. Company I, 2 officers and 53 enlisted men, reached Fort Yuma after I had inspected that post. Company K, 2 officers and 59 men, reached Fort Miller after I had inspected that post. Major Thoma's field and staff number 2 assistant surgeons, one lieutenant, and 9 enlisted men. Thus increasing the number of officers present to 92, and companies to 25, and enlisted men to 1,229—and requiring 873 recruits to fill up the companies.

The ordnance in the department embraces an invoice that had been shipped but not yet arrived. The number of small arms seem all sufficient for this department, but the field artillery and the sea coast guns are too limited, particularly if a war should suddenly break out with a power in command of the sea. It would be impossible to ship guns to Benecia. I would therefore recommend that 200 heavy sea coast guns and mortars be shipped to Benecia Arsenal as soon as convenient, and suitable field Batteries, to prepare that department to resist any sudden and unlooked for collision with Great Britain or France. Either of these powers could land an army on that coast, which should be met in the field to save the country.

« *General Remarks Relative to the Troops* »

With respect to the troops, I should observe that two companies should occupy the Mission of San Diego, three companies and one of them mounted on mules should occupy Fort Yuma, one mounted company occupy the post at the Tejon, one company occupy Fort Miller, one company occupy Benecia Barracks with such other troops as may be in reserve, two companies occupy Fort Reading and one of them mounted on mules, one company occupy Fort Jones, one mounted company occupy Fort Lane, two companies occupy Fort Vancouver with reserve troops, two companies occupy Fort Dalles and one of them mounted on mules, two companies occupy Fort Steilacoom and one of them mounted on mules, one company occupy Fort Humbolt, [and] one company occupy the Presidio of San Francisco; and I would recommend the establishment of a one-company post at Billingham Bay, thus disposing of 21 companies, provided they were full, which would leave four companies for reserve to move forward to establish posts towards El Paso and over the Rocky Mountains. And I will here add that in case further troops should be required at any time for the field, they could be withdrawn from Benecia, Presidio of San Francisco, Fort Humbolt, and Fort Miller without exposing the country to much damage from the friendly Indians.

There was a great deficiency of musicians for companies. There was none at Fort Yuma, only one at the Mission of San Diego, none at the Presidio of San Francisco, three at Fort Miller with two companies, one at Benecia, one at Fort Reading, two at Fort Humbolt with two companies, one only at Fort Vancouver with three companies, none at Fort Dalles, one at Fort Steilacoom with two companies, none at Fort Jones, two at Fort Lane with two companies.

The armament of the troops is well with the exception of the musketoon. I cannot regard it as fit for any arm of the service. There is a deficiency of horses for the dragoons, which must come from east of the Rocky Mountains till a supply can be raised in this department, towards which a beginning has already been made in the Willamette Valley.

The instruction of the troops will hereafter advance as the labour of erecting log houses &c will comparatively cease, and the rank and file, being better paid, will be filled up of better material. The drill as skirmishers generally was indifferent, and there seems to have been little or no practice at target firing beyond the mere discharge of the old guard. And no drill at the bayonette exercise.

I would here suggest that the certificate of the commanding officer of a post be sufficient to enable the acting commissary to draw his pay without application to Washington City.

« *Remarks for Immediate Consideration* »

First, there is in dispute the boundary and dividing line from the parallel of 49° to the Straits of Fuca. The English claim one channel, whereas the Americans claim another as the boundary, the bone of contention being several large islands.[103]

Second, a steamer revenue cutter of the propeller model should be on Puget Sound to act in concert with the troops and keep up a communication with the mouth of the Columbia River by water.

Third, the fortifications at the mouth of the Columbia River should be immediately commenced.[104]

Fourth, a mail from Fort Vancouver to Cascade City and another from Stockton to Millerton near Fort Miller are necessary for the population and would greatly benefit the military posts.

Fifth, appropriations should be asked for the Cañon and Grave Creek Hill, on the military road from Rogue River to Myrtle Creek; for a military road from Fort Vancouver to Fort Dalles; for a military road from Fort Dalles to Steilacoom; for a military road from Fort Steilacoom to Fort Vancouver; for repair of the military road from San Diego to Fort Yuma.[105]

---

[103] Mansfield refers to the San Juan Island dispute which was settled by arbitration in favor of the United States in 1872.

[104] See note 49 on page 115.

[105] A Congressional Act of January 7, 1853, required the construction of two military roads in Oregon Territory (actually Washington Territory was created about a month after the act was passed). The commencement of one of these, the road from Myrtle Creek to Camp Stuart, was delayed by the difficulties with the Rogue River Indians, but a contract was made for a road from Fort Walla Walla (the Hudson's

Sixth, a rail road across the Rocky Mountains is indispensable to the preservation by the U.S. of the Pacific state and territories in time of war with either France or England, and of vast importance to commerce and trade.

All which is respectfully submitted,

Jos. K. F. MANSFIELD
Colonel and Inspector General, U.S.A.

MIDDLETOWN, CONNECTICUT
1t March, 1855

« *Copies of Reports to Brevet Major General J. E. Wool,*
Commanding Pacific Department, of the 7th June,
1t July and 29h September, 1854. Made
agreeably to his request. »

Bay post) to Fort Steilacoom. This road was supposed to be made passable by October 15, 1853. Report of the Secretary of War, 1853, in 33 Cong., 1 sess., *Sen. Exec. Doc. 1*, II, p. 29. On May 9, 1853, Captain George B. McClellan was ordered to survey the route from Fort Walla Walla to Fort Steilacoom and to do such work on the most difficult portions as to make the road usable by fall. For the purpose twenty thousand dollars was allocated. McClellan accomplished very little, though more was achieved by private enterprise (see note 53 on page 118. Some further work on the road was undertaken by the army in 1854, but after that date the government did nothing more with the Naches Pass route. Thomas W. Prosch, "The Military Roads of Washington Territory," *Washington Historical Quarterly*, Vol. II (January, 1908), 120–21. In 1854, Congress appropriated additional funds to extend the military road from Myrtle Creek to Scottsburg, which was considered to be the head of navigation on the Umpqua River. Davis to Lieutenant John Withers, August 2, 1854, in 33 Cong., 2 sess., *Sen. Exec. Doc. 1*, II, p. 41. The military road from Cowlitz Landing to Fort Steilacoom was opened in 1857. At that time transportation from Monticello to Cowlitz Landing, a distance of thirty miles, was still by canoe. The military road from Fort Vancouver to Fort Dalles was completed by 1856, but portions of it washed away during the winter, necessitating extensive repair work in 1857. Mendell to Major Hartman Bache, Topographical Engineers, September 1, 1857, in 35 Cong., 1 sess., *Sen. Exec. Doc. 11*, II, pp. 521–23.

FORT YUMA, 7h June, 1854

Brevet Major General J. E. Wool
Commanding Pacific Department
U.S. Army

SIR:

I have inspected the post at the mission commanded by Captain H. S. Burton. This post is situated on the San Diego River 6 miles from Old San Diego and 9 miles from the quartermaster's depot at New San Diego and 11 miles from the playa at the entrance of the harbour.

I look upon this post as necessary to the proper occupancy of this section of the frontier, on account of its vicinity to the harbour and fortifications that will eventually be erected, and the availability of the troops here stationed to take the field against the Indians. Further there is abundant water and grazing for the animals and of land for garden purposes, and it is perfectly healthy. The site of the old mission buildings is beautiful, and the cathedral is now being converted into excellent quarters for two companies of soldiers and likewise accommodates the sick extremely well. Some considerable expenditure must further be made to make the other accommodations of the post convenient and suitable. The quarters now occupied by the officers are wholly unfit and are only suitable to adjutant's, quartermaster's, commissary offices & c. It will therefore be necessary to erect soon entirely new quarters by the quartermaster for the officers. The remaining buildings of the mission now falling to pieces are not even suitable for the laundresses and must be levelled and cleared away. The plans of Captain Burton are good; and in due time with such aid as should be furnished by the Quartermaster's Department, he will accomplish, himself, all but the quarters suitable for officers.

The depot at New San Diego labours under the disadvantage

[187]

of no water, and water is brought from Old San Diego, a distance of three and one-half miles, daily to supply the U.S. officials. An artesian well was commenced by Major McKinstry and carried to a depth of over one hundred feet when the contractor absconded; I would recommend the continuance of this effort for water to a satisfactory conclusion as to water or no water by this means.

A small map of this locality I presume you already have.

I have also inspected Fort Yuma & c. It seems that this post too is indispensable to the proper occupancy of this section of the country, in reference to the Indians and the emigrant route from New Mexico. The site itself is beautiful at the junction of the Gila with the Colerado and 80 feet above the surrounding country perfectly secure against freshets and overflows and 225 miles by wagon road from San Diego and 600 miles from El Paso. This road, however, is wholly out of the question for transportation of supplies and should not be relied upon at all for that purpose, nor can an appropriation of moderate amount make it suitable or profitable across the desert. The Colerado, however, is a beautiful river at this time and at all times is navigable for boats of light draft of water to this place, and all supplies should be brought here by water. There is now a fine little steamer here ready for the transportation of goods, and a contract has been judiciously made by the Quartermaster's [Department] with the proprietors, and I would recommend that all supplies be sent by water.

The water is good here and wood abundant. There are now no quarters nor buildings here fit for any purpose except the commanding officer's which is about half finished. All others are mere brush sheds and not even suitable for the protection and preservation of public property. The ammnuition of the post is piled up on the parade and covered by a tarpaulin. I would therefore recommend the immediate construction of suitable quarters and store houses & c for three companies, agreeably to the plans considered and recommended by Brevet Major Heintzelman and

Brevet Major McKinstry as in every respect adapted to this peculiar position. All materials therefor, except adobes and stone and sand, must be brought to this place by water.

I take pleasure in adding that I have found the troops here in excellent condition and creditable to the service and to the officer in command. There are, however, but 112 all told.

I would recommend the employment of citizen labourers and mechanics in the construction of these quarters, generally.

I have the honour to be,
very respectfully,
your obedient servant,

Jos. K. F. MANSFIELD
Colonel and Inspector General

MERCEDE RIVER, EAST OF SNELLINGS
1t July, 1854

Brevet Major General John E. Wool
Commanding Pacific Department
U.S.A.

SIR:

I last wrote you from Fort Yuma. Since then I have visited the Indian reservation under Mr. Beale at Tejon. This point appears to have been in the route of the wild Indians from east of the Sierra, say Owen's Lake, when on expeditions of depredations on the inhabitants west of the coast range. There are many trails over the mountains and can all be intercepted by troops occupying this locality. The Tejon Pass, however, is nothing more than a road over the mountains. The pass into this valley from the south is that of Las Uvas thro' which the communication is kept up with Los Angeles, a city of 2,100 population, and with Los Angeles County, 7,000 population, about equally divided between the

American and native Californian races. There is but little American population in the southern part of the San Joaquine Valley that needs protection, but the friendly Indians in this quarter number over 2,000 or 500 warriors. Thus it seems that the principal population to be protected against the depredations of the wild Indians are the inhabitants of Los Angeles, Santa Barbara, and San Luis Obispo, and the friendly Indians on the reserve of Tejon. Now the people of Los Angeles are strong in themselves and therefore less liable to depredations. Those of the other counties will be effectually protected when the passes across the San Joaquine Valley are intercepted to the Indians, and the friendly Indians of that valley will be protected by a force of one company of good troops stationed at the Tejon on the spot selected by Mr. Beale and Captain Jordan. And this position will effectually control the entrance into this valley on the south of Tula River, whilst Fort Miller controls all north of that river. Further, should depredations be committed in Los Angeles County, an express from that county thro' Uvas Pass would reach the troops in time for them to move over the Sierra and intercept the Indians on their return, and troops here would be an effectual guarantee against any combinations between the wild Indians and the friendly Indians on the reserve. It appears, therefore, that a military post at this reserve is indispensable as a guarantee against Indian depredations, and I accordingly would recommend it. A glance at the map, too, would indicate that the chain of posts at the foot of the Sierra towards San Diego will be incomplete without it.

As to the proper time to establish this post, you will judge. Mr. Beale, however, is desirous it should be deferred till next spring, and in the mean time, retain there the present guard of 12 dragoons. His reason for deferring to so late a period may be connected with the establishment of the Indians permanently on the reserve, the only place suitable for them in the part of the state I have passed over. His success thus far is quite promising, and his means of subsisting all Indians that will come in and plant, abundant.

As to the particular spot marked out for the troops, there can be no exception. It is beautifully located among large oak trees near the mountains and with abundant water, wood, and grazing near. The labour of erecting quarters is a matter that rests with the quartermaster. My opinion is that no calculations should be made on the Indians, even if well paid, as they have not as yet good houses built for themselves, and I know Mr. Beale intends they shall erect good tenements for themselves and prepare fields for next year. It is possible the Indians near Fort Miller might be hired to go there and work at adobes.

I have also inspected Fort Miller. The quarters for two companies are not sufficient for the rank and file, and the officers will be crowded. Resort will have to be had to the French bell tent to supply immediate demand. This post is beautifully situated and cannot, for the present, in my opinion, be broken up.

In a few days I shall have the pleasure of seeing you.

I am, Sir, very respectfully,
Your obedient servant,

Jos. K. F. Mansfield
Colonel and Inspector General

San Francisco, Calif.
29h September, 1854

Brevet Major General John E. Wool
Commanding the Pacific Department
U.S.A.

Sir:

I arrived at Fort Reading on the 18h July. I found that post well commanded by Colonel Wright, and the troops in excellent condition. It is pleasantly situated on Cow Creek, an eastern tributary of the Sacramento River, and about [25] miles from Red Bluff in a grove of oak trees & c. The quarters are good, and there is an excellent stable and the store houses & c, ample. Yet it is unhealthy, and Dr. Tenbroek has made to me an official report against it on that account. The prevailing complaint is the ague and fever. The same complaint is common to all the country in that locality.

Another objection to the post is that its locality is not, in my opinion, of importance to suppress Indian depredations. A more suitable point for that object would probably be found near the junction of Pitt River and McLeod's Fork, thus placing the troops between the wild Indians and the population. A suitable reconnaissance would test this point. There is no necessity for this post as a depot of supplies for Fort Jones, as that post is only accessible over a mule trail from Shasta City of about 95 miles, in addition to 25 miles wagon road to Shasta City. Whereas Fort Jones should be supplied with such articles as must come from the sea board, via Scottsburg at the mouth of the Umpqua River, and Fort Lane or Jacksonville over a good wagon road, say 140 miles to Fort Lane and 84 miles thence to Fort Jones. This I have no doubt will be found to be the least costly mode of supplying both Forts Jones and Lane. The mode of packing now adopted is extremely expensive. The articles of fresh beef, flour, oats, and hay can undoubtedly now be furnished by the mills and farmers in the immediate neighbourhood of these posts and of the best quality.

There is now a stage line from the southern extremity of Scotts Valley via Fort Jones and Yreca to Jacksonville in Oregon and one organized from Jacksonville via Fort Lane to Scottsburg, and there seems to be no obstacle to transportation wagons in the dry season.

From Fort Reading we took mules and packs and proceeded

over the mountains via Shasta City, Weaversville, Trinity River, Mad River to Union at the head of Humbolts Bay. Thence a steamer conveyed us to Bucksport (Fort Humbolt), a distance of 185 miles from Fort Reading and most of it an extremely difficult mule trail over and along the sides of mountains. Here I found the command in excellent order under Colonel Buchanan. This is a very eligible locality for a post of one company and the quarters ample and the reservation of 640 acres well selected for all purposes. It should not be abandoned.

From Fort Humbolt we proceeded to Fort Jones via Union, Red Wood River, Klamath River, Salmon Mountain and River, Scotts Mountain into Scotts Valley, a distance of 138 miles. Here I found the command in good order under Lieutenant Bonneycastle. This post appears judiciously selected with a reservation of 640 acres. It should not be broken up for some time to come. It is on Scott's River and 18 miles from its junction with the Klamath, and the supplies can undoubtedly be had as heretofore suggested.

From Fort Jones we proceeded over a good wagon road via Yreka, across Klamath River, over the Siskiow Mountain and Jacksonville 84 miles to Fort Lane, under the command of Captain Smith of the 1t Dragoons. The troops were in good order.

This post is very judiciously selected on the south side of Rogue River opposite the Indian reservation and at the junction of Bear (Stewarts) Creek with the Rogue. A reservation of 640 acres has been well made, but lays over the whole claim of Mr. Jennison. This reservation occurred in this way. Mr. Jennison settled here in the fall of 1852, built a house, put up fences and ploughed about 30 acres, and had cut grass and stacked 25 or 3[0] tons of hay near his house, and had a corral. He left t[his] place in August, 1853, on account of Indian difficulties and took his family to Jacksonville, intending to return after the difficulties were over. In the mean time the Indians burnt his house and hay and corral. Peace with the Indians was made 14h September, 1853. Captain Smith took possession 25h September, 1853. Mr. Jennison returned to his claim prior to the 1t October, before Captain Smith had put up any buildings. Captain Smith then warned him he had taken possession for a reservation and that he must look to the law of Congress for any redress. Mr. Jennison has since, I understand, taken another claim. There is no place so well calculated for a military post in this locality as this. It places the military between the citizens and the Indian reservation on the north side of the river, and Captain Smith has done well in so doing. The damage sustained by Mr. Jennison, whatever it may be, will of course be settled under the laws of Congress. This post should not be broken up for several years to come, although one company may be all sufficient if full. It can readily be supplied as heretofore stated.

At this post there are one 12-pounder mountain and one 12-pounder field howitzer and caisson that require painting.

The Indian Agent here, Mr. S. H. Culver, is a very efficient and useful man, and commands the respect of the Indians. There was a little excitement at the time I visited this post occasioned by shooting two of the Indians by the whites, but I presume in this it is all over.

From Fort Lane we proceeded via Evan's Ferry across the Rogue River, Grave Creek, Cow Creek, the Cañon, south fork of the Umpqua, Myrtle Creek, Deer Creek, Winchester on the north fork of the Umpqua, Callapooya Creek and Mountain, along the valley of the Willamette to Corvallis, Salem, Oregon City, Portland, to Fort Vancouver, 285 miles over a good wagon road almost the entire distance. Here the troops were in excellent order under Lieutenant Colonel Bonneville. [Thi]s locality, under the circumstances, is probably the best for a depot in [this] section of the country. It undoubtedly would have been better further down the river opposite or below the mouth of the Willamette, in as much as in such a place it would be on the route of all steamers bound up the Willamette as well as Columbia River. But I am not able to say if such a position can now be had. Another objection is that this reservation of 640 acres lays over the claims of the Hudson Bay Company, and in addition, the quartermaster is paying that company an annual rent of 540 dollars for the use of a miserable building for a hospital and 900 dollars for the use of a building for store house. Further the log buildings occupied by the officers and soldiers are poor structures to keep out the wind and cold. This post, or a new one further down the river, cannot be dispensed with, as a depot in this section of the country is indispensable.

From Fort Vancouver we proceeded by steamer to the Cascades; thence over a portage of 5 miles; then by steamer to Fort Dalles, say 95 miles from Fort Vancouver. This post is well commanded by Major Rains and, from its locality, should be preserved as a two company station for some years to come. The reservation here is 640 acres but lays over a Methodist Mission claim. The recent attacks of the Indians on the emigrants near Fort Boissé demonstrates the necessity of another post in that locality of infantry and dragoons which could probably be supplied from the Mormon settlements at Salt Lake.

From Fort Dalles we returned to Vancouver and thence proceeded to Fort Steilacoom via the Cowlitz River and Olimpia, say 160 miles from Fort Vancouver and one and one-half miles from the town of Steilacoom on the Sound. The troops here were in good order under the command of Lieutenant Russell, and a post in this neighbourhood indispensible for several years to come. The emigrant road now open to Walla Wa[lla] thro' the Nachess Pass terminates here and at Olimpia. Th[is] post is located on the land claimed by the Puget S[ound] Agricultural Company, and the quartermaster is paying 600 dollars per annum for four miserable old log buildings. All the buildings at this post are of logs and worthless to keep out the cold and winds.

The garden is the best I have seen in this department, and is 5 miles to the north east of the quarters, and the only nearest suitable spot for that purpose, and on the Walla Walla road. There is at the garden a beautiful elevated and extended plateau for buildings, and I would earnestly recommend, as no suitable reservation has yet been made, that one be made immediately at this garden of 640 acres and, as lumber is abundant here, that plank buildings be put up suitable for a command of one full company which will not cost over 10,000 dollars, and each officer can have his own little building to himself. The reservation made on Whidby's Island, 6 miles from the main in Puget Sound, is entirely out of place and should not be occupied.

I must here recommend that another post for one full company be established at Bellingham Bay as indispensable, say 160 miles from Steilacoom.

At Port Orford I found the troops in good order under 2d Lieutenant Kautz of the 4th Infantry. The necessity of this post depends on the apprehensions of attacks by Indians on the limited population here. Perhaps in a short time there will be no further call for a station here.

I have now, in connection with my prior reports, completed, agreeably to your request, a brief notice of all the posts under your command in this department, and have to remark generally in regard to the troops that I am of opinion that the practice of target firing by the soldiers at long distances to familiarize them with the use of the ball cartridge is by no means sufficient for their pro[per] instruction, and that at some of the posts the drill [as skir]mishers is quite indifferent. I am also of opinion that the musketoon is a worthless arm for the dragoons. I would recommend, in its stead, sharps short rifle carbine as the only efficient arm for the dragoons.

I am also of opinion that a paymaster should be stationed at Fort Vancouver.

I shall leave your department for head quarters of the army in the steamer of tomorrow, and regret your absence in the Sacramento Valley will prevent the pleasure of a personal interview at this time. Yet I must express to you my obligations for the favours and facilities you have afforded me in the prosecution of my duties.

With my best wishes for your success in the arduous duties of your command.

I subscribe myself very respectfully
your obedient servant,

Jos. K. F. M[ANSFIELD]
Colonel and Inspector General

Military Personnel
Named in the Reports

In the two inspection reports, Mansfield gives the names of 231 officers. A number of these men were not stationed in the western departments, 2 were dead, and one, Ulysses S. Grant, had recently resigned from the army. Of those named, 23 were surgeons, 3 were chaplains, 3 were military storekeepers, and one was an ordnance sergeant. Eliminating these, there remain 201, of whom 167 were graduates of the United States Military Academy, while 3 others had attended the academy but had not graduated, leaving but 31 officers without any academy training. Thirty-two of the officers named died prior to the Civil War. Only 10, including 2 of the chaplains, served on neither side in the war. Those who remained loyal to the Union numbered 148, though a number of those who did, resigned or retired in the early months of the war. Only 42 cast their lot with the Confederacy. One must be counted on both sides: Lloyd Beall held the rank of captain in the Union army until he was dismissed in September, 1862. For the remainder of the war, he served as a private in Confederate ranks.

The following list includes all of the officers named by Mansfield. U.S.M.A. indicates that the officer attended the United States Military Academy, and the figure in parentheses designates class standing. Regular rank, date of achievement, service unit, and brevet rank at the time of Mansfield's inspection follow. U.S.A. indicates that the officer remained loyal to the

Union; C.S.A., that he served with the Confederacy. The next rank given is the highest attained, either regular or brevet, if it differs from the rank at the time of the report. d. refers to the date of death where known. This information is taken from Robert M. Danford, ed., *Register of Graduates and Former Cadets, United States Military Academy* (New York, 1953); Francis B. Heitman, *Historical Register and Dictionary of the United States Army*; and *Army Register*, 33 Cong., 2 sess., *House Exec. Doc. 58.*

Abadie, Eugene H. Major Surgeon (July 24, 1853). U.S.A. Lieutenant Colonel. d.December 22, 1874.

Abbott, Robert O. Assistant Surgeon (November 23, 1849) with the rank of First Lieutenant. U.S.A. Major Surgeon. d.June 16, 1867.

Adams, Wylly C. First Lieutenant (July 1, 1852), Second Artillery. Dismissed August 16, 1854.

Alexander, Edmund B. U.S.M.A. (33). Major (November 10, 1851), Eighth Infantry, and Brevet Lieutenant Colonel. U.S.A. Brevet Brigadier General. d.January 3, 1888.

Alexander, Newton F. U.S.M.A. (2). Brevet Second Lieutenant (July 1, 1852), Corps of Engineers. Second Lieutenant. d. October 10, 1858.

Allen, Robert. U.S.M.A. (33). Captain (May 11, 1846), Assistant Quartermaster, and Brevet Major. U.S.A. Brevet Major General. d.August 5, 1886.

Alley, John W. U.S.M.A. (32). Second Lieutenant (March 5, 1851), Third Infantry. U.S.A. Captain. Dismissed October 20, 1863. d.February 5, 1890.

Alvord, Benjamin. U.S.M.A. (22). Major Paymaster (June 22, 1854). U.S.A. Brigadier General. d.October 16, 1884.

Anderson, George B. U.S.M.A. (10). Brevet Second Lieutenant (July 1, 1852), Second Dragoons. Resigned April 25, 1861.

C.S.A. Brigadier General. d.October 16, 1862, of wounds received in the Battle of Antietam.

Arnold, Richard. U.S.M.A. (13). First Lieutenant (March 17, 1854), Third Artillery. U.S.A. Brevet Major General. d. November 8, 1882.

Auger, Christopher C. U.S.M.A. (16). Captain (August 1, 1852), Fourth Infantry. U.S.A. Major General, Volunteers. d.January 16, 1898.

Ayres, Romeyn B. U.S.M.A. (22). First Lieutenant (March 16, 1852), Third Artillery. U.S.A. Brevet Major General. d. December 4, 1888.

Backus, Electus. U.S.M.A. (28). Major (June 10, 1850), Third Infantry. U.S.A. Colonel. d.June 7, 1862.

Baldwin, Briscoe G. Military Storekeeper (October 3, 1851), Ordnance. Resigned April 22, 1861. C.S.A. Lieutenant, Ordnance.

Barnard, John G. U.S.M.A. (2). Captain (July 7, 1838), Corps of Engineers, and Brevet Major. U.S.A. Brevet Major General. d.May 14, 1882.

Bates, Francis H. U.S.M.A. (23). Second Lieutenant (April 15, 1852), Fourth Infantry. U.S.A. Brevet Major. d.August 12, 1895.

Beall, Lloyd First Lieutenant(June 30, 1851), Second Artillery. U.S.A. Captain. Dismissed September 12, 1862. C.S.A. Private, Artillery.

Bee, Barnard E. U.S.M.A. (33). First Lieutenant (March 5, 1851), 5th Infantry, and Brevet Captain. Resigned March 3, 1861. C.S.A. Brigadier General. Killed at Bull Run, July 21, 1861.

Bell, David. U.S.M.A. (18). Second Lieutenant (October 9, 1852), Second Dragoons. First Lieutenant. d.December 2, 1860.

Bingham, Thomas. U.S.M.A. (29). Second Lieutenant (November 10, 1851), Second Dragoons. Resigned March 21, 1854. C.S.A. d.October 13, 1913.

Blake, George A. H. Major (July 25, 1850), First Dragoons. U.S.A. Brevet Brigadier General. d.October 27, 1884.

Bonneau, Richard V. U.S.M.A. (42). Brevet Second Lieutenant (July 1, 1852), Third Infantry. Resigned March 2, 1861. C.S.A. Major. d.January 28, 1899.

Bonneville, Benjamin L. E. U.S.M.A. Lieutenant Colonel (May 7, 1849), Fourth Infantry U.S.A. Brevet Brigadier General. d.June 12, 1878.

Bonnycastle, John C. U.S.M.A. (did not graduate). First Lieutenant (August 5, 1853), Fourth Infantry. Resigned May 30, 1861. d.October 29, 1884.

Bowen, Isaac. U.S.M.A. (15). Captain (September 27, 1850), Commissary of Subsistence. d.October 3, 1858.

Bowman, Andrew W. U.S.M.A. (40). Captain (June 6, 1852), Third Infantry. U.S.A. Lieutenant Colonel. d.July 17, 1869.

Brent, Thomas Lee. U.S.M.A. (55). Captain (March 3, 1847), Assistant Quartermaster. d.January 11, 1858.

Brice, Benjamin W. U.S.M.A. (40). Major Paymaster (February 9, 1852). U.S.A. Brevet Major General. d.December 4, 1892.

Brooks, Horace. U.S.M.A. (9). Captain (June 18, 1846), Second Artillery, and Brevet Lieutenant Colonel. U.S.A. Brevet Brigadier General. d.January 13, 1894.

Brooks, William T. H. U.S.M.A. (46). Captain (November 10, 1851), Third Infantry. U.S.A. Brigadier General, Volunteers. d.July 19, 1870.

Brown, Nathan W. Major Paymaster (September 5, 1849). U.S.A. Brigadier General. dMarch 4, 1893.

Buchanan, Robert C. U.S.M.A. (31). Captain (November 1,

1838), Fourth Infantry, and Brevet Lieutenant Colonel. U.S.A. Brevet Major General. d.November 29, 1878.

Buford, Abraham. U.S.M.A. (51). Captain (July 15, 1853), First Dragoons. Resigned October 22, 1854. C.S.A. Brigadier General. d.June 9, 1884.

Burton, Henry S. U.S.M.A. (9). Captain (September 22, 1847), Third Artillery. U.S.A. Brevet Brigadier General. d.April 4, 1869.

Byrne, Bernard M. Major Surgeon (March 31, 1853). d.September 6, 1860.

Byrne, John. Assistant Surgeon (March 2, 1849) with the rank of Captain. Resigned October 11, 1857.

Calhoun, Patrick, U.S.M.A. (37). Captain (September, 6 1853), Second Dragoons. d.June 4, 1858. Calhoun was the son of John C. Calhoun.

Campbell, John. Assistant Surgeon (December 13, 1847) with the rank of Captain. U.S.A. Brevet Colonel.

Campbell, Reuben P. U.S.M.A. (27). Captain (August 8, 1851), Second Dragoons. Resigned May 11, 1861. C.S.A. Colonel. Killed on June 27, 1862, in the Battle of Gaines's Mill, Virginia.

Carleton, James H. Captain (February 16, 1847), First Dragoons, and Brevet Major. U.S.A. Brevet Major General. d. January 7, 1873.

Castor, Thomas F. U.S.M.A. (28). First Lieutenant (October 9, 1851), First Dragoons. d.September 8, 1855.

Chandler, Daniel T. Captain (September 21, 1846), Third Infantry, and Brevet Lieutenant Colonel. Retired February 27, 1862, C.S.A. Lieutenant Colonel. d.October 14, 1877.

Churchill, Charles G. First Lieutenant (June 30, 1852), Third Artillery. U.S.A. Captain. Retired February 28, 1862.

Clary, Robert E. U.S.M.A. (13). Captain (July 7, 1838), Assistant Quartermaster. U.S.A. Brevet Brigadier General. d. January 19, 1890.

Collins, Joseph B. First Lieutenant (July 7, 1853), Fourth Infantry. U.S.A. Brevet Colonel. d.December 20, 1888.

Crane, Charles H. Assistant Surgeon (February 14, 1848) with the rank of Captain. U.S.A. Brevet Brigadier General. d. October 10, 1883.

Crook, George. U.S.M.A. (38). Second Lieutenant (July 7, 1853), Fourth Infantry. U.S.A. Major General. d.March 21, 1890.

Cross, Osborne. U.S.M.A. (26). Major (July 24, 1847), Quartermaster. U.S.A. Brevet Brigadier General. d.July 15, 1876.

Cunningham, Francis H. Major Paymaster (March 2, 1849). U.S.A. d.August 14, 1864.

Daniel, Junius. U.S.M.A. (33). Second Lieutenant (November 10, 1851), Third Infantry. Resigned January 14, 1858. C.S.A. Brigadier General. Killed May 12, 1864, in the Battle of Spottsylvania, Virginia.

Davidson, Delozier. Captain (January 1, 1849), Second Infantry. U.S.M.A. Major. Resigned March 9, 1863. d.July 17, 1888.

Davis, Matthew L. U.S.M.A. (21). Second Lieutenant (July 1, 1852), Third Infantry. Resigned May 13, 1861. C.S.A. Colonel. d.April 23, 1862.

Davis, Nelson H. U.S.M.A. (49). First Lieutenant (June 8, 1849), Second Infantry. U.S.A. Brigadier General. d.May 15, 1890.

Day, Edward H. U.S.M.A. (10). Second Lieutenant (June 30, 1852), Third Artillery. First Lieutenant. d.January 2, 1860.

De Lano, Horace F. U.S.M.A. (20). Second Lieutenant (January 13, 1850), Second Dragoons. d.May 24, 1854.

De Leon, David C. Assistant Surgeon (August 21, 1838) with

the rank of Captain. Resigned February 19, 1861. C.S.A.
Surgeon. d.September 3, 1872.

Derby, George H. U.S.M.A. (7). Second Lieutenant (August
4, 1851), Topographical Engineers. Captain. d.May 15, 1861.
Derby was well known for his writings as a humorist under the
pseudonym, John Phoenix.

Dryer, Hiram. First Lieutenant (September 29, 1853), Fourth
Infantry. U.S.A. Brevet Lieutenant Colonel. d.March 5,
1867.

Du Barry, Beekman. U.S.M.A. (7). First Lieutenant (December 24, 1853), Third Artillery. U.S.A. Brigadier General.
d.January 12, 1901. Du Barry, at the time of Mansfield's
inspection, was acting assistant professor of the French language, United States Military Academy.

Duncan, Johnson K. U.S.M.A. (5). First Lieutenant (December 24, 1853), Third Artillery. Resigned January 31, 1855.
C.S.A. Brigadier General. d.December 18, 1862.

Dye, William McEntire. U.S.M.A. (32). Brevet Second Lieutenant (July 1, 1853), Fourth Infantry. U.S.A. Brevet Brigadier General. d.November 13, 1899.

Easton, Langdon C. U.S.M.A. (22). Captain (March 3, 1847),
Assistant Quartermaster. U.S.A. Brevet Major General. d.
April 29, 1884.

Eaton, Amos B. U.S.M.A. (36). Captain (July 7, 1838), Commissary of Subsistence, and Brevet Major. U.S.A. Brevet
Major General. d.May 21, 1877.

Eaton, Joseph H. U.S.M.A. (43). Captain (June 18, 1846),
Third Infantry, and Brevet Lieutenant Colonel. U.S.A. Brevet Brigadier General. d.January 20, 1896.

Eckerson, Theodore J. Military Storekeeper (September 16,
1853), Ordnance. U.S.A. Major, Quartermaster.

Eddy, Asher R. U.S.M.A. (5). First Lieutenant (August 19,

1847), First Artillery. U.S.A. Brevet Colonel. d.January 27, 1879.

Edwards, John. U.S.M.A. (15). Second Lieutenant (March 16, 1852), Third Artillery. U.S.A. Brevet Lieutenant Colonel. d.October 12, 1881.

Evans, George F. U.S.M.A. (36). Second Lieutenant (October 18, 1847), First Dragoons, and Brevet First Lieutenant. d. March 29, 1859.

Evans, Nathan G. U.S.M.A. (36). Second Lieutenant (September 30, 1849), Second Dragoons. Resigned February 27, 1861. C.S.A. Brigadier General. d.November 30, 1868.

Ewell, Richard S. U.S.M.A. (13). Captain (August 4, 1849), First Dragoons. Resigned May 7, 1861. C.S.A. Lieutenant General. d.January 25, 1872.

Fitzgerald, Edward H. Captain (August 23, 1849), First Dragoons, and Brevet Major. d.January 9, 1860.

Floyd-Jones, De Lancey. U.S.M.A. (45). Captain (July 31, 1854), Fourth Infantry. U.S.A. Colonel. d.January 19, 1902. The name was changed from Delancey F. Jones.

Folsom, Joseph L. U.S.M.A. (36). Captain (September 10, 1846), Assistant Quartermaster. d.July 19, 1855.

Forsythe, Benjamin D. U.S.M.A. (13). First Lieutenant (March 27, 1854), 4th Infantry. d.January 31, 1861.

Fraser, William D. U.S.M.A. (1). Captain (July 7, 1838), Corps of Engineers, and Brevet Major. d.July 27, 1856.

Fry, Cary H. U.S.M.A. (20). Major Paymaster (February 7, 1853). U.S.A. Brevet Brigadier General. d.March 5, 1875.

Gardiner, John W. T. U.S.M.A. (26). Captain (October 9, 1851), First Dragoons. U.S.A. Brevet Lieutenant Colonel. d.September 27, 1879.

Garland, John. Colonel (May 7, 1849), Eighth Infantry, and Brevet Brigadier General. U.S.A. d.June 5, 1861.

Garrard, Kenner, U.S.M.A. (8). Brevet Second Lieutenant (February 20, 1852), First Dragoons. U.S.A. Brevet Major General. d.May 15, 1879. Mansfield spells Garrard's name in several ways, but never correctly.

Gordon, William H. Captain (September 21, 1846), Third Infantry, and Brevet Major. U.S.A. Major. d.December 7, 1865.

Graham, Lawrence P. Captain (August 31, 1843), Second Dragoons, and Brevet Major. U.S.A. Brigadier General.

Graham, Lorimer. Second Lieutenant (February 2, 1848), First Dragoons, and Brevet Captain. Resigned October 31, 1853.

Grant, Ulysses S. U.S.M.A. (21). Captain (August 5, 1853), Fourth Infantry. Resigned July 31, 1854. U.S.A. General. d.July 23, 1885.

Green, Duff C. U.S.M.A. (29). Second Lieutenant (May 22, 1850), Third Infantry. Resigned December 31, 1856. C.S.A. Quartermaster General, Alabama. d.November 9, 1865.

Grier, William N. U.S.M.A. (54). Captain (August 23, 1846), First Dragoons, and Brevet Major. U.S.A. Brevet Brigadier General. d.July 8, 1885.

Griffin, Charles, U.S.M.A. (23). First Lieutenant (June 30, 1849), Second Artillery. U.S.A. Brevet Major General. d. September 15, 1867.

Haller, Granville O. Captain (January 1, 1848), Fourth Infantry, and Brevet Major. U.S.A. Colonel. d.May 2, 1897.

Hamilton, John. U.S.M.A. (2). First Lieutenant (February 13, 1850), Third Artillery. U.S.A. Colonel. d.July 15, 1900.

Hammond, John F. Assistant Surgeon (February 16, 1847) with the rank of Captain. U.S.A. Colonel Surgeon. d.September 29, 1886.

Hardie, James A. U.S.M.A. (11). First Lieutenant (March 3, 1847), Third Artillery. U.S.A. Brevet Major General. d. December 14, 1876.

Hatheway, John S. U.S.M.A. (32). Captain (March 3, 1847), First Artillery, and Brevet Major. d.March 31, 1853.

Heintzelman, Samuel P. U.S.M.A. (17). Captain (November 4, 1838), Second Infantry, and Brevet Lieutenant Colonel. U.S.A. Major General, Volunteers. d.May 1, 1880.

Henry, Thomas C. Assistant Surgeon (March 1, 1853) with the rank of First Lieutenant. Resigned October 15, 1855. U.S.A. Brevet Lieutenant Colonel, Volunteers. d.January 5, 1877.

Hill, Bennett H. U.S.M.A. (21). Captain (January 12, 1848), First Artillery, U.S.A. Brevet Brigadier General. d.March 24, 1886.

Hitchcock, Ethan Allen. U.S.M.A. Colonel (April 15, 1851), Second Infantry, and Brevet Brigadier General. U.S.A. Major General, Volunteers. d.August 5, 1870.

Hodges, Henry C. U.S.M.A. (32). Second Lieutenant (August 1, 1852), Fourth Infantry. U.S.A. Brigadier General. d. November 3, 1917.

Hood, John B. U.S.M.A. (44). Brevet Second Lieutenant (July 1, 1853), Fourth Infantry. Resigned April 16, 1861. C.S.A. General. d.August 30, 1879.

Howe, Marshall S. U.S.M.A. (did not graduate). Major (July 13, 1848), First Dragoons. U.S.A. Colonel. d.December 8, 1878.

Hunt, Lewis C. U.S.M.A. (33). First Lieutenant (April 15, 1852), Fourth Infantry. U.S.A. Brigadier General, Volunteers. d.September 6, 1886.

Ingalls, Rufus. U.S.M.A. (32). First Lieutenant (February 16, 1847), First Dragoons. U.S.A. Brevet Major General. d. January 15, 1893.

Jackson, Andrew. Second Lieutenant (December 30, 1847), Third Infantry. Dismissed June 6, 1861. C.S.A. Lieutenant Colonel.

Johns, William B. U.S.M.A. (39). Captain (December 4, 1847), Third Infantry. Dismissed April 11, 1861. d.October 19, 1894.

Johnston, Robert. U.S.M.A. (28). Second Lieutenant (February 1, 1853), First Dragoons. Resigned April 25, 1861. C.S.A. Colonel. d.July 8, 1902.

Jones, David Rumple. U.S.M.A. (41). First Lieutenant (May 7, 1849), Third Infantry, and Brevet Captain. Resigned February 15, 1861. C.S.A. Major General. d.June 16, 1863.

Jordan, Thomas. U.S.M.A. (41). Captain (March 3, 1847), Assistant Quartermaster. Resigned May 21, 1861. C.S.A. Brigadier General. d.November 27, 1895.

Judah, Henry M. U.S.M.A. (35). Captain (September 29, 1853), Third Infantry. U.S.A. Brigadier General, Volunteers. d.January 14, 1866.

Judd, Henry B. U.S.M.A. (14). Captain (February 13, 1850), Third Artillery. U.S.A. Brevet Colonel. d.July 27, 1892.

Kane, Elias K. U.S.M.A. (47). Captain (January 12, 1848), Second Dragoons. d.July 9, 1853.

Kautz, August V. U.S.M.A. (35). Second Lieutenant (March 24, 1853), Fourth Infantry. U.S.A. Brevet Major General. d.September 4, 1895.

Keeney, Charles C. Assistant Surgeon (March 19, 1845) with the rank of Captain. U.S.A. Colonel. d.January 30, 1883.

Kellogg, John U.S.M.A. (16). First Lieutenant (December 24, 1853), Third Artillery. U.S.A. Lieutenant Colonel. d. April 25, 1865.

Kendrick, Henry L. U.S.M.A. (16). Captain (June 18, 1846), Second Artillery, and Brevet Major. U.S.A. d.May 24, 1891.

Kendrick was a professor of chemistry, mineralogy, and geology at the United States Military Academy from 1835 to 1847 and again from 1857 to 1880.

Kerren, Richard. Ordnance Sergeant.

Keyes, Erasmus Darwin. U.S.M.A. (10). Captain (November 30, 1841), Third Artillery. U.S.A. Major General, Volunteers. d.October 14, 1895.

Langworthy, Elisha P. Assistant Surgeon (May 16, 1850) with the rank of First Lieutenant. Resigned April 30, 1861. C.S.A. Surgeon. d.March 8, 1862.

Larnard, Charles H. U.S.M.A. (16). Captain (February 25, 1841), Fourth Infantry, and Brevet Major. Drowned in Puget Sound on March 27, 1854. Name changed from Larned.

Latimer, Alfred E. U.S.M.A. (38). Brevet Second Lieutenant (July 1, 1853), Fourth Infantry. U.S.A. Brevet Lieutenant Colonel. d.March 19, 1905.

Laub, Charles H. Assistant Surgeon (November 30, 1836) with the rank of Captain. U.S.A. Lieutenant Colonel. d.December 2, 1876.

Lendrum, John H. First Lieutenant (March 24, 1848), Third Artillery, and Brevet Captain, U.S.A. Captain. d.October 26, 1861.

Leonard, Hiram. Major Paymaster (March 2, 1849). U.S.A. Brevet Brigadier General. d.December 21, 1883.

Long, Armistead L. U.S.M.A. (17). Second Lieutenant (June 30, 1851), Second Artillery. Resigned June 10, 1861. C.S.A. Brigadier General. d.April 20, 1891.

Lyon, Nathaniel. U.S.M.A. (11). Captain (June 11, 1851), Second Infantry. U.S.A. Brigadier General. Killed August 10, 1861 at Wilsons Creek, Missouri.

McCall, George A. U.S.M.A. (26). Colonel (June 10, 1850),

Inspector General. U.S.A. Major General, Volunteers. d. February 25, 1868.

McCarty, John. Chaplain. McCarty had served briefly as chaplain in the U.S. Navy, 1825–26, and as brigade chaplain in the army, 1847–48. He was chaplain at Jefferson Barracks, Missouri, 1848–52, and at Fort Vancouver and Fort Steilacoom, 1853–67. d.May 10, 1881.

McConnell, Thomas R. U.S.M.A. (50). First Lieutenant (October 8, 1848), Fourth Infantry. Captain. Resigned March 11, 1856. d.April 20, 1861.

McCook, Alexander McD. U.S.M.A. (30). Brevet Second Lieutenant (July 1, 1852), Third Infantry. U.S.A. Major General. d.June 12, 1903.

Macfeely, Robert. U.S.M.A. (31). Second Lieutenant (July 13, 1852), Fourth Infantry. U.S.A. Brigadier General. d. February 21, 1901.

McFerran, John C. U.S.M.A. (34). First Lieutenant (October 22, 1847), Third Infantry. U.S.A. Brevet Brigadier General. d.April 25, 1872.

McKinstry, Justus, U.S.M.A. (40). Captain (March 3, 1847), Assistant Quartermaster, and Brevet Major. U.S.A. Brigadier General, Volunteers. Dismissed January 28, 1863. d.December 11, 1897.

McLean, Nathaniel H. U.S.M.A. (27). First Lieutenant (January 8, 1853), Second Infantry. U.S.A. Lieutenant Colonel. d.July 5, 1884.

Macrae, Nathaniel C. U.S.M.A. (33). Captain (December 18, 1839), Third Infantry. U.S.A. Brevet Colonel. Retired September 25, 1861. d.February 5, 1878.

Magruder, David L. Assistant Surgeon (February 1, 1850) with the rank of First Lieutenant. U.S.A. Colonel.

Magruder, John B. U.S.M.A. (15). Captain (June 18, 1846),

First Artillery, and Brevet Lieutenant Colonel. Resigned April 20, 1861. C.S.A. Major General. d.February 19, 1871.

Maloney, Maurice. First Lieutenant (May 6, 1848), Fourth Infantry, and Brevet Captain. U.S.A. Colonel, Volunteers. d.January 8, 1872.

Marshall, Louis H. U.S.M.A. (41). Second Lieuteant (March 5, 1851), Third Infantry. U.S.A. Colonel. d.October 8, 1891.

Mason, James L. U.S.M.A. (2). Captain (April 24, 1847), Corps of Engineers, and Brevet Lieutenant Colonel. d.September 5, 1853.

Mason, John S. U.S.M.A. (9). First Lieutenant (September 7, 1850), Third Artillery. U.S.A. Brigadier General, Volunteers. d.November 29, 1897.

Maxwell, Joseph E. U.S.M.A. (42). Second Lieutenant (March 5, 1851), Third Infantry. Killed by Apaches near Fort Union on June 30, 1854.

Mendell, George H. U.S.M.A. (3). Brevet Second Lieutenant (July 1, 1852), Topographical Engineers. U.S.A. Colonel. d.October 19, 1902.

Miles, Dixon S. U.S.M.A. (27). Lieutenant Colonel (April 15, 1851), Third Infantry. U.S.A. Colonel. Killed at Harpers Ferry on September 16, 1862.

Milhau, John J. Assistant Surgeon (April 30, 1851) with the rank of First Lieutenant. U.S.A. Brevet Brigadier General. d.May 8, 1891.

Miller, Morris S. U.S.M.A. (14). Captain (September 13, 1845), Assistant Quartermaster. U.S.A. Brevet Brigadier General. d.March 11, 1870.

Montgomery, Thomas J. U.S.M.A. (26). Captain (March 27, 1854), Fourth Infantry. d.November 22, 1854.

Moore, John C. U.S.M.A. (17). Second Lieutenant (September 10, 1850), Second Artillery. Resigned February 28, 1855. C.S.A. Brigadier General. d.December 31, 1910.

Moore, Isaiah M. U.S.M.A. (14). Second Lieutenant (February 21, 1853), First Dragoons. U.S.A. Captain. d.January 16, 1862.

Moore, Tredwell. U.S.M.A. (26). First Lieutenant (June 11, 1851), Second Infantry. U.S.A. Brevet Brigadier General. d.May 29, 1876.

Morris, Gouverneur. U.S.M.A. (did not graduate). Major (January 31, 1850), Third Infantry. U.S.A. Lieutenant Colonel. Retired September 9, 1861. d.October 18, 1868.

Nauman, George. U.S.M.A. (8). Major (December 24, 1853), Third Artillery, and Brevet Lieutenant Colonel. U.S.A. Colonel. d.August 11, 1863.

Nichols, William A. U.S.M.A. (19). Brevet Captain (July 29, 1852), Assistant Adjutant General, and Brevet Major. U.S.A. Brevet Major General. d.April 8, 1869.

Norris, Charles E. U.S.M.A. (24). Second Lieutenant (July 9, 1853), Second Dragoons. U.S.A. Lieutenant Colonel, Volunteers. Dismissed February 10, 1870. d.October 31, 1875.

Nugen, John. U.S.M.A. (28). Second Lieutenant (September 29, 1853), Fourth Infantry. d.October 22, 1857.

O'Bannon, Lawrence W. Second Lieutenant (March 3, 1848), Third Infantry. Resigned March 31, 1861. C.S.A. Lieutenant Colonel, Quartermaster. d.June 2, 1882.

O'Connell, John D. U.S.M.A. (27). Second Lieutenant (July 31, 1853), Second Infantry. U.S.A. Brevet Colonel. d.September 16, 1867.

Ogle, Charles H. U.S.M.A. (29). Second Lieutenant (August 4, 1849), First Dragoons. U.S.A. Major, Volunteers. d. March 7, 1863.

Ord, Edward O. C. U.S.M.A. (17). Captain (September 7, 1850), Third Artillery. U.S.A. Major General. d.July 22, 1883.

Paige, George H. U.S.M.A. (26). First Lieutenant (February 23, 1852), Second Infantry. Captain. d.April 18, 1859.

Parke, John G. U.S.M.A. (2). Second Lieutenant (April 18, 1854), Topographical Engineers. U.S.A. Major General, Volunteers. d.December 16, 1900.

Patten, George W. U.S.M.A. (36). Captain (June 18, 1846), Second Infantry, and Brevet Major, U.S.A. Lieutenant Colonel. d.April 28, 1882.

Patterson, Francis E. First Lieutenant (October 29, 1848), First Artillery. U.S.A. Brigadier General, Volunteers. d.November 22, 1862.

Pleasonton, Alfred. U.S.M.A. (7). First Lieutenant (September 30, 1849), Second Dragoons. U.S.A. Major General, Volunteers. d.February 17, 1897.

Pope, John. U.S.M.A. (17). First Lieutenant (March 3, 1853), Topographical Engineers, and Brevet Captain. U.S.A. Major General. d.September 23, 1892.

Potts, Richard. Assistant Surgeon (September 16, 1853) with the rank of First Lieutenant. Resigned May 7, 1861. C.S.A. Surgeon.

Prime, Frederick E. U.S.M.A. (1). Second Lieutenant (September 13, 1853), Corps of Engineers. U.S.A. Brevet Brigadier General. d.August 12, 1900.

Radford, Richard C. W. U.S.M.A. (31). First Lieutenant (October 24, 1848), First Dragoons. Resigned November 30, 1856. C.S.A. Colonel. d.November 2. 1885.

Raines, Gabriel J. U.S.M.A (13) Major (March 9, 1851), Fourth Infantry. Resigned July 31, 1861. C.S.A. Brigadier General. d.August 6, 1881.

Ransom, Robert. U.S.M.A. (18). Second Lieutenant (October 9, 1851), First Dragoons. Resigned May 24, 1861. C.S.A. Major General. d.January 14, 1892.

Reynolds, John. Chaplain (December 31, 1850). Reynolds remained as chaplain at the Post of San Diego until August 31, 1854. Perhaps his lack of popularity with the officers, which Mansfield reported, was a factor in his departure from the position.

Reynolds, Joseph J. U.S.M.A. (10). Second Lieutenant (May 11, 1846), Third Artillery. U.S.A. Brevet Major General. d.February 25, 1899. Reynolds was assistant professor of natural and experimental philosophy, United States Military Academy, at the time of Mansfield's inspection.

Richardson, Israel B. U.S.M.A. (38). Captain (March 5, 1851), Third Infantry, and Brevet Major. Resigned September 30, 1855. U.S.A. Major General. Volunteers. d.November 3, 1862, of wounds received at Antietam.

Robertson, Beverly H. U.S.M.A. (25). Second Lieutenant (July 25, 1850), Second Dragoons. Dismissed August 8, 1861. C.S.A. Brigadier General. d.November 12, 1910.

Rundell, Charles H. U.S.M.A. (25). Second Lieutenant (August 5, 1853), Fourth Infantry. Dismissed June 6, 1861. C.S.A. Captain. d.in 1864 in Peru.

Russell, David A. U.S.M.A. (38). Captain (June 22, 1854), Fourth Infantry. U.S.A. Brevet Major General. Killed September 19, 1864, in the Battle of Opequan, Virginia.

Schroeder, Henry B. U.S.M.A. (22). First Lieutenant (December 4, 1847), Third Infantry. Resigned May 30, 1861. Captain. d.December 21, 1904.

Scott, Henry L. U.S.M.A. (41). Captain (February 16, 1847), Fourth Infantry. U.S.A. Colonel. Retired October 31, 1862. d.January 6, 1886.

Shaw, John M. Chaplain (October 12, 1852). Resigned September 30, 1856.

Shepherd, Oliver M. U.S.M.A. (33). Captain (December 1,

1847), Third Infantry, and Brevet Major. U.S.A. Brevet
Brigadier General. d.April 15, 1894.

Shoemaker, William R. Master Storekeeper (August 3, 1841),
Ordnance. U.S.A. Captain. d.September 16, 1886.

Sibley, Ebenezer S. U.S.M.A. (1) Captain (July 7, 1838),
Assistant Quartermaster, and Brevet Major. U.S.A. Brevet
Colonel. Resigned April 15, 1864. d.August 14, 1884.

Simpson, Josiah. Assistant Surgeon (July 11, 1837) with the
rank of Captain. U.S.A. Brevet Colonel. d.March 3, 1874.

Slaughter, William A. U.S.M.A. (21). First Lieutenant (June
22, 1854), Fourth Infantry. Killed December 4, 1855, in
action against the White River Indians, Brannan's Prairie,
Washington Territory.

Slemmer, Adam J. U.S.M.A. (12). First Lieutenant (April 30,
1854), First Artillery. U.S.A. Brigadier General, Volunteers.
d.October 7, 1868.

Smith, Albert J. Major Paymaster (June 1, 1849). Dismissed
June 20, 1861. C.S.A. Lieutenant Colonel, Paymaster. d.
March 28, 1871.

Smith, Andrew J. U.S.M.A. (36). Captain (February 16,
1847), First Dragoons. U.S.A. Brevet Major General. d.
January 28, 1897.

Smith, William D. U.S.M.A. (35). First Lieutenant (August
8, 1851), Second Dragoons. Resigned January 28, 1861.
C.S.A. Brigadier General. d.October 4, 1862.

Sorrel, Francis. Assistant Surgeon (June 29, 1849) with the
rank of First Lieutenant. Resigned June 27, 1856, C.S.A.
Surgeon.

Stanley, David S. U.S.M.A. (9). Brevet Second Lieutenant
(July 1, 1852), Second Dragoons. U.S.A. Major General,
Volunteers. d.March 13, 1902.

Stanton, Henry W. U.S.M.A. (45). Captain (July 25, 1854)

First Dragoons. Killed January 20, 1855, by Apaches in the Sacramento Mountains, New Mexico.

Steele, William. U.S.M.A. (31). Captain (November 10, 1851), Second Dragoons. Resigned May 30, 1861. C.S.A. Brigadier General. d.January 12, 1885.

Steen, Alexander E. Second Lieutenant (June 30, 1852), Third Infantry. Resigned May 10, 1861. C.S.A. Brigadier General. Killed November 27, 1862, in the Battle of Kane Hill, Arkansas.

Steen, Enoch. Major (July 15, 1853), Second Dragoons. U.S.A. Lieutenant Colonel. Retired September 23, 1863. d.January 22, 1880.

Stone, Charles P. U.S.M.A. (7). First Lieutenant (February 26, 1853), Ordnance, and Brevet Captain. U.S.A. Brigadier General, Volunteers. d.January 24, 1887.

Stoneman, George. U.S.M.A. (33). First Lieutenant (July 25, 1854), First Dragoons. U.S.A. Major General, Volunteers. d.September 5, 1894. After his retirement from the army in 1871 Stoneman resided in California where he served as governor of the state, 1883–87.

Sturgis, Samuel D. U.S.M.A. (32). First Lieutenant (July 15, 1853) First Dragoons. U.S.A. Brevet Major General. d. September 28, 1889.

Suckley, George. Assistant Surgeon (December 2, 1853) with the rank of First Lieutenant. U.S.A. Brevet Colonel. d.July 30, 1869.

Summers, John E. Assistant Surgeon (December 13, 1847) with the rank of Captain. U.S.A. Colonel Surgeon. Retired January 24, 1886.

Sumner, Edwin V. Lieutenant Colonel (July 13, 1848), First Dragoons, and Brevet Colonel. U.S.A. Major General, Volunteers. d.March 21, 1863.

Sutherland, Charles. Assistant Surgeon (August 5, 1852) with the rank of First Lieutenant. U.S.A. Brigadier General, Surgeon General (1890–93). d.May 10, 1895.

Sykes, George. U.S.M.A. (39). First Lieutenant (September 21, 1846), Third Infantry. U.S.A. Major General, Volunteers. d.February 8, 1880.

Taylor, Oliver H. P. U.S.M.A. (31). First Lieutenant (February 21, 1853), First Dragoons, and Brevet Captain. Killed May 17, 1858, by Spokane Indians, Washington Territory.

Ten Broeck, Peter G. S. Assistant Surgeon (December 13, 1847), with the rank of Captain. U.S.A. Brevet Lieutenant Colonel. d.December 19, 1867.

Thomas, George H. U.S.M.A. (12). Captain (December 24, 1853), Third Artillery, and Brevet Major. U.S.A. Major General. d.March 28, 1870.

Thompson, Philip R. U.S.M.A. (36). Captain (June 30, 1846), First Dragoons, and Brevet Major. Dismissed September 4, 1855. d.June 24, 1857.

Tidball, John C. U.S.M.A. (11). First Lieutenant (March 31, 1853), Second Artillery. U.S.A. Brevet Major General, Volunteers. d.May 15, 1906.

Tower, Zealous B. U.S.M.A. (1). First Lieutenant (April 24, 1847), Corps of Engineers, and Brevet Major. U.S.A. Brevet Major General. d.March 20, 1900.

Townsend, Edward D. U.S.M.A. (16). Brevet Major (July 15, 1852), Assistant Adjutant General. U.S.A. Brevet Major General. d.May 11, 1893.

Trevitt, John. U.S.M.A. (12). First Lieutenant (December 1, 1847), Third Infantry. Captain. Resigned April 17, 1861. d.March 24, 1893.

Tripler, Charles S. Major Surgeon (July 7, 1838). U.S.A. Brevet Brigadier General. d.October 20, 1866.

Underwood, Edmund. First Lieutenant (March 3, 1848), Fourth Infantry. U.S.A. Major. Retired February 27, 1862. d.September 5, 1863.

Van Horne, Jefferson. U.S.M.A. (30). Captain (December 1, 1840), Third Infantry, and Brevet Major. d.September 28, 1857.

Van Voast, James. U.S.M.A. (8). Second Lieutenant (August 22, 1853), Third Artillery. U.S.A. Brigadier General. d.July 16, 1915.

Wallen, Henry D. U.S.M.A. (34). Captain (January 31, 1850), Fourth Infantry. U.S.A. Brevet Brigadier General. d.December 2, 1886.

Ward, James N. U.S.M.A. (28). First Lieutenant (March 5, 1851), Third Infantry. Captain. d.December 6, 1858.

Webb, William A. U.S.M.A. (35). Brevet Second Lieutenant (July 1, 1853), Fourth Infantry. U.S.A. Colonel, Volunteers. d.December 24, 1861.

Welker, William T. U.S.M.A. (4). Second Lieutenant (June 26, 1853), Ordnance. Dismissed July 22, 1861. C.S.A. Captain. d.November 3, 1900.

Wessels, Henry W. U.S.M.A. (29). Captain (February 16, 1847), Second Infantry, and Brevet Major. U.S.A. Brigadier General, Volunteers. d.January 12, 1889.

Whipple, Amiel W. U.S.M.A. (5). First Lieutenant (April 24, 1851), Topographical Engineers. U.S.A. Major General, Volunteers. d.May 7, 1863, of wounds received at Chancellorsville, Virginia.

Whipple, William D. U.S.M.A. (31). Second Lieutenant (September 9, 1851), Third Infantry. U.S.A. Brevet Brigadier General. d.April 1, 1902.

Whistler, Joseph N. G. U.S.M.A. (47). First Lieutenant (June

6, 1852), Third Infantry. U.S.A. Brevet Brigadier General. d.April 20, 1898.

Whistler, William. Colonel (July 15, 1845), Fourth Infantry. U.S.A. Retired October 9, 1861. d.December 4, 1863.

White, William J. H. Assistant Surgeon (March 12, 1850) with rank of First Lieutenant. U.S.A. Major Surgeon. Killed September 17, 1862, at Antietam.

Whiting, William H. C. U.S.M.A. (1). First Lieutenant (March 16, 1853), Corps of Engineers. Resigned February 20, 1861. C.S.A. Major General. d.March 10, 1865, of wounds received while a prisoner of war.

Wilkins, John D. U.S.M.A. (46). First Lieutenant (November 10, 1851), Third Infantry. U.S.A. Colonel. d.February 20, 1900.

Williamson, Robert S. U.S.M.A. (5). Second Lieutenant (October 26, 1853), Topographical Engineers. U.S.A. Lieutenant Colonel. d.November 10, 1882.

Winder, Charles S. U.S.M.A. (22). First Lieutenant (April 5, 1854), Third Artillery. Captain. Resigned April 1, 1861. C.S.A. Brigadier General. Killed August 9, 1862, in the Battle of Cedar Mountain, Virginia.

Winship, Oscar F. U.S.M.A. (22). Captain (June 30, 1851), Second Dragoons, and Brevet Major. d.December 13, 1855.

Withers, John, U.S.M.A. (23). Second Lieutenant (January 21, 1850), Fourth Infantry. Brevet Captain. Resigned March 1, 1861. C.S.A. Lieutenant Colonel, Assistant Adjutant General. d.February 3, 1892.

Wood, William H. U.S.M.A. (37). First Lieutenant (September 9, 1851), Third Infantry. U.S.A. Colonel. d.January 1, 1887.

Wool, John E. Brigadier General (June 25, 1841) and Brevet Major General. U.S.A. Retired August 1, 1863. d. November 10, 1869.

Wright, George. U.S.M.A. (24). Major (January 1, 1848),
Fourth Infantry, and Brevet Colonel. U.S.A. Brigadier General, Volunteers. Drowned in a shipwreck, July 30, 1865.

Wright, Thomas. U.S.M.A. (19). Second Lieutenant (October
16, 1849), Second Infantry. First Lieutenant. d.October 12,
1857.

Wyse, Francis O. U.S.M.A. (43). Captain (March 3, 1847),
Third Artillery, and Brevet Major. U.S.A. Lieutenant Colonel. Resigned July 25, 1863. d.January 21, 1893.

Tabular Statement of the Number of Troops & Horses Present &
Absent for Duty in New Mexico at Each Post, & of All the Small
Arms & Artillery Fit for Service in the Field, from 1st August to
1st September 1853.[1]

FORT UNION

1st Dragoons, Company K
  Officers present, 1; absent, 2
  Enlisted men present, 41; ab-
    sent, 9
  Dragoon horses serviceable,
    29; unserviceable, 13
  Musketoons, 28; Percussion
    Rifles, 30; Percussion Pis-
    tols, 37; Colts Revolvers,
    47
  Dragoon Sabres, 53
  Mountain Howitzers, brass, 2
2nd Artillery, Company D
  Officers present, 1; absent, 2
  Enlisted men present, 66; ab-
    sent, 10

  Percussion Rifles, 78; Per-
    cussion Pistols, 15
  Horse Artillery Sabres, 1;
    Infantry Swords, 7
  12 pounder Mountain Howit-
    zers, brass, 4
3rd Infantry, Company D
  Officers present, 1; absent, 2
  Enlisted men present, 55; ab-
    sent, 15
  Percussion Muskets, 74
Quartermaster's Department
  Officers present, 1
  Citizens employed, 28
Ordnance Department
  Enlisted men present, 12
  Military Store Keeper, 1

[1] The Tabular Statements presented here are modifications of the tables in the
original manuscript.

Citizens employed, 1

Percussion Muskets, 642; Flint Muskets, 273; Musketoons, 494; Percussion Rifles, 1331; Sharps Rifles, 30; Percussion Carbines, 179; Percussion Pistols, 575; Colts Revolvers, 121

Dragoon Sabres, 600; Artillery Sabres, 153; Infantry Swords, 139

12 pounder Mountain Howitzers, brass, 6; 24 pounder Field Howitzers, brass, 2; 6 pounder Field Guns, brass, 3

Commissary Department
Officers present, 1

Medical Department
Citizen employee, 1

FORT MASSACHUSETTS
Field Officer present, 1
Mountain Howitzer, brass, 1

1st Dragoons, Company F
Officers present, 1; absent, 2
Enlisted men present, 66; absent, 12
Dragoon Horses serviceable, 48; unserviceable, 6
Musketoons, 88; Percussion Rifles, 4; Percussion Pistols, 34; Colts Revolvers, 39
Dragoon Sabres, 61

3rd Infantry, Company H
Officers present, 1; absent, 2
Enlisted men present, 57; absent, 14
Percussion muskets, 86; Musketoons, 6
Infantry Swords, 3

Medical Department
Officers present, 1

CANTONMENT BURGWIN

1st Dragoons, Company J
Officers present, 1; absent 2
Enlisted men present, 40; absent, 32
Dragoon Horses serviceable, 44; unserviceable, 14
Musketoons, 45; Percussion Carbines, 1; Percussion Pistols, 48; Colts Revolvers, 19
Dragoon Sabres, 77

FORT MARCY
Commandant
12 pounder Mountain Howitzer, brass, 1; 6 pounder Field Gun, brass, 1

3rd Infantry, Company G
Officers present, 2; absent, 1
Enlisted men present, 73; absent, 8
Percussion Muskets, 85
Infantry Swords, 8

Medical Department
Officers present, 1

SANTA FE PAY DEPARTMENT
Officers present, 2
Civilians employed, 2

ALBUQUERQUE
Headquarters
Officers present, 3
2nd Dragoons, Company H
Officers present, 1; absent, 3
Enlisted men present, 59;
absent, 17
Dragoon Horses serviceable,
55; unserviceable, 7
Musketoons, 72; Percussion
Carbines, 3; Percussion
Pistols, 65; Colts Revol-
vers, 39
Dragoon Sabres, 101
Quartermaster's Department
Citizens employed, 13
Medical Department
Officers present, 1

FORT DEFIANCE
2nd Artillery, Company B
Officers present, 4; absent 0
Enlisted men present, 68;
absent, 15
Percussion Muskets, 9; Mus-
ketoons, 91; Percussion
Rifles, 37; Percussion
Pistols, 10; Colts Revol-
vers, 8

Horse Artillery Sabres, 9
12 pounder Field Howitzers,
brass, 1; 12 pounder Moun-
tain Howitzers, brass, 4;
6 pounder Field Guns,
brass, 1; Rifle Wall Piece, 1
3rd Infantry, Company B
Officers present, 2; absent, 1
Enlisted men present, 55;
absent, 23
Percussion Muskets, 79;
Musketoons, 1; Percussion
Rifles, 10
3rd Infantry, Company F
Officers present, 2; absent, 1
Enlisted men present, 54;
absent, 28
Percussion Muskets, 90;
Percussion Rifles, 1
Infantry Swords, 5
Medical Department
Officers present, 1

LOS LUNAS
1st Dragoons, Company G
Officers present, 1; absent 2
Enlisted men present, 72;
absent, 9
Dragoon Horses serviceable,
40; unserviceable, 19
Percussion Rifles, 12; Sharps
Rifles, 5; Percussion Car-
bines, 74; Percussion
Pistols, 71; Colts Revol-
vers, 2

Dragoons Sabres, 80

FORT CONRAD
Commandant
12 pounder Mountain Howitzers, brass, 2
2nd Dragoons, Company K
Officers present, 1; absent, 3
Enlisted men present, 41; absent, 6
Dragoon Horses serviceable, 48; unserviceable, 6
Musketoons, 66; Percussion Rifles, 10; Percussion Pistols, 36; Colts Revolvers, 53
Dragoon Sabres, 88; Horse Artillery Sabres, 4
3rd Infantry, Company I
Officers present, 1; absent, 2
Enlisted men present, 53; absent, 27
Percussion Muskets, 74; Percussion Rifles, 4; Colts Revolvers, 2
Infantry Swords, 11
Medical Department
Citizen employee, 1

FORT WEBSTER
Commandant
12 pounder Mountain Howitzers, brass, 1
1st Dragoons, Company H
Officers present, 1; absent, 3

Enlisted men present, 65; absent, 0
Dragoon Horses serviceable, 41; unserviceable, 2
Musketoons, 85; Percussion Rifles, 30; Percussion Carbines, 21; Colts Revolvers, 12
Dragoon Sabres, 112
2nd Dragoons, Company E
Officers present, 2; absent, 2
Enlisted men present, 63; absent, 2
Dragoon Horses serviceable, 28; unserviceable, 14
Musketoons, 73; Percussion Pistols, 10; Colts Revolvers, 26
Dragoon Sabres, 97
3rd Infantry, Company K
Officers present, 2; absent, 1
Enlisted men present, 74; absent, 0
Percussion Muskets, 67
Infantry Swords, 2
Medical Department
Officers present, 1

FORT FILLMORE
Field Officer present, 1
12 pounder Mountain Howitzers, brass, 2
2nd Dragoons, Company D
Officers present, 0; absent, 3

Enlisted men present, 61; absent, 5

Dragoon Horses serviceable, 50; unserviceable, 1

Musketoons, 55; Percussion Pistols, 9; Colts Revolvers, 62

Dragoon Sabres, 78

3rd Infantry, Company A

Officers present, 2; absent, 2

Enlisted men present, 64; absent, 8

Percussion Muskets, 79; Percussion Rifles, 4

Infantry Swords, 9

3rd Infantry, Company C

Officers present, 2; absent, 0

Enlisted men present, 69; absent, 10

Percussion Muskets, 95; Percussion Rifles, 2

Infantry Swords, 8

3rd Infantry, Company E

Officers present, 2; absent 2

Enlisted men present, 75; absent, 5

Percussion Muskets, 90; Musketoons, 2

Medical Department

Officers present, 1

Pay Department

Officers present, 1

Citizens employed, 1

Total for the Department[2]

Officers present, 47

Officers absent, 38

Enlisted men present, 1283

Enlisted men absent, 256

Dragoon Horses serviceable, 383

Dragoon Horses unserviceable, 82

Militery Store Keeper, 1

Citizens employed, 42

Percussion Muskets, 1470

Flint Muskets, 273

Musketoons, 1106

Percussion Rifles, 1553

Sharps Rifles, 35

Percussion Carbines, 278

Percussion Pistols, 910

Colts Revolvers, 430

Dragoon Sabres, 1347

Horse Artillery Sabres, 167

Infantry Swords, 192

12 pounder Field Howitzers, brass, 1

12 pounder Mountain Howitzers, brass, 20

24 pounder Field Howitzers, brass, 2

6 pounder Field Guns, brass, 5

Mountain Howitzer, brass, 3

Rifle Wall Piece, 1

[2] Not all of the figures in the table agree with the figures in the body of the report. Also, a few errors in addition occur in the table.

Pacific Department. Tabular Statement of the Posts, Companies, Departments, Commissioned Officers Present & Absent, Enlisted Men Present & Absent, Military Store Keepers & Citizens Employed, Serviceable Small Arms and Artillery from the 4h May to 30h September 1854.

SAN FRANCISCO

Headquarters of the Department
Commissioned Officers
present, 5
Enlisted men present, 2
Quartermaster's Department
Commissioned Officers
present, 2
Citizens employed, 5
Subsistance Department
Commissioned Officers
present, 1
Citizens employed, 2
Pay Department
Commissioned Officers
present, 2
Medical Department
Commissioned Officers
present, 1
Topographical Department
Commissioned Officers
present, 2
Military Engineers
Commissioned Officers
present, 5
Citizens employed, 2 +

PRESIDIO OF SAN FRANCISCO
3rd Artillery, Company M

Commissioned Officers
present, 1; absent, 3
Enlisted men present, 55;
absent, 9
Percussion Muskets, 82;
Percussion Rifles, 6; Colts
Revolvers, 19
Non-Commissioned Officers
Swords, 6

MONTEREY
Military Store Keeper, 1
Percussion Muskets, 48
Artillery Swords, 200

NEW SAN DIEGO
Quartermaster's Sub Depot
Commissioned Officers
present, 1
Enlisted men present, 1
Citizens employed, 23
Subsistence Sub Depot
Commissioned Officers
present, 1
Citizens employed, 2
Pay Department
Commissioned Officers
present, 1

OLD SAN DIEGO
Topographical Department

Commissioned Officers
present, 1

MISSION OF SAN DIEGO
Ordnance Sergeant, 1
Percussion Rifles, 100
1st Artillery, Company I
Commissioned Officers
present,1; absent, 3
Enlisted men present, 36;
absent, 46
Percussion Muskets, 96;
Percussion Rifles, 4; Mus-
ketoons, 73; Percussion
Pistols, 13
Non-Commissioned Officers
Swords, 6; Artillery
Swords, 39; Artillery
Sabres, 25
6 pounder Brass Field Guns,
2; 12 pounder Brass How-
itzers, 2
3rd Artillery, Company F
Commissioned Officers
present, 1; absent, 3
Enlisted men present, 28;
absent, 57
Percussion Muskets, 26
Medical Department
Officers present, 1

FORT YUMA
Colts Revolvers, 73
12 pounder Brass Mountain
Howitzers, 2

2nd Infantry, Company D
Commissioned Officers
present, 3; absent, 0
Enlisted men present, 38;
absent, 0
Percussion Muskets, 78;
Percussion Rifles, 5
Non-Commissioned Officers
Swords, 6
1st Artillery, Company I
(detachment)
Commissioned Officers
present, 1
Enlisted men present, 16
Percussion Muskets, 32;
Percussion Rifles, 5
Non-Commissioned Officers
Swords, 4
3rd Artillery, Company F
(detachment)
Commissioned Officers
present, 1
Enlisted men present, 50
Percussion Muskets, 116;
Percussion Rifles, 8; Colts
Revolvers, 1
Non-Commissioned Officers
Swords, 8
Medical Department
Commissioned Officers
present, 1

TEJON RESERVATION
1st Dragoons, Company A
(detachment)

Enlisted men present, 12

FORT MILLER
1st Dragoons, Company A
Commissioned Officers
present, 1; absent, 2
Enlisted men present, 41;
absent, 19
Musketoons, 70; Percussion
Pistols, 3
Calvary Sabres, 62
2nd Infantry, Company G
Commissioned Officers
present, 1; absent, 2
Enlisted men present, 32;
absent, 0
Percussion Muskets, 149;
Percussion Rifles, 9
Non-Commissioned Officers
Swords, 13
Medical Department
Commissioned Officers
present, 1
Quartermaster's Department
Commissioned Officers
absent, 1
Citizens employed, 17

BENICIA
Field Staff, 3rd Artillery
Commissioned Officers
present, 2; absent, 0
Enlisted men present, 14;
absent, 1
Non-Commissioned Officers

Swords, 28; Artillery
Sabres, 2
3rd Artillery, Company B
(Barracks)
Commissioned Officers
present, 2; absent 2
Enlisted men present, 41;
absent, 23
Percussion muskets, 58
Non-Commissioned Officers
Swords, 10
Ordnance Depot
Commissioned Officers
present, 2; absent 0
Enlisted men present, 38;
absent, 6
Citizens employed, 4
Percussion Muskets, 12,212;
Percussion Rifles, 5738;
Musketoons, 1061; Car-
bines, 200; Percussion Pis-
tols, 1199; Colts Revolv-
ers, 280
Non-Commissioned Officers
Swords, 687; Calvary
Sabres, 702; Artillery
Sabres, 303
6 pounder Brass Field Guns,
11; 12 pounder Brass How-
itzers, 6; Sea Coast Guns,
47; Mortars, 3
Quartermaster's Depot
Commissioned Officers
present, 1
Citizens employed, 26

Subsistence Depot
Commissioned Officers
present, 1
Citizens employed, 3

FORT READING
Field and Staff, 4th Infantry
Commissioned Officers
present, 2
12 pounder Brass Mountain
Howitzers, 1
3rd Artillery, Company D
Commissioned Officers
present, 1; absent, 3
Enlisted men present, 47;
absent, 0
Percussion Muskets, 74;
Percussion Rifles, 3
Non-Commissioned Officers
Swords, 4
4th Infantry, Company D
Commissioned Officers
present, 3; absent 1
Enlisted men present, 41;
absent, 1
Percussion Muskets, 100;
Percussion Rifles, 4; Per-
cussion Pistols, 4; Colts
Revolvers, 1
Non-Commissioned Officers
Swords, 12
Quartermaster's Department
Commissioned Officers
present, 1

FORT HUMBOLDT
12 pounder Brass Mountain
Howitzer, 1
4th Infantry, Company B
Commissioned Officers
present, 1; absent, 0
Enlisted men present, 36;
absent, 1
Percussion Muskets, 69
Non-Commissioned Officers
Swords, 6
4th Infantry, Company F
Commissioned Officers
present, 2; absent, 0
Enlisted men present, 27;
absent, 1
Percussion Muskets, 65
Non-Commissioned Officers
Swords, 6
Medical Department
Commissioned Officers
present, 1

FORT JONES
Colts Revolvers, 7
4th Infantry, Company E
Commissioned Officers
present, 3; absent 1
Enlisted men present, 27;
absent, 0
Percussion Muskets, 50
Non-Commissioned Officers
Swords, 6

Medical Department
Commissioned Officers
present, 1

FORT LANE
Percussion Muskets, 15;
Percussion Rifles, 3; Colts
Revolvers, 5
12 pounder Brass Howitzer, 1
1st Dragoons, Company C
Commissioned Officers
present, 1; absent 2
Enlisted men present, 19;
absent, 1
Horses, 28
Musketoons, 43; Percussion
Pistols, 8; Colts Revolvers,
1
Calvary Sabres, 49
1st Dragoons, Company E
Commissioned Officers
present, 1; absent, 2
Enlisted men present, 28;
absent, 3
Horses, 30
Musketoons, 33; Percussion
Muskets, 5; Percussion
Pistols, 30
Calvary Sabres, 42
Medical Department
Commissioned Officers
present, 1

FORT VANCOUVER
Field and Staff, 4th Infantry

Commissioned Officers
present, 3; absent 1
Enlisted men present, 16;
absent, 1
3rd Artillery, Company L
Commissioned Officers
present, 1; absent, 3
Enlisted men present, 61;
absent, 4
Percussion Muskets, 74;
Musketoons, 4; Colts
Revolvers, 4
Non-Commissioned Officers
Swords, 7
4th Infantry, Company G
Commissioned Officers
present, 1; absent, 2
Enlisted men present, 20;
absent, 5
Percussion Muskets, 66
Non-Commissioned Officers
Swords, 6
4th Infantry, Company H
Commissioned Officers
present, 1; absent, 2
Enlisted men present, 37;
absent, 1
Percussion Muskets, 75
Non-Commissioned Officers
Swords, 6
Quartermaster's Depot
Commissioned Officers
present, 1
Citizens employed, 4

Subsistence Sub Depot
  Commissioned Officers
    present, 1
  Citizens employed, 1
Ordnance Depot
  Military Store Keeper, 1
  Percussion Muskets, 292;
    Percussion Rifles, 9; Colts
    Revolvers, 24
  Non-Commissioned Officers
    Swords, 20
  6 pounder Brass Field Guns,
    2; 12 pounder Brass How-
    itzers, 1

FORT DALLES
Field and Staff, 4th Infantry
  Commissioned Officers
    present, 2
  Percussion Rifles, 17; Colts
    Revolvers, 2
  6 pounder Brass Field Guns, 1
4th Infantry, Company K
  Commissioned Officers
    present, 2; absent, 1
  Enlisted men present, 22;
    absent, 6
  Citizens employed, 1
  Percussion Muskets, 70
  Non-Commissioned Officers
    Swords, 6
4th Infantry, Company I
  Commissioned Officers
    present, 2; absent, 1

Enlisted men present, 21;
  absent, 6
Percussion Muskets, 80
Non-Commissioned Officers
  Swords, 6

FORT STEILACOOM
12 pounder Brass Mountain
  Howitzers, 2
4th Infantry, Company A
  Commissioned Officers
    present, 2; absent, 1
  Enlisted men present, 23;
    absent, 0
  Percussion Muskets, 61
  Non-Commissioned Officers
    Swords, 6
4th Infantry, Company C
  Commissioned Officers
    present, 3; absent, 0
  Enlisted men present, 26;
    absent, 0
  Percussion Muskets, 61
  Non-Commissioned Officers
    Swords, 6
Medical Department
  Commissioned Officers
    present, 1

PORT ORFORD
Ordnance Sergeant, 1
4th Infantry (post commander)
  Commissioned Officers
    present, 1

3rd Artillery, Company M
(detachment)
Enlisted men present, 23;
absent, 0
Percussion Muskets, 23
Non-Commissioned Officers
Swords, 1

BREVET MAJOR
G. H. THOMAS' COMMAND
3rd Artillery, Not Inspected
Field and Staff
Commissioned Officers
present, 4
Enlisted men present, 9
Company G
Commissioned Officers
present, 1
Enlisted men present, 49
Company I
Commissioned Officers
present, 1
Enlisted men present, 53
Company K
Commissioned Officers
present, 2
Enlisted men present, 59
Total Percussion Muskets,
170

Totals for the Department[1]

Officers present, 92
Officers absent, 37
Enlisted men present, 1038
Enlisted men absent, 191
Military Store Keepers and
Ordnance Sergeants, 4
Citizens employed, 99
Horses, 58
Percussion Muskets, 14,247
Percussion Rifles, 5009
Musketoons, 1284
Carbines, 200
Colts Revolvers, 417
Percussion Pistols, 1257
Non-Commissioned Officers
Swords, 866
Calvary Sabres, 855
Artillery Sabres, 330
6 pounder Brass Field Guns,
16
12 pounder Brass Howitzers,
12
12 pounder Brass Mountain
Howitzers, 6
Sea Coast Guns, 47
Mortars, 3

[1] The figures in the tabular statement do not always agree with the figures given in the body of the report, and there are errors in addition in the table.

Bibliography

« I. UNPUBLISHED MATERIAL »

Farmer, Malcolm F. "New Mexico Camps, Posts, Stations, and Forts." Mimeographed list provided by the Library of the Museum of New Mexico, Santa Fe, New Mexico.

Hill, Gertrude. "Military Forts of New Mexico, a Bibliography." Mimeographed list provided by the Library of the Museum of New Mexico, Santa Fe, New Mexico.

Ledbetter, William Glen. "Military History of the Oregon Country, 1804–1859." M.A. thesis, University of Oregon, Eugene, 1935.

Littleton, John O. "Frontier Military Posts of the Southwest, 1848–1860." Mimeographed list provided by the National Park Service, Region Three Office, Santa Fe, New Mexico, 1953.

McCall, George A. "McCall's Inspection Report, Department of New Mexico, 1850." Records of the Office of the Adjutant General, Record Group 94, the National Archives, Washington, D.C.

———. "McCall's Inspection Report, Department of the Pacific, 1852." Records of the Office of the Adjutant General, Record Group 94, the National Archives, Washington, D.C.

Mansfield, Joseph K. F. "Report of Inspection of the Department of New Mexico, 1853." Records of the Office of the Adjutant General, the National Archives, Washington, D.C.

———. "Report of Inspection of the Department of the Pacific, 1854." Records of the Office of the Adjutant General, the National Archives, Washington, D.C.

« II. GOVERNMENT PUBLICATIONS »

Abel, Annie Heloise, ed. *The Official Correspondence of James S. Calhoun while Indian Agent at Santa Fé and Superintendent of Indian Affairs in New Mexico.* Washington, D.C., 1915.

Army Register. 33 Cong., 2 sess., *House Exec. Doc. 58.* Washington, D.C., 1854. For the fiscal year ending June 30, 1854.

Boundary Between Texas and the Territories. 33 Cong., 2 sess., *House Exec. Doc. 89.* Washington, D.C., 1855.

Buchanan, James. *Message of the President of the United States to the Two Houses of Congress.* 35 Cong., 1 sess., *Sen. Exec. Doc. 11.* Washington, D.C., 1858.

———. *Message of the President of the United States to the Two Houses of Congress.* 35 Cong., 2 sess., *House Exec. Doc. 2.* Washington, D.C., 1859.

California and New Mexico. 31 Cong., 1 sess., *House Exec. Doc. 17.* Washington, D. C., 1850.

Coolidge, Richard H., comp. *Statistical Report on the Sickness and Mortality in the Army of the United States, Compiled from the Records of the Surgeon General's Office; Embracing a Period of Sixteen Years, from January, 1839, to January, 1855.* 34 Cong., 1 sess., *Sen. Exec. Doc. 96.* Washington, D.C., 1856.

Conrad, Charles M. *Report of the Secretary of War Communicating, in Compliance with a Resolution of the Senate, Colonel McCall's Reports in Relation to New Mexico.* 31 Cong., 2 sess., *Sen. Exec. Doc. 26.* Washington, D.C., 1851. The document contains reports on conditions in New Mexico, one to Secretary of War George W. Crawford, July 15, 1850, and one to Adjutant General Roger Jones, December 26, 1850. It does not include McCall's inspection reports.

Crawford, George W. *Reports of the Secretary of War, with Reconnaissances of Routes from San Antonio to El Paso.* 31 Cong., 1 sess., *Sen. Exec. Doc. 64.* Washington, D.C., 1850. The document also contains: "Report of Captain R. B. Marcy's Route from Fort Smith to Santa Fe," "Report of Lieutenant J. H. Simpson of an Expedition to the Navajo Country," and "Report of Lieutenant

W. H. C. Whiting's Reconnaissances of the Western Texas Frontier."

Davis, Jefferson. *Report of the Secretary of War Communicating the Several Pacific Railway Explorations.* 33 Cong., 1 sess., *House Exec. Doc. 129.* 3 vols. and atlas. Washington, D.C., 1855.

Emory, Lieutenant Colonel W. H. *Notes of a Military Reconnoissance, from Fort Leavenworth in Missouri, to San Diego, in California, Including Part of the Arkansas, del Norte, and Gila Rivers.* 30 Cong., 1 sess., *House Exec. Doc. 41.* Washington, D.C., 1848. The document also includes: "Notes by Lieutenant J. W. Abert," "Report of Lieutenant J. W. Abert, of His Examination of New Mexico, in the Years 1846–47," "Report of Lieutenant Colonel P. St. George Cooke of His March from Santa Fé, New Mexico, to San Diego, Upper California," and "Journal of Captain A. R. Johnston, First Dragoons."

Fillmore, Millard. *Message from the President of the United States, to the Two Houses of Congress.* 31 Cong., 2 sess., *Sen. Exec. Doc. 1.* Washington, D.C., 1850.

———. *Message from the President of the United States, to the Two Houses of Congress.* 32 Cong., 1 sess., *Sen. Exec. Doc. 1.* Washington, D.C., 1851.

———. *Message from the President of the United States, to the Two Houses of Congress.* 32 Cong., 1 sess., *House Exec. Doc. 2.* Washington, D.C., 1851.

———. *Message from the President of the United States, to the Two Houses of Congress.* 32 Cong., 2 sess., *House Exec. Doc. 1.* Washington, D.C., 1852.

Heitman, Francis B. *Historical Register and Dictionary of the United States Army, from Its Organization, September 29, 1789, to March 2, 1903.* 2 vols. Washington, D.C., 1903.

Hodge, Frederick W., ed. *Handbook of American Indians North of Mexico.* 2 vols. Washington, D.C., 1912.

Kappler, Charles J. *Indian Affairs, Laws and Treaties.* 2 vols. Washington, D.C., 1904.

Kennedy, Joseph C. G. *Preliminary Report on the Eighth Census: 1860.* 37 Cong., 2 sess., *Sen. Doc.* Washington, D.C., 1862.

McDowell, Irwin. *Outline Descriptions of Military Posts in the Military Division of the Pacific.* San Francisco, 1879.

Marcy, Randolph B. *Outline Description of the Posts and Stations of Troops in the Geographical Divisions and Departments of the United States.* Washington, D.C., 1872.

Pierce, Franklin. *Message from the President of the United States to the Two Houses of Congress.* 33 Cong., 1 sess., *House Exec. Doc. 1.* Washington, D.C., 1853.

———. *Message from the President of the United States to the Two Houses of Congress.* 33 Cong., 1 sess., *Sen. Exec. Doc. 1.* Washington, D.C., 1853.

———. *Message from the President of the United States to the Two Houses of Congress.* 33 Cong., 2 sess., *House Exec. Doc. 1.* Washington, D.C., 1854.

———. *Message from the President of the United States to the Two Houses of Congress.* 33 Cong., 2 sess., *Sen. Exec. Doc. 1.* Washington, D.C., 1854.

———. *Message from the President of the United States to the Two Houses of Congress.* 34 Cong., 1 sess., *Sen. Exec. Doc. 1.* Washington, D. C., 1855.

Polk, James K. *Message from the President of the United States to the Two Houses of Congress.* 30 Cong., 2 sess., *House Exec. Doc. 1.* Washington, D. C., 1848.

Reports of Explorations and Surveys to Ascertain the Most Practicable and Economical Route for a Railroad from the Mississippi River to the Pacific Ocean. 33 Cong., 2 sess., *Sen. Exec. Doc. 78.* 10 vols. Washington, D.C., 1855–59.

Reports of Explorations and Surveys to Ascertain the Most Practicable and Economical Route for a Railroad from the Mississippi River to the Pacific Ocean. 33 Cong., 2 sess., *House Exec. Doc. 91.* 10 vols. Washington, D.C., 1855–58.

Reports of Explorations and Surveys to Ascertain the Most Prac-

ticable and Economical Route for a Railroad from the Mississippi River to the Pacific Ocean. 36 Cong., 1 sess., *House Exec. Doc. 56.* Vol. 12 in 2 parts. Washington, D. C., 1860.

Thian, Raphael P. *Notes Illustrating the Military Geography of the United States.* Washington, D.C., 1881.

U.S. War Department, Surgeon General's Office. *A Report on Barracks and Hospitals with Descriptions of Military Posts.* Circular No. 4. Washington, D. C., 1870.

———. *A Report on the Hygiene of the United States Army, with Descriptions of Military Posts.* Circular No. 8. Washington, D.C., 1875.

« III. OTHER PUBLISHED MATERIAL »

Abel, Annie Heloise, ed. "Indian Affairs in New Mexico Under the Administration of William Carr Lane," *New Mexico Historical Review,* Vol. XVI (April, 1941), 206–32; (July, 1941), 238–58.

Bailey, Walter. "The Barlow Road," *Quarterly of the Oregon Historical Society,* Vol. XIII (September, 1912), 287–96.

Bancroft, Hubert Howe. *Works.* 39 vols. San Francisco, 1882–90.

Barnes, Will C. *Arizona Place Names.* Tucson, 1960. Revised and enlarged by Byrd H. Granger.

Bartlett, John Russell. *Personal Narrative of Explorations and Incidents in Texas, New Mexico, California, Sonora, and Chihuahua, Connected with the United States and Mexican Boundary Commission during the Years 1850, '51, '52, and '53.* 2 vols. in 1. New York, 1856.

Bender, Averam B. "Frontier Defense in New Mexico, 1846–1853," *New Mexico Historical Review,* Vol. IX (July, 1934), 249–72.

———. "Frontier Defense in New Mexico, 1853–1861," *New Mexico Historical Review,* Vol. IX (October, 1934), 345–73.

———. *The March of Empire: Frontier Defense in the Southwest, 1848–1860.* Lawrence, Kansas, 1952.

———. "Military Posts in the Southwest 1848–1860," *New Mexico Historical Review,* Vol. XVI (April, 1941), 125–47.

Bennett, James A. *Forts and Forays.* Albuquerque, 1948. Clinton E.

Brooks and Frank D. Reeve, eds. Journal of a dragoon in New Mexico, 1850–56.

Bieber, Ralph P., ed. *Exploring Southwestern Trails*. Glendale, 1938.

Binkley, William C. "The Question of Texan Jurisdiction in New Mexico Under the United States, 1848–1850," *Southwestern Historical Quarterly*, Vol. XXVI (July, 1920), 1–38.

Bledsoe, A. J. *Indian Wars of the Northwest: A California Sketch*. San Francisco, 1885.

Brackett, R. W. *A History of the Ranchos of San Diego County, California*. San Diego, 1939.

Carey, Charles H. *A General History of Oregon Prior to 1861*. 2 vols. Portland, Oregon, 1936.

Caughey, John W. *California*. New York, 1940.

Clark, Robert Carlton. "Military History of Oregon, 1849–1859," *Oregon Historical Quarterly*, Vol. XXXVI (March, 1935), 14–59.

Coan, C. F. "The Adoption of the Reservation Policy in the Pacific Northwest, 1853–1855," *Quarterly of the Oregon Historical Society*, Vol. XXIII (March, 1922), 1–38.

Conkling, Roscoe P., and Margaret B. Conkling. *The Butterfield Overland Mail, 1857–1869*. 3 vols. Glendale, 1947.

Coues, Elliott, trans. and ed. *On the Trail of a Spanish Pioneer: The Diary and Itinerary of Francisco Garcés*. 2 vols. New York, 1900.

Cowan, Robert G. *Ranchos of California: A List of Spanish Concessions, 1775–1822, and Mexican Grants, 1822–1846*. Fresno, California, 1956.

Crimmins, M. L., ed. "Colonel J. K. F. Mansfield's Report of the Inspection of the Department of Texas in 1856," *Southwestern Historical Quarterly*, Vol. XLII (October, 1938), 122–48; (January, 1939), 215–57; (April, 1939), 351–87.

———. "Fort Fillmore," *New Mexico Historical Review*, Vol. VI (October, 1931), 327–33.

———. "Fort Massachusetts, First United States Military Post in Colorado," *The Colorado Magazine*, Vol. XVI (July, 1937), 128–33.

———. "W. G. Freeman's Report on the Eighth Military Department," *Southwestern Historical Quarterly*, Vol. LI (July, 1947), 54–58; (October, 1947), 167–74; (January, 1948), 252–58; (April, 1948), 350–57; Vol. LII (July, 1948), 100–108; (October, 1948), 227–33; (January, 1949), 349–53; (April, 1949), 444–47; Vol. LIII (July, 1949), 71–77; (October, 1949), 202–208; (January, 1950), 308–19; (April, 1950), 443–73.

Cullimore, Clarence. *Old Adobes of Forgotten Fort Tejon.* 2nd ed. Bakersfield, California, 1949.

Danford, Robert M., ed. *Register of Graduates and Former Cadets, United States Military Academy.* New York, 1953.

Davis, W. W. H. *El Gringo: or, New Mexico and Her People.* New York, 1857.

DeBow, J. D. B. *Statistical View of the United States.* Washington, D.C., 1854.

Domenech, Abbé Em. *Seven Year's Residence in the Great Deserts of North America.* 2 vols. London, 1860.

Edgar, William F. "Historical Notes of Old Land Marks in California," *Publications of the Historical Society of Southern California,* Vol. III (1893), 22–30. Edgar was post surgeon at various posts in California in the 1850's. His account includes sketches of Forts Miller, Reading, and Tejon.

Eccleston, Robert. *The Mariposa Indian War, 1850–1851.* Salt Lake City, 1957. C. Gregory Crampton, ed.

Englehardt, Zephyrin. *San Diego Mission.* San Francisco, 1920.
———. *San Luis Rey Mission.* San Francisco, 1921.

Foreman, Grant. *Marcy and the Gold Seekers.* Norman, 1939.

Fuller, George W. *A History of the Pacific Northwest.* New York, 1931.

Garber, Paul Neff. *The Gadsden Treaty.* Philadelphia, 1923.

Giffen, Helen F. "Fort Miller and Millerton," *The Quarterly,* Historical Society of Southern California, Vol. XXI (March, 1939), 5–16.

Glisan, R. *Journal of Army Life.* San Francisco, 1874. Glisan was post surgeon at Fort Orford, 1855–1856.

Gorman, Mrs. Samuel. "Samuel Gorman," *Old Santa Fe,* Vol. I (January, 1914), 308–31. Mrs. Gorman was Samuel Gorman's third wife.

Gudde, Erwin G. *California Place Names.* Berkeley and Los Angeles, 1949.

Hafen, LeRoy R. "Status of the San Luis Valley, 1850–1861," *The Colorado Magazine,* Vol. III (May, 1926), 46–49.

Haley, J. Evetts. *Fort Concho and the Texas Frontier.* San Angelo, Texas, 1952.

Hall, Martin Hardwick. *Sibley's New Mexico Campaign.* Austin, 1960.

Hamersley, Thomas H. S. *Complete Regular Army Register of the United States for One Hundred Years (1779–1879).* Washington, D.C., 1880.

Hazeltine, Jean. "The Discovery and Cartographical Recognition of Shoalwater Bay," *Oregon Historical Quarterly,* Vol. LVIII (September, 1957), 251–63.

Heizer, R. F., and M. A. Whipple, eds. *The California Indians.* Berkeley and Los Angeles, 1960.

Hewett, Edgar Lee. *Ancient Life in the American Southwest.* Indianapolis, 1930.

Huggins, Dorothy H., comp. *Continuation of the Annals of San Francisco, Part 1, From June 1, 1854, to December 31, 1855.* San Francisco, 1939.

Johnson, Henry Warren. "Where Did Frémont Cross the Tehachapi Mountains in 1844?" *Publications of the Historical Society of Southern California,* Vol. XIII (1924), 365–73.

Kip, William Ingraham. *A California Pilgrimage.* Fresno, California, 1921.

Leavitt, Francis Hale. "Steam Navigation on the Colorado River," *California Historical Society Quarterly,* Vol. XXII (March, 1943), 1–25; (June, 1943), 151–74.

McArthur, Lewis A. *Oregon Geographic Names.* 3rd ed. Portland, Oregon, 1952.

Marshall, William I. *Acquisition of Oregon.* 2 vols. Seattle, 1911.

Meeker, Ezra. *Pioneer Reminiscences of Puget Sound*. Seattle, 1905.

Mills, Anson. *My Story*. 2nd ed. Washington, D.C., 1921.

Möllhausen, Baldwin. *Diary of a Journey from the Mississippi to the Coast of the Pacific with a United States Government Expedition*. 2 vols. London, 1858.

Pancoast, Charles Edward. *A Quaker Forty-Niner*. Philadelphia, 1930. Anna Paschall Hannum, ed.

Prince, LeBaron Bradford. *Old Fort Marcy, Santa Fe, New Mexico*. Santa Fe, 1912.

Prosch, Thomas W., "The Military Roads of Washington Territory," *Washington Historical Quarterly*, Vol. II (January, 1908), 118–26.

Rickard, Thomas A. *A History of American Mining*. New York, 1932.

Rolle, Andrew F. "William Heath Davis and the Founding of American San Diego," *California Historical Society Quarterly*, Vol. XXXI (March, 1952), 33–48.

Rosborough, Alex. J. "A. M. Rosborough, Special Indian Agent," *California Historical Society Quarterly*, Vol. XXVI (September, 1947), 201–207.

Scammell, J. M. "Military Units in Southern California, 1853–1862," *California Historical Society Quarterly*, Vol. XXIX (September, 1950), 229–49.

Scott, Leslie M., *History of the Oregon Country*. 6 vols. Cambridge, 1924.

———. "Indian Diseases as Aides to Pacific Northwest Settlement," *Oregon Historical Quarterly*, Vol. XXIX (June, 1928), 144–61.

Settle, Raymond W. *The March of the Mounted Riflemen*. Glendale, 1940.

Stanley, F. [Stanley Francis Louis Crocchiola]. *The Fort Conrad New Mexico Story*. Dumas, Texas, 1961.

———. *Fort Union (New Mexico)*. N.p., 1953.

Stevens, Hazard. *The Life of Isaac Ingalls Stevens*. 2 vols. Boston and New York, 1900.

Thomlinson, M. H. *The Garrison of Fort Bliss, 1849–1916*. El Paso, 1945.

Twitchell, Ralph Emerson. *The Leading Facts of New Mexican History*. 5 vols. Cedar Rapids, Iowa, 1911–17.

Whiting, J. S., and Richard J. Whiting. *Forts of the State of California*. Longview, Washington, 1960.

Winther, Oscar O. *Express and Stagecoach Days in California from the Gold Rush to the Civil War*. Stanford, California, 1936.

———. *The Old Oregon Country*. Bloomington, 1950.

Woodward, Arthur. *Feud on the Colorado*. Los Angeles, 1955.

———, ed. *Journal of Lt. Thomas W. Sweeny, 1849–1853*. Los Angeles, 1956.

« IV. MAPS »

"A Map of the Territory of New Mexico." Compiled by Brevet Second Lieutenant John G. Parke, Topographical Engineers, 1851.

"A Map of the Territories of New Mexico and Arizona." Prepared in the Office of the Chief of Engineers, U.S.A., 1879.

United States Geological Survey Maps. Washington, D.C., latest editions.

Index

Abadie, Eugene H.: 20n., 44, 199
Abbott, Robert O.: 146, 147, 199
Abert, James W.: 23n.
Abiquiu, New Mexico, Post of: *xvi*n., *xix*
Adams and Company: 127n., 131n., 177
Adams, Wylly C.: 32, 33, 199
Adjutant General's Department, Pacific Department: 126
Aguirre, José Antonio: 105n.
Albuquerque, New Mexico, described: 20n.
Albuquerque, Post of: *xvi*n., *xix*, 68; department headquarters at, *xvii*, 20, 30, 43; discussed, 20–21, 43–46; established, 20n.; personnel and property at, 222
Alcatraz Island, California: reservation of, 121n., 122; lighthouse on, 133; discussed, 134–35
Alemany, Joseph Sadoc, Bishop: 106n.
Alexander, Edmund B.: 15, 199
Alexander, Newton F.: 132, 199
Algodones, Lower California: 83n. 84, 109
Algodones, New Mexico, sub-depot at: *xix*
Allen, Robert: 126–27, 128, 199
Alley, John W.: 47, 199
Almaden, California: 96n.
Alvord, Benjamin: 175, 199
American population: in New Mexico, 5n., 6, 11–12; in California, 103; in Oregon country, 103
Anderson, George B.: 50, 199–200
Angel Island, California, reservation of: 121n.
Ankrim, Joel R.: on New Mexico-Texas boundary, 4; on Indian depredations, 70–75
Apache Indians: 10–11, 23; Jicarilla, 10, 15, 17; Gila, 11, 25, 27; Sacramento Mountain, 11, 76; White Mountain, 11, 25, 27, 76
Armijo, Rafael: 75
Arnold, Richard: 135, 200
Arapho Indians: 10, 13
Astoria, Post of, Oregon: *xxvi*
Auger, Christopher C.: 171, 200
Ayres, Romeyn B.: 154, 200

Babacomeri Ranch, San Ignacio de: 125n.
Backus, Electus: 21, 27, 30, 54, 200
Baldwin, Briscoe G.: 137, 138, 200
Baptist missionaries in New Mexico: 6, 8
Barclay's Fort, New Mexico: 13, 37
Barlow Road: 179n.
Barnard, John G.: 132, 133, 200
Bartlett, John Russell: estimates of Indian population, 11n.; and Indian depredations, 71n.; escort provided for, 73; mentioned, 77
Bates, Francis H.: 159, 200

silla Valley, 12n.; estimates population of Albuquerque, 20n.

Day, Edward H.: 137, 171, 172, 203

De Lano, Horace F.: 50, 203–204

Department of New Mexico: *see* Military Department No. 9

Department of the Pacific: established, *xxii;* extent, *xxii,* 91; desertions in, *xxiv;* inspected by McCall, *xxvii, xxviii*n.; supplies for, *xxviii;* costs and expenses in, *xxviii, 126–27, 133,* 139–40, 148n., 152ff., 177, 180–81; population of classified, 97–105; departmental headquarters, 125–32; Adjutant General's Department, 126; Quartermaster General's Department, 126–29; Subsistence Department, 129; Pay Department, 130–31; Medical Department, 131; personnel and property in, 182–83, 225–31; recommended distribution of troops in, 183–84

Derby, George H.: 141–42, 204

Desertions, effect of gold discovery on: *xxiv,* 167

Diegueño Indians: 83n., 107n.

Domenech, Abbé Emmanuel: estimates Pueblo Indian population, 7n.; estimates population of Albuquerque, 20n.

Doña Ana, Post of, New Mexico: *xvi, xix*

Doniphan, Alexander: 72n.

Dryer, Hiram: 171, 204

Du Barry, Beekman: 143, 204

Duncan, Johnson K.: 171, 204

Dye, William McE.: 160, 204

Easton, Langdon C.: 31, 204

Eaton, Amos B.: 126, 129, 158, 164, 169, 172, 181, 204

Eaton, Joseph H.: 21, 46, 204

Eckerson, Theodore J.: 170, 172–73, 204

Eddy, Asher R.: 138, 139, 140, 142, 204–205

Edwards, John: 154, 205

Elguea, Francisco Manuel, and Santa Rita copper mines: 26n.

Elías, Ignacio Eulalia: 125n.

El Paso County, Texas: created, 4n.; trade routes through, 12; mentioned, 64; Indian depredations in, 70–75

El Paso del Norte, Chihuahua: 28, 70ff.

Evans, George F.: 150, 205

Evans, Nathan G.: 52, 205

Ewell, Richard S.: 48, 49, 205

Extra daily duty, Jesup's recommendations on: 65n.

False Bay (Mission Bay), California: 142

Farming, military, in New Mexico: regulations concerning, 34, 62n.; indebtedness, 34, 37, 63; failure of, 46, 48, 51, 62–64

Ferrell, William C.: 105n.

Fillmore, Millard: post named for, 26n.

Fitzgerald, Edward H.: 167, 205

Floyd–Jones, De Lancy: 179, 180, 205

Flour mills: Hart's Mill, 28n., 62; near Taos, 36, 39; on Moro River, 36; in California, 87, 166, 192; in Oregon, 169

Folsom, Joseph L.: 126, 135, 136, 205

Forsythe, Benjamin D.: 170, 176, 205

Fort, designation defined: *xxiv*n.

Fort Atkinson, Kansas: 13

Fort Bellingham, Washington: 124n.

Fort Bidwell, California: *xxv*

Fort Bliss, Texas: 28n., 71n.

Fort Boise, in present Idaho (army post): 123n.

Fort Boise, in present Idaho (Hudson's Bay post): 176, 195

Fort Breckenridge, in present Arizona: 124n.

Fort Brown, Texas: *xiv*

Mansfield on the Condition of the Western Forts

has been set in 12-point Linotype Caslon Old Face, a present-day reproduction of the hand-set Caslon designs which originated in England two centuries ago. Had Mansfield's letters been printed in his own time, his publisher would probably have used a Caslon type, available then in most American printing houses. The historical flavor imparted by Caslon, together with its timeless readability, makes the selection doubly appropriate for this volume.

University of Oklahoma Press

Norman